The SNOWS of SUMMER

The **SNOWS** of **SUMMER**

A NOVEL OF THE FUTURE

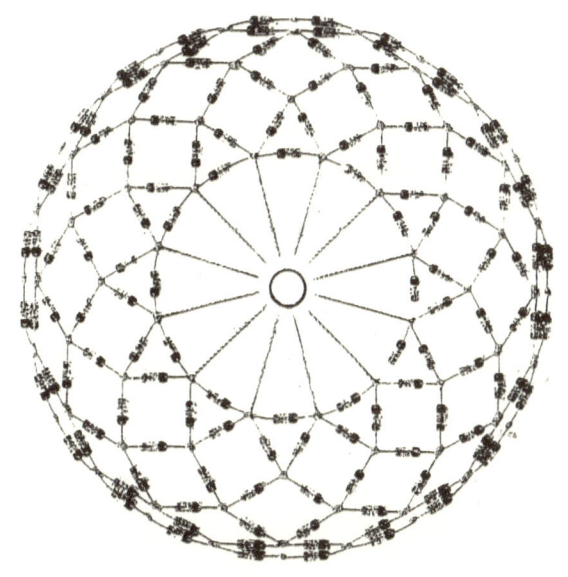

William H. Isely

To order additional copies of this book, contact:
Xlibris LLC
1-888-795-4274
www.Xlibris.com
Orders@Xlibris.com
131927

CONTENTS

To

Doris, Rick, Eva, Toni, Larry, Josephine, John, and Nancy
without whose inspiration and assistance
I would never have completed this story.

ACKNOWLEDGMENTS

I would like to acknowledge John D. Hamaker as the originator of the concept of glaciation caused by demineralization of the soils and subsequent carbon dioxide buildup and Don Weaver for his part in publishing Hamaker's book, which I refer to in the story, *The Survival of Civilization*. The resulting oscillation between glacial and interglacial periods I have termed the 110,000-year biomass oscillation, which the earth has been experiencing for over a million years. Whether mankind will prevent the next 100,000-year glacial cold period is yet to be determined.

FOREWORD

This novel of the future was originally created in response to a competition to submit novels of the future which emphasized problems of the environment and their solutions. It was emphasized in the competition that the novel be easily adapted to a movie format. Unfortunately, the criteria were abandoned by the judging committee, and this novel in an earlier version of over twenty years ago was relegated to a high storage shelf.

In the interim, the problems of climate change, a center piece of *The Snows of Summer*, have been further aggravated by our continued dependence on fossil fuels, with a critical threat to the environment involving tar sands and fracking for natural gas and oil. With a prospect of fifty more years of cheap energy, the start toward an environmental friendly energy society seems to be coming to an end, making climate change more likely.

The *Snows of Summer* has been updated to include events that have transpired since its original writing to act as a belated warning that our environment has become fragile enough and industry-powerful enough that a continued ignoring of humanity's effects on the environment may put the future of our species at risk.

Beginnings

The UN Secretary-General, Hamar Arundel, sat in his office, waiting for a phone call from an assistant who was investigating a crisis in a third world country. Hamar reflected on the state of the world. While a student of psychology and politics, with some sociology thrown in, he had his experts in technology who assured him that there were technical solutions to just about all the world's problems. For instance, by making the needed capital investment, the world could be weaned away from fossil fuels to renewable and sustainable sources, and that would solve many problems, including the frequent fighting over the oil in the Mideast. The easily produced, French-invented abortion pill could bring the continuing explosive population growth under control, if people could be motivated to use it. Most diseases of an infectious nature were under control. It had been found that most degenerative health problems were a matter of diet and that low cost supplements, when added to a proper diet, could prevent most of these conditions. Still, the majority of the world's population continued to eat as it always had. The list of problems and their technical solutions went on and on, but in most cases, the solutions went unimplemented. Even food was not really a problem, although a lot of people were still starving. Hamar supposed that somewhere there were probably people who had a solution to the big problem of the greenhouse effect, which many expected would adversely affect the world's climate.

Hamar sighed. He was a realist and knew that the lack of solving humanity's problems was tied up in human nature. Except when immediate survival was at stake, most humans were motivated by greed, attachment to things, with a lust for indulging the senses. The worst, Hamar thought, were pride and a thirst for power. When these negative human tendencies became concentrated by organizations and institutions, there was no stopping them. The result was war over oil, food, and the other resources valued by humans. Besides pollution of the planet, there was large-scale starvation, lack of basic health needs, holy wars, and brother against brother.

Hamar's reflections were interrupted by the phone call he was expecting. It was a depressing, negative report. The initiative he was hoping to introduce would have to be delayed. The individuals in power were afraid that to try to make the desired improvements in their family-planning programs at this time would trigger violent reactions from the conservative religious forces. The political situation in the countries involved was very unstable. They would have to wait for a more propitious time.

Hamar thought as he hung up the phone that humanity seemed to have lost its will, its collective will, to make the world a livable planet.

*   *   *

Two climatologists were arguing in Cambridge, England. The first said, "I still hold to the conventional view on the greenhouse effect. It's only common sense that the earth's temperature must rise when more of the heat received from the sun is trapped in the atmosphere by the increasing carbon dioxide. Records over the last hundred years show that the average world temperature has risen nearly a degree. As the carbon dioxide increases from burning of all kinds of fuels, mostly fossil, this average temperature is bound to rise still more. With the melting of the large ice fields, there is bound to be flooding of all the coastal plains where the bulk of humanity lives, a great catastrophe."

The other shook his head. "The key to what is going to happen to the climate is in understanding that word *average.* You are taking too simplistic a view. I grant you there has been an increase in the average temperature, but its effect is not distributed evenly. There has been an increase in the tropics which is of more significance than increases anywhere else. The increase in the tropics will cause more evaporation from the oceans, moving more snow water vapor to the Polar Regions. This could cause a buildup of ice rather than a melting, potentially a much worse catastrophe than the coastal plain flooding you are worrying about."

The first climatologist spoke again. "Well, none of the models properly represent the effect of heat storage in the oceans or of the transfer of heat by ocean currents. Also the proper modeling of the cloud cover is yet to be achieved. Until we can afford bigger and faster computers, who can be sure of the future? It will remain one of the great questions facing humanity. When the answer is known, perhaps it will then be too late to do anything about it."

*   *   *

Gertrude Vogel checked her data for the fourth time before sealing it in an envelope and sending it to the new Germany Forestry Research Department. She thought of the four years of back-breaking work it represented on her part in an out-of-the-way post in the Black Forest. At the very least, it should get her a promotion and a transfer closer to civilization, maybe somewhere where there was some social life, maybe even some suitable male company. Not being able to satisfy her natural, lusty nature was the hard part of her isolation. Present conditions would change, she was sure, when her boss realized that she had discovered a simple way to bring back the forests that were dying everywhere. That would be the first step to getting a man to marry her and satisfy her desire to have a family. Maybe eventually a position as a department head, or even an assistant minister, posted to Berlin!

*   *   *

Olav Kerensky hurried through the Kremlin halls in answer to a summons from the Russian Prime Minister, Ivan Petrovich. As Olav arrived, the Prime Minister motioned him to a chair and spoke hurriedly, "Olav, I am concerned that we have not made the expected progress on our Project ARARAT that we had planned. I worry at night before falling asleep that the Americans will be successful first. I have decided to transfer the project to your personal management, and I want you to give it your close attention. I have already authorized an increase in two levels of priority for the project. You are, of course, generally familiar with the project. Do you have any suggestions?"

"Yes, Ivan," Olav replied. "The project cannot succeed in a reasonable time period unless a computer with the greatest capacity and speed is utilized. There are only three such computers in all of the Russia. They are currently assigned to the Strategic Rocket Forces."

The President responded, "We are not currently likely to need them in that fashion. I will speak to General Metchnikoff, and you will have one of his computers as soon as you want it."

*   *   *

Wong Lee rose from his meditation pad and searched out a companion monk in a Confucian monastery near Shanghai. Wong said to his friend, "It was harder today than usual to try to still my mind. One would think that after twenty years it would get easier, but somehow that doesn't seem to be so. Just when I begin to see some light and hear some sounds, my body gets tired and demands attention, and my mind loses its concentration. What is to be done?"

His companion was somewhat older and had a more resigned attitude. "We must be patient. It is all in the hands of Heaven, and it cannot be rushed whatever we do. It is our duty to meditate whether we make any apparent spiritual progress or not. When the Time is right, Heaven will shower its grace."

*   *   *

Mikhail Zellov, supreme commander of military forces in Kazakhstan, was with his security chief in a very private meeting. "Andrei," Mikhail said, "before the Soviet breakup, how was it that the central KGB in Moscow never learned that we were boyhood friends? If they had known, they would never have assigned us to the same command."

Andrei smiled, "When I was new in the KGB, and neither of us was yet important to anyone, I made sure to delete that information from both of our files. Being boyhood friends, we can trust each other, something that was rare in the old Soviet Union. Now, of course, we are free of them, and we have great opportunities in this Republic we control."

"Yes," said Mikhail, "but for us to be successful, you and I must continue to have our first loyalties to each other. There are many here who still have their first loyalties to Mother Russia, forgetting that the old days are gone forever. They would block our plans to take Kazakhstan out of Russian influence. Russia will still try to have her way with us, and many here will help her. We must always be on guard against those who would try to put the old empire back together."

Using a secret monitoring device, Viktor Andropov listened to the conversation of the commander and security chief with interest. He was really not that surprised. Why otherwise would he have been assigned as a special agent, reporting directly to Moscow, to spy on them? This was the first conversation he had been able to overhear since planting his bug. His cover as an orderly at staff headquarters had been arranged before the breaking away of the Republics. The new realities of separation, however, did not make provision for frequent reporting to Moscow to whom he felt an overriding loyalty. He would have to think carefully about how to report what he had just learned and what he would no doubt learn in the future. So far, besides the bugging, the only other successful accomplishment of his mission had been the planting of an electronic module in the general's staff car. He had not been informed of its function but assumed it was not an explosive device because of its small size.

* * *

The Alaska drill ship, North Explorer, had just finished its last run across the channel between the Bering Strait and St. Lawrence Island. As it headed for its home port at anchorage,

Geologist Sam Trevor examined the last cores that had been brought up from the bottom. Sam discovered that near the bottom of the last hole they had drilled, they had passed through material that was highly fractured, an indication of a geological fault. Sam was surprised, because his maps did not show faulting in that area. He decided that it really didn't matter, because none of the core samples anywhere nearby had shown any promising signs of possible oil-bearing strata. Still there were other people outside his oil company who might be interested in the discovery of a new fault line, so Sam decided to include it in his report.

*   *   *

Buddy Rustler looked up from his notes; not a bad day at all. In fact, it had been a very good day. He has sold five new cars, most of them heavies, and by a fluke, he had also sold the rebuilt light truck for the used car department, the one with the tricky four-wheel drive.

Suckers, he thought of the young couple who had bought the truck. Probably wouldn't even find out that the four-wheel drive needed a thousand-dollar repair job before their warranty ran out. Buddy thought about the truck that had an old style manual shift. It had probably been damaged on a demo drive by being put into low range by some fool who didn't know you had to be stopped to do it.

The wall clock showed past closing time, and Buddy got up to leave. Not a bad life, he thought. With the world full of suckers, he could always make a good living. He decided to stop off at the Central Bar and Grill. Maybe he would find a chick looking for some action.

*   *   *

The phone rang shrilly for the fourth time before Larry Owens bestirred himself to answer. "Hello, this is Larry," he said, not expecting anything good.

"Say, Larry," was the response from the other end. "This is George Fox down at the Craft House, remember? You left me those funny art designs made out of those electronic parts that look like glass beads with wires through them."

"Oh yeah," Larry managed, "did you sell any of them?"

"Not exactly," George said apologetically, "But one couple seem quite interested. They would like to borrow them for some kind of experiment. Also they are anxious to meet you sometime. How about letting me lend them out? They are reliable people over at the university. Who knows, they might end up buying?"

"OK," Larry ended. "And let me know when they can get together."

*   *   *

The sign on the door said, "Range Safety Project Office." Inside, the office looked run-down, like it had seen better days. It had been a long day, and Red Kelley was finally getting to the bottom of his mail. He glanced at a memo, with a blueprint attached, subject, "Destruct Package Wiring Change."

Ah, he thought. That looks like an interesting item, one that will take some study, and no doubt some actions to be taken by the office. He filed it in his bottom desk drawer where he could get it easily some afternoon when he had two or so hours to devote to it.

The next day, Red was riding his motorcycle in a Florida afternoon thunderstorm, skidded, went off the road, and broke his neck when he collided with a palm tree. He was dead on arrival at the Brevard County Hospital. No one else in his office understood his filing system.

Chapter 1

Another Record Year

Roger shifted his attention from the computer displays to the sound of the paging system. "Roger Foreman, please call your office, Roger Foreman, please call your office . . ."

He picked up his cell phone and soon had his secretary, Michelle, telling him, "You have a meeting with the boss in twenty minutes." Then she added, guardedly, "His secretary said you are the only one invited."

"That's fine," he said, "I'll go straight from here."

His thoughts drifted, contemplating that the past year had been a record year, certainly for weather. Three major hurricanes, each with winds over 160 miles per hour, had hit Florida, with a total of estimated damages of over 250 billion dollars. One month before, in December, the last hurricane had been the worst of the three, arriving after the official hurricane season was over. It had also been a record year for tornadoes, and frosts in June and August had killed much of the Canadian and plain states' grain harvest.

Roger had moved from Colorado and expected the Washington, DC, weather to be milder, but that had not happened. Arctic cold had repeatedly swept down from Canada, pulling moist air up from the Gulf to dump unusual amounts of snow along the seacoast. As a Federal employee at the National Oceanic and Atmospheric Administration, called NOAA for short, Roger had been excused from work on several occasions already this winter because of snarled traffic.

NOAA kept tabs on the weather all over the world, and Roger was keenly aware that wild weather patterns were a world-wide phenomenon. The Arctic ports had frozen solid a month earlier than usual. Bangladesh earlier had flooding over 50 percent of its land, although strangely the monsoons had largely failed over India proper. The Indians were facing starvation, since most world surplus food stocks had already been sent to central Africa, where millions were actually starving.

Roger's thoughts turned to the project he was leading at NOAA, the simulation of the climate, and the fact that the simulations had so far been dramatically unsuccessful. He could not understand how their models, generated by the world's best climatic scientists using the latest computer technology, were doing so poorly. Unexpected random events could cause the actual weather to deviate from the simulations, but one and two percent probability events being repeated so often in the real weather just was not logical. Somewhere his team must be missing something very basic.

Roger looked at the display screens which showed the results of the run that had just been finished before he was paged. It was similar to all the other runs that had been made for the past year, starting in January with real-world initial conditions. Random events were introduced into each run so that they differed somewhat, but even with the inclusion of volcanic eruptions, none resembled the actual weather that had been experienced. On average, only one hurricane hit Florida each year in the simulations, and in no run were the total damages greater than thirty-five million dollars. There had been no early or late frost damages to crops. This could be expected with a general warming trend due to the greenhouse effect, which had been carefully included. In the simulation runs, the tornadoes had only been of usual intensity, and the monsoons had behaved as well as the Indians could hope.

As the time for his meeting approached, Roger's thoughts shifted to his boss, Dr. Leon Strongfellow, Department Head for NOAA Climate Simulation and Research. Roger disliked Dr. Strongfellow personally because of his arrogance and lack of consideration for others. He did feel, however, that

Dr. Strongfellow was a good bureaucrat and did a good job of protecting the project from rival organizations and the ever-present budget cutters. While it had been years since Dr. Strongfellow had done any true scientific work, Roger felt he was a good communicator and could quickly get those who worked for him to address the important issues.

Meanwhile, while waiting for Roger, Leon was also reminiscing, with his thoughts going back to the long trail that had brought him to this point. He had done rather brilliantly in school but recognized it had been at some cost to his personal relationships. He knew he had a very strong desire to be the best, to beat out the other guys, and that he was generally thought of as arrogant, not liked by anyone. He accepted it as the price of getting ahead.

So far his career was right on track. With a Ph. D in physics and a master of business administration from Harvard, Leon knew he had the right credentials academically for going to the top in NOAA. When NOAA had been brought into the newly-created Department of Science and Technology and moved back to Washington, Leon had been very happy, because it meant he was back near the center of power where he would get more exposure. The administrators above him in NOAA were either close to retirement or considered weak and not promotable. His schedule called for moving into the top NOAA position in five years. He knew his performance record was well-known by both political parties. Perhaps even the position of the secretary of Science and Technology could be his someday. There was only one last hurdle, and he would be on a greased track to the top. He had to pull off Project NOAH, the name that had been given to the climate simulation effort. The only problem was that time was running out.

This shortage of time was the reason for the meeting with Roger. Leon knew that he personally contributed next to nothing to the project, very little even in the way of management, actually, and that Roger and his team were what would make it successful. Hard as they were working, they would have to be pushed harder if they were going to finish before the bureaucrats lost interest and reprogrammed their resources. Leon sensed that with some creative thinking, a breakthrough should be possible, and that they could succeed.

When Roger came in and sat down, Leon got right to the point. "The Assistant Secretary for Science and Technology is starting to put pressure on due to our lack of success in being able to model the climate accurately. We are a line item in the budget, costing him four million dollars a year, which might get him more visibility if spent on something else. If we don't get positive results in the next several months, Project NOAH will go down the tubes. Without results there will be no more support from Congress either."

Roger started to respond with something about how hard the team had been working, but Leon cut him off short. "I've scheduled a meeting for next Wednesday with our in-house scientists from the research side. Also some outside folks will be coming. I want a brain-storming session, no bullshit or ego touting, just calling a spade a spade. Maybe we can get a handle on what we have missed. Roger, I want you to start off the meeting with a summary of how your computer simulation runs differ from the actual weather records to see if the main trends can be identified. How many runs do you have in the database as of now?"

Roger could have given the answer right off, but he wanted time to see if he should be playing a political angle, so he keyed Leon's terminal for the data instead. He looked at the screen and summarized for Leon. "As you know, Project NOAH's original goal was to predict climate trends five years in advance, at least that was in the plan we sold to Congress to get the funding. After we moved everything from Colorado and got the bugs out of the system, we started making five-year runs, ten of which were completed. Analysis quickly showed that, after three months into a run, there was little correlation between it and the actual real weather records, so we dropped back to limiting the runs to a single year at a time. We just ran the forty-fifth."

Leon looked like Roger had told him all he wanted to know and said quickly, as he indicated the meeting was over, "Well, get the team together first thing in the morning and get humping. You have just a week to get ready for the meeting."

Back in his office, the eight-to-five crowd was just leaving for the day. Roger thought about how things had changed with NOAA since the creation of the new administrative Department of Science and Technology. Before, NOAA had been part of the Department of Commerce with its labs and offices scattered around the country. The new Secretary, to make NOAA a showpiece, had physically centralized all of NOAA in or around the Washington area. Roger didn't like the change in moving to Washington, since it seemed now that more decisions above him were made for political reasons to suit the politicians. He also missed the winter outdoor sports of Colorado and didn't enjoy the traffic snarls in Washington which could result from just four inches of snow.

When he too quit for the day, Roger had recovered from his meeting with Leon. He knew deep down in his heart that he had a job on the cutting edge of science, and he wouldn't trade it for anything. He knew that when they found the problem with Project NOAH, it would all be worth it.

* * *

Across the Atlantic, in due course of time, Gertrude's report arrived at its destination, but her supervisor, Rudolph Meyer, was on holiday and didn't see it for a month. When he did, he thought, "Rubbish. She is always doing something dramatic to try to get posted away from the Black Forest. I'll look into it on my annual tour." The report languished in his "To be looked at later" file.

* * *

Even farther east, General Zellov and his security chief, Andrei, were meeting again in private. Andrei was concerned. "My counter-intelligence staff has intercepted a communication to Moscow Center from someone who must be attached to our staff headquarters. We have been unable to decode the message or identify its sender."

General Zellov looked pensive. "I am not surprised. We must assume that this is not the first time. Under no circumstances should you or I agree to leave Kazakhstan, certainly not for a trip to Russia. Also I think it is time to move the command center frequently."

Andrei nodded his agreement. "And we will do what we can to find the spy. With our plan coming to fruition first to gain control in Turkmenistan, and with the help of the Chinese to eventually take over Iran, we must have no premature leaks back to Moscow."

"Yes, certainly," said General Zellov. "But soon it will not matter. The technicians are nearly finished with their work on the SS-18 missiles."

CHAPTER 2

Brainstorm

Leon and Dr. Meriwether, an independent consultant, were the first ones to arrive at the meeting. While Dr. Meriwether had been well recommended, Leon had not previously had the opportunity to get to know him. After exchanging names, Leon asked, "While we are waiting for the others, why don't you tell me something about your background and work?"

When asked about his background, Meriwether always took a few moments to think about what to say. He had been born to an American couple, at the time living in Beirut, Lebanon. Because of this circumstance, on initial recitation, his listeners would first think he was Lebanese. For those unfamiliar with the law in such circumstances, he would then explain that one would normally take the citizenship of the country of one's parents. Often, however, there was an option upon reaching one's majority to take the citizenship of the country of one's birth. Meriwether had not been aware of all these nuances of the laws (in some circumstances one could have dual citizenship), and so he was surprised a few years later, when he applied for a security clearance, that his citizenship was indeterminate. It took nearly a year of assembling documents, a hearing before the Immigration Service, and then court action before he received a paper, certifying as to his American citizenship. He never had understood why the Immigration Service had jurisdiction since his category was not that of a naturalized citizen. Whether he could legally be elected to the office of the President of the

United States as an American by birth, but born abroad, had never been ruled on by the Supreme Court.

Deciding that the complications of his citizenship could come out later, Meriwether said, "I was born in Beirut when my parents were there teaching at the American University of Beirut. I lived in Beirut through my first two years of high school, going to the American Community School. In those days, before the fighting started, Beirut was an ideal place to live. Then my parents sent me back to the States to complete my education, which eventually included a BS in physics from Northwestern and a PhD from the University of Pittsburgh. Early on, I specialized in climatology and set up a private consulting service."

Quite impressed with his background, Leon asked, "What are some of the important contributions you feel you have made to the field of climatology?"

Meriwether smiled. "Well, of course, some of what I consider of a unique nature has been for private clients and cannot be discussed in public. In the public area, however, my most controversial and important contribution has been related to the effects of the greenhouse phenomenon. In general, I disagree with all the widely distributed predictions on the grounds that the models on which they are based are flawed."

"In what way?" Leon asked.

"Generally," responded Meriwether firmly, "the conventional experts don't include the effects of ocean currents properly nor the significantly increased moisture that will be evaporated from the tropical oceans as a result of the extra energy absorption in the tropics. When the world's climatologists come up with proper models, I suspect we will be in for some surprises."

"I presume you already have the answers," Leon responded.

"Only intuitively," said Meriwether. "It takes an organization with resources, such as yours, to be able to afford the computing power required to properly model the problem."

The other participants began to arrive, and soon the conference room buzzed with small talk over the serving of coffee and sweet rolls. Roger glanced over the attendance sheet to see what surprises Leon had arranged. He saw that he had previously met all of the attendees except a Dr. Lloyd Harrison of MIT, a Chen Chew from Stanford, and a distinguished looking elderly gentleman who was talking with Leon. Roger assumed the elderly gentleman must be a Dr. Jim Meriwether, who had listed "self" as his organizational affiliation.

Before Roger could speculate further, Leon stood up at the front end of the conference room and went through introductions. After being introduced as the opening presenter, Roger started toward the front but then sat down again as he saw that Leon was not going to miss an opportunity to impress a captive audience.

Leon moved with vigor into his standard spiel about the NOAA overall charter and then onto the importance of the work of the Climate Simulation and Research Section, of which he was the head. He then spoke of Project NOAH, particularly stressing the budget levels by year. Roger's mind began to wander as he had heard all this many times before. He thought about the last seven days and how the presentation he was about to give had only come together the day before. Leon had been too busy to review it, so he would be seeing it for the first time along with all the others. Roger felt it was a good presentation and that the exercise of preparing it had been well worthwhile, in that they had not taken the time before to look at the broad picture. Some trends and correlations had appeared that had not been noticed before.

Suddenly Roger realized that Leon was looking at him, saying, " . . . Roger will summarize for you where we are at this time on Project NOAH, as well as cover some of the remaining problems on which we are working."

Roger moved into his presentation with no preliminaries. First, he covered all the major assumptions of the model that were based on the scientific studies of the research branch. These included the thermodynamics of how heat moves from the tropics to the Polar Regions; the interplay between air, land, and water, cloud cover, cloud reflections and absorptions of heat; the greenhouse effect; the momentum of the rotation of air masses; and on and on over the minutiae of the science called climatology. Next, with a small show of pride, he went into the architecture of the Project NOAH simulation: The various sizes of the cells used; the iteration period; the methods of handling random events; the setting up of initial conditions for the start of a run; and all the other details that computer buffs could wallow in for days. He made a big point of the state-of-the-art computer hardware and software that were employed, with the conclusion that Project NOAH had the most advanced computing facility in the world.

Roger noticed that he was beginning to lose the attention of some of his audience and so hurried on to his conclusions before Leon could interrupt him to make the suggestion.

His conclusions showed that the model results deviated from the real weather records so that after three months, there was almost no correlation between the two. The rate of deviation was greater in runs that represented recent history. Worst and last, the simulations did not predict any of the wild weather swings which were characteristic of the weather of the past five years. Roger handed out a thick packet of graphs and charts, documenting his presentation, a signal that the formal part of the meeting was over.

At this point, Leon called for a break to allow for coffee refills and for finishing the rolls. Roger, a strict health-food addict, thought all government refreshment offerings to be pure poison. Nevertheless, he welcomed the break before what he knew would probably be the most difficult part of the meeting for him. He did take the opportunity to ask Leon who Dr. Jim Meriwether was. Leon answered that Meriwether ran an independent weather service with a private clientele of rich businessmen who stood to lose or make a lot of money due to the ups and downs of the weather. Meriwether had a reputation for being more accurate on long-range forecasts than the US weather service.

The questions started out from the visiting scientists who knew their reputations depended on appearing to be knowledgeable. The questions were easily answered by Roger or one of the members of his staff who were there for that purpose. The questions largely delved further into the assumptions or mechanizations of the simulations but did not seem to be productive toward shedding light on the problems Roger had summarized. The general tone of the experts, while not directly stated, seemed to be that, on a very complex simulation such as this was, you couldn't venture much of an opinion unless you became involved full-time for a long period. This was no more than Roger had expected.

Meriwether had stayed out of the direct questions, but as the open discussion seemed to be winding down, he got Roger's eye. "Do I recall your assumptions on global warming that the main driver is the difference between the average temperature in the tropics and the average temperature at the poles?"

Roger nodded. "Yes," he said, "We are using the average values generally accepted by the climatic community."

With a glint in his eye Meriwether responded, "But the real driver is how much energy is absorbed in the tropics and how it divides between warming ocean water and how much fresh water gets to the North Atlantic to drive the ocean currents. Also there is a big question as to whether historical temperatures and ice core samples are accurate."

Roger knew he didn't have good answers, but gave him the truth. "When we began Project NOAH, global warming effects were very uncertain, and we concentrated on temperature which is what everyone, including the media could relate to. We didn't make energy balance our main thrust because we couldn't get support for it. I would also like to have made a more complete analysis of all the fresh water being transported to the North Atlantic, including rain in storms, which is continually dropping and being carried aloft by updrafts. I suspect this could be as much as is transported as very fine drops in clouds. We also did not include earth's heating from radioactivity in its core." Meriwether seemed undeterred and said, "I agree. The temperature in the tropics may not be as big a driver as how the absorbed energy from the sun is being divided. The energy that vaporizes water actually cools the surroundings in the process to somewhat balance the energy from the sun that would otherwise directly raise the temperature of the surroundings. A model is suspect unless it accounts for every known fact."

Meriwether had obviously polarized himself from the rest of the group who had long identified themselves with the scenario of melting ice caps and flooding of the coastal plains, a belief widely held and one largely responsible for the funding of Project NOAH. The politicians were really concerned about global warming and felt it would be useful to know how bad the weather changes might be in the future and if flooding would happen while they were still in office. The meeting had obviously come to its useful end, and out-of-town attendees began to shuffle toward their coats, murmuring about having to catch the only flight that could yet get them home that day.

Leon thanked everyone, obviously glad not to have to continue into the controversial area broached by Meriwether, one which did not show the project in a good light. As he left, Meriwether handed both Roger and Leon his rainbow-colored business card and, with a pleasant good-bye, indicated he had a few open hours for consulting if needed in the next several months.

Roger went back to his office and wondered if Meriwether was right and if their problem was in the improper modeling of the energy flows resulting from greenhouse effects. He went over Meriwether's arguments, looking for a hole somewhere but couldn't find one. They could find out by changing the model to be compatible with Meriwether's approach, but that would never happen because it would be outside their resources. His thoughts were rudely interrupted by Michelle stating that Leon had reconvened the meeting he had just come from for all in-house attendees, and he would have to leave immediately to arrive on time.

Leon came right to the point. "I didn't want to air our dirty linen in public, but Meriwether seems to have made a good point we can't afford to ignore. I would like to hear first from our in-house climatologists on what they make of Meriwether's position."

The scientists looked around at each other, none wanting to be the first to speak. The branch chief in charge of satellite temperature mapping finally spoke, "Well, having a proper energy distribution due to the greenhouse effect should certainly improve the model. But, based on our original studies, which didn't show it to be important, I can't imagine it would make enough difference to account for our present discrepancies.

Still, it is true that there are nonlinear effects involved that don't yield to simple analysis." This generality broke the ice, and the others chimed in. Most felt that at least no harm could result in changing the model this way but to expect improvement was unlikely.

Leon nodded and said, "Are there any other bright suggestions? I didn't notice any of you making any earlier." No one said anything.

Leon then turned to Roger. "How long would it take to put Meriwether's suggestion into the model?"

Roger knew that the question was coming and was able to respond immediately. "It will take roughly four thousand lines of code to change the program and then three months to get it debugged, checked out and running as well as what we have today. What really worries me is that the run time for a year's simulation will take a week of computer run time, ten times longer than at present." Roger knew his answer would not be acceptable to Leon.

And he was right. Leon responded with, "Get your staff together tomorrow and see what they think can be done in a month. That's all the time there is. Also I want to see you meet our original goal of being able to run a five-year simulation in no more than twelve computer run hours." He ended the meeting by walking out the door.

The next day, Roger met with his team and agreed on how to change the model. Since the tropics were not heated as much as assumed, more absorbed energy must be going into evaporating tropical seawater which was then being carried to the North Atlantic, mainly as rain. The model evaporated amount was to be increased to a level where a balance of energy was achieved. One of the experts pointed out that at that level, the gravity pump driving the warm-water circulation from the gulf would probably not be working, and any current flow was likely due to momentum only. It was agreed that the energy of the current momentum as well as the heat of radioactivity from the earth's core would also be included in the energy balance.

Chapter 3

The Next Glacial Period

It had been a hard three and a half weeks, but Roger felt that the worst was over as they incorporated Meriwether suggestions. They did a more thorough energy balance of the energy received from the sun, the energy stored in earth, air, and water, and the energy reradiated to outer space. They then confirmed that more energy than they had previously allowed for was being used to evaporate tropical seawater, which was being transported to the North Atlantic. The tropics were then cooler in temperature, and furthermore, the additional heat given off when this additional vapor condensed into water and snow in the Polar Regions made the Polar Regions warmer.

The significant increase in precipitation from water vapor moved to the North Atlantic, so diluted the ocean water that the downward pumping action of sinking dense water was no longer active to energize the motion of the ocean currents of which the "Gulf Stream" was a part. That the currents still flowed was entirely due to the mechanical momentum of the great mass of the ocean current that was equal to five hundred large surface rivers and wound itself around the earth nearly twice. It was uncertain how many years this current would continue to flow and transport heat to the northern regions, but when it finally wound down, the transformation to a glacial cold period would be complete. Even the summers would be cold enough in the northern regions than any vapor condensed as snow or ice would not melt, but rather would add to the thickness of the ice.

The team had also come up with some real software innovations that made meeting Leon's demands within reach. George Noble, Roger's supervisor for requirements, had reviewed all the specifications they had previously been working to and found many were over specified for the amount of error contributed. Redistributing the error budget allowed great reductions in the computation load in many critical areas, greatly speeding up the run time. Martin Valdez, his chief for the coding section, had introduced the new code in what a purist would claim was highly inelegant, but nevertheless minimized the changes to the existing code. This had resulted in a reduced code, debug, and check-out cycle. Lucille Van Brunt, his supervisor for computer operations and support, using the good-old-girl grapevine, had located another computer operation in the science and technology department which was temporarily short of work, and agreed to have their personnel used as a second shift on the NOAH simulations.

There were still patches in the code and places needing some cleanup which would happen with the next assembly run, but Roger was confident that he had a good operational program. He and Fred Willow, his deputy, were looking at the results of the last three two-year weather simulation runs. In strong contrast to the work of the previous month, the new runs almost perfectly straddled the actual weather records for the same period. In fact, the correlation with the actual records was better than the specified requirements. Stated mathematically, all parameters were within the design tolerances greater than 80 percent of the time.

As the fourth run came to its end, and the results were displayed and printed out, Fred said to Roger. "If I had this as a private weather service and also had a little investment capital, I could be a billionaire in just a few years, investing in the futures markets."

Roger responded, "Yeah, but that will never happen. When this thing is checked out a little further, NOAA will go public with all its long-range forecasts so that everyone can benefit, including the rest of the world. Just think, you will be able, six months ahead of time, to make reservations at a ski resort and not be disappointed with a warm spell. Governments and others will know when to buy grain ahead of time to avoid shortages and high prices due to drought periods and crop failures. Even planning for severe hurricane damage could be done six months or more in advance."

It was still hard for Fred to believe all such advances would soon be accepted as commonplace even though he had been on the project almost from the beginning. Reaching the end of the tunnel had always seemed to be in the distant future, and actually being there was just beginning to sink in. He turned to Roger and asked, "Does Leon know where we are?"

Roger grunted, "Yeah."

"What about on up the line? Do you think that the administrator knows?"

"Nope," Roger said, "While Leon gave us a one-month deadline, he probably really had three months from his boss before a cutoff would have been implemented. I don't know exactly. Leon never tells you something he doesn't have to. If I know Leon, though, he will have saved at least half the time he had as a cushion to be sure everything is right before any word goes on up the chain."

Fred gave Roger a sidelong glance and said almost to himself, "Then we have at least a month during which we could play the market."

Larry laughed. "One month is probably not long enough for Project NOAH results to give you a clear-cut advantage. Some investors are using private weather services, which over only a month's time are nearly as good."

"But," Fred went on, "we could run the program out into the future for, say, five years and make some sound long-term investments."

Roger had to agree. "Yes, that would certainly be stacking the odds in your favor, but if it ever came out, the situation is probably covered by the Insider Trader Laws, and you would probably end up in jail." Fred looked crushed.

Privately Roger decided that it was time to tighten up security on Project NOAH, with limited access as well as automated logging of system use to prevent exactly the things Fred had been suggesting. It crossed Roger's mind briefly that something of the sort could already be happening. He trusted most of his staff but certainly had less confidence in the ethics of the people Lucille had borrowed. He knew them hardly at all, and no security clearances were required on the project.

Michelle came by with the message that Leon wanted a meeting with him at two o'clock that afternoon.

Roger wondered what the meeting was about because as he walked into Leon's office, Leon first carefully looked outside his door and then closed it carefully.

"Please tell me where we are right now," he said.

"Since we talked last," Roger said, "we have made one more two-year run with comparable results to the others. The statisticians in the research branch say that our runs couldn't come closer to the real weather by more than 1 percent even if they were perfect because of the random events in the real world as well as the random events we insert into the simulations. So, in effect, we are within our tolerance limits on all parameters 82 percent of the time.

"Having a true energy balance and getting all sources of fresh water going into the North Atlantic right with better simulation of the effects of the ocean currents seems to have done the trick." His voice trailed off as he saw that Leon was not listening but was thinking of something else.

Leon broke the long silence and moved to the real reason for the meeting. "Roger, before the end of the day, I want you to give my secretary a list of everybody who knows that we now have successful runs on the project. If there are others you're not sure about, but who might possibly know, I want their names on a second list. We can't go up the chain with this until we have done a thorough checking," he paused, "we can't stand a leak in the interim."

Roger asked, "What do you mean by 'thorough checking'?"

Leon said, "Our promise to Congress is to be able to predict the weather five years in advance, so we should run five-year simulations from the time good weather records were kept. 1920 should be about the time to start. We should have at least four runs for each five-year period."

"That will take nearly a month, even with our two shifts," Roger complained.

"That's how I came up with the number of runs," Leon smiled.

It seemed to Roger that the meeting had come to an end, and he started to get up, but Leon motioned Roger to stay. "About security," he said, "I guess the only way to avoid a leak is to assign a security classification to Project NOAH of 'Secret,' so treat it that way from now on."

"How can you do that?" Roger questioned. "The project was set up in the open, with no authorization for classification. No security clearances have been processed on any of the staff."

"Don't worry," Leon countered. "I'll talk to the administrative people, and I am sure they can work it out. In the bureaucracy, you can do a lot of things if you just know the right people." And that was the end of the meeting.

Three weeks later, Roger was back in Leon's office, this time with Fred and an array of charts showing the results of the concentrated work of the recent past. Roger was saying, "So you see that the conclusions of three weeks ago are borne out by all these additional runs except that we have a greater confidence factor. Also we have demonstrated a five-year capability. Except for duplicating these originals, we are ready to go public or, at least, go up the line with our success," Roger paused, but not as if he was finished.

"Well," Leon asked, "What else do you have?"

"We had time for a few extra runs before this meeting. Since the whole purpose of Project NOAH is to predict the climate in the future, we thought it would be very interesting to make runs into the future. Yesterday, on the first and second shifts, we made two back-to-back runs going ten years into the future."

Roger glanced at Fred who was staring at the wall. Roger continued, "Look at these graphs of the pertinent parameters. They represent a classic transition into a glacial period. Within two years, field crops will not be able to be grown in Canada or northern Europe. In five years, the crop line will have moved south to the Missouri-Arkansas border and down into the northern Mediterranean countries in Europe. Almost no food at all will be grown in Russia, except in the southern Ukraine, and you notice that all of Northern China is also affected. And it doesn't stop there. That is just the first five years."

Leon finally just said, "That's impossible!"

Roger responded, wishing it weren't true, "It's not only possible, but what will actually happen, at least in the broad picture. We made these last two runs with exactly the same program as we made the others that matched the actual weather so well. The only difference was the starting dates. The second five-year run, of course, did not have real world initial conditions, but the statisticians say that would make only a few percent differences in the results in the second five-year run."

Leon could think of nothing to say, so Roger continued. "I'm sure you don't know it, but one of my hobbies when I have any extra time is the glacial period climate. The simulation transition to a glacial period fits the records we have of past transitions. On an average, a glacial period lasts one hundred thousand years, and then there is an inter glacial period, a warm period, that lasts maybe ten thousand years. There seems to be no agreement as to what causes the switch between one and the other, but lake sediments now indicate that the transition can take only a couple of decades. The climate switches quickly. It takes a long time to build up the ice caps and glaciers. The present warm period started about eleven thousand years ago, so actually on averages we are overdue. The transition periods are marked by wild swings in the weather, just what we have been seeing. Some climatologists have estimated that with our present agricultural systems, the earth, when it really gets into a full glacial period, will only support a few billion people." On that note, Roger fell silent.

It took another minute for Leon to come out of his shock and start thinking like a good bureaucrat. "How many people know about this?"

"Just we three," Roger said.

Somewhat relieved, Leon continued his questioning. "Is this all the data?"

"There is some more locked in my desk," Roger said. "We copied the system data onto hard disks and dumped the hot data.

The operations crew knows the dates we were running but not the results. When we saw how the runs were going, we kept the data from being added to the database."

"You did well," Leon said with obvious relief. "Bring me the rest of the data, and I am locking it all up for now, classified 'Top Secret,' access on a need-to-know basis only. For the time being, I don't want any more runs made. If this were to get out and be believed, it would be dynamite. We could have mobs in the streets, and governments would fall."

Roger said, "But shouldn't something be done? People need to be warned . . ."

Leon interrupted. "Yes, of course. But the timing has to be right. The people will have to be prepared so that there is no panic. We will have to be very careful how we go with this. I will think about it and figure out where in the government the key people are who need to be brought in first." Leon had almost forgotten that Roger and Fred were there in his preoccupation with the political opportunities the situation presented. Maybe a special new department would be created to deal with the catastrophe. Who else better qualified than himself? The meeting was obviously over, and Roger and Fred left without saying anything more.

When Roger got back to his office, Michelle gave him a message that Dr. Meriwether had called and had requested he be called back. Roger decided that since Meriwether had steered them in the right direction, he certainly owed him a call, even, in spite of the security invoked by Leon, if he couldn't say anything.

"Hello, Dr. Meriwether," he said when he got him back, "what can I do for you?"

Dr. Meriwether replied heartily, "I presume putting in the energy balance, the actual vapor transfers and ocean currents fixed your program?"

Roger said nothing.

"Oh," Meriwether went on, "So you aren't allowed to talk about it. It doesn't surprise me a bit. I've been dealing with bureaucrats for years, and I figured if they got something significant, they would classify it. Have you run into the coming glacial period yet?"

Roger blurted out, "What do you mean?"

Meriwether laughed. "Well, if your program is any good, and you have run it some years into the future, I would expect you would find that we are in a transition into a glacial period, and so you would know when it is going to affect life on the planet in a major way. There are a number of us independent climatologists who think a glacial period is coming soon. We just don't know when. I had hoped you would tell me."

Again Roger had nothing to say.

Dr. Meriwether then finished the conversation with, "I predict that before long, you will be asked to make differential analyses with your program. I'm very good at setting those up, so if I can help, please get in touch with me." With that, he hung up. Roger told no one about the call.

CHAPTER 4

The Russian Bombshell

Ray Carr, deputy chief of staff to President Morgan, sat in the anteroom of the oval office, waiting for his first meeting that morning. It was unusually early for a meeting with the President, and none of the regular Whitehouse staffers were about yet. It was certainly not usual to be called for a meeting with the President before breakfast, although Ray was used to unusual things with the President, his lifelong friend.

Ray was the queen-piece of Morgan's staff, to use a chess term. Ray had no regular assignments and actually never stood in for George Sherwood, Morgan's regular chief of staff. There was in fact another deputy who did the normal things expected of a regular deputy. Sherwood never gave Ray any assignments; Ray always worked directly under the President. It was understood by those close to the President that Ray was Morgan's man to do whatever or go wherever the President needed him to for very high priority purposes, those the President could not handle himself. For those in the know, Ray spoke for the President and could commit the President when he felt it was necessary. Without exception, the President had always backed any action Ray had taken. Had he not done so, Ray's value would have been compromised. Their close bond went back to college, and each trusted the other absolutely.

This relationship was well guarded, and to the public and the press, Ray was just another member of Morgan's staff, just another of the many trappings of the bureaucracy, someone with an obscure position about whom no one cared. Ray liked it that way. It gave him room to maneuver.

Ray began to realize that something really important was up as he noted the other attendees who that had collected so far. Basil Harwood, head of the CIA; General Wiley Brooks, of the Joint Chiefs of Staff; Ulysses Gonzalez, head of the arms reduction negotiating team; Bull Adams, Secretary of State; Paul Cummings, secretary of defense; Lynda Smith of the defense communications agency (DCA); and Wayne Turley, Secretary of the recently created Department of Science and Technology.

As the group was ushered into the Oval Office, Ray began to think that perhaps something had happened to derail the upcoming summit with the Russians on arms reductions. Ray was aware that, with the dissolution of their communist empire decades ago, the Russians still did not appear realistic about reducing their military forces, still hoping to influence their neighbors with shows of force even if they were no longer welcome. Certainly the fact that the meeting had been called on almost no notice implied some sudden, unexpected developments. As Gil Powers of the Office of the Management and Budget came in, the President's office secretary, Marty, returned with quickly pulled together coffee and sweet rolls. The coffee seemed freshly brewed, but Ray thought that the rolls were probably left over from the previous day. Most had not had time for breakfast and ate the rolls anyway.

As security finished making a sweep of the office, Marty announced that the President was coming, and everyone stood up as President Robert Morgan entered. He quickly asked everyone to be seated and moved around behind his desk but remained standing. President Morgan was a tall and commanding figure, characteristics that had been very helpful in winning the past election. As was his normal way, he began the meeting immediately and got right to the point.

"Earlier today, at approximately 9:00 a.m. Moscow time, our Ambassador, Will Commons, was called to a private meeting with the Russian Prime Minister, Ivan Petrovich. He was given a written message to convey to the US government, to which an answer is required in three days. I will ask Bull to read the message, because Will called it to him by scrambler phone. Bull took it down in his own handwriting, which only he can read. Bull." The President smiled as if at a private joke, which in actuality it was, since Bull's handwriting was excellent.

The President sat down as Bull pulled his notes from an inner pocket. Apologizing, he said, "The original given to Will was plaintext English, most unusual. When compared to previous notes from the Russian Prime Minister, it's clear it was drafted by the Petrovich himself. I read it back to Will over the phone twice to be sure that it is exactly correct." The letter Bull proceeded to read consisted of five numbered paragraphs:

My friend, President Morgan,

1. I am using this form of communication, considering the urgency of this matter as you will see, and the need for utmost secrecy.
2. Since you started Project NOAH, the Russian services have had what they tell me is a computer tap on your project. Even between friendly nations, which I hope we are, we would not normally admit such a tap. What is that old saying of your State Department? "Gentlemen read not each other's mail?" Our scientists have been able to recreate all your data runs, including those classified secret and top secret. It is a puzzle to us why there has been no activity for the past few weeks on your project after such a great discovery. Without independent confirmation of your Project NOAH, we couldn't take action for fear of being wrong.
3. As the leader of a responsible major power, I have, of course, for some time ordered that the Russians should also have our project which we call Project ARARAT. Without your fast computers, our project has been slow and less ample, but we have made steady progress. Just yesterday, I was informed that our independent researchers have come to the same conclusions as your Project NOAH, except that we have, of course, more

interest in the detailed damage to be expected to the Russian homeland and our neighbors.

4. In view of this great threat, the differences in the positions of our two countries to be talked about in our summit meeting are no longer important to us. The Russian Republic accepts all of your proposals, and ours are hereby withdrawn. I suggest at the summit that our assistants work out all the details on all items on the arms-reduction agenda for our signatures. I understand that, for your side, your Senate will have to approve, but since we are conceding all your proposals, surely that will happen.

5. As for you and me at the summit, I propose that we talk only about your NOAH and my ARARAT, and the actions we should agree on as the world's major atomic powers. Surely between us, we should be able to see how survival is possible.

Your friend, Ivan Petrovich

While normally a much disciplined group, comments were immediately forthcoming from nearly everybody.

"Gentlemen, gentlemen, please, let's have an orderly meeting." As relative quiet returned, the President continued, "Our first item of priority is to find out something about this Project NOAH of ours. Is there anyone who has any information?" He was greeted with silent stares. President Morgan turned toward the Secretary for Science and Technology, "Wayne, the sense of the letter implies that Project NOAH is a scientific matter. Does it ring any bells?"

"President Morgan, you know I have only begun to digest all the cats and dogs that were pulled together to form my department. In the process, so far I can't remember coming across anything called NOAH. I presume it is NOAH and not NOAA, the National Oceans and Atmospheric Administration?"

Secretary Adams nodded. "I thought of that during the phone call from Will and made a specific point to be sure."

President Morgan then took the lead again. "There aren't too many government bodies authorized to classify anything 'top secret.' That alone should narrow things down."

The head of the CIA said, "I regularly review the list of every CIA top-secret project in the shop, and NOAH is not one of them." The DCA chief, the secretary of defense, and head of the Joint Chiefs made similar comments.

Suddenly Will Powers of OMB came to life. "Wait a minute. I seem to remember an item in the budget that the Department of Science and Technology carried over from Commerce, specifically NOAH, yeah, Project NOAH. Its name was supposed to be a pun on the great flood. This one was forced on us by Congress for the past five years. I never heard that they had achieved anything useful, just wasting money, and five million a year at that. You know the environmentalists are worried about the global warming effect and eventual flooding of the coastal areas. Something to worry about, I suppose, if you have to be elected every two years. Probably won't happen in a hundred years, something this administration doesn't need to take seriously. I think this was a job to simulate the climate changes coming as the result of the hypothetical global warming, nothing that we can seriously plan to do anything about, but with a project like this going, we and the Congress can claim we are concerned." Will ran down and turned quiet.

Secretary Cummings injected, "It must be a rogue classification, if it is part of NOAA, NOAA is supposed to be unclassified. We and the military don't use the same weather satellites just for that reason. This is truly amazing."

President Morgan decided that it was time to reassert his leadership. "Gentlemen, we have apparently gone as far as we can for the moment in locating where Project NOAH is in the government. Why don't we adjourn and reconvene at nine thirty, and I'm sure by then that we can have an appropriate member of Project NOAH give us a briefing."

As the group filed out of the Oval Office, Marty came in, and the President gave her instructions on contacting NOAA for a one-hour briefing to be held later that morning.

Using her directory of federal organizations, Marty worked her way down from secretary to secretary in the NOAA organization. She soon got the impression that nobody worked there until she got to Michelle, Roger's secretary. What Marty didn't know was that most of the NOAA managers belonged to the same skiing club and were off in Vermont for a week. This included Leon, who had used his inside information to pick a particularly good week for the skiing club.

Michelle told Marty that her boss, Roger Foreman, probably knew just about everything there was to know about Project NOAH and would be the right person to make the desired briefing. "Great," Marty said, "Please put him on." It was only eight-thirty in the morning, and Roger was having coffee with his staff. Since Leon had shut down the operation a few weeks before, there hadn't been much to do but sit around and gossip. Roger and Fred had talked a number of times about Leon apparently doing nothing, but what could they do about it? Everyone knew that generally unpleasant things happened to whistle blowers.

Suddenly Roger's secretary appeared. "Roger," she almost screamed, "President Morgan's secretary, a Marty something or other, is on line six for you. She says the President has asked for a one-hour presentation on Project NOAH for this morning at nine thirty."

All four coffee drinkers said, "What?" in unison, and Roger picked up the phone. "This is Roger Foreman speaking."

Marty repeated what she had already told Michelle and then asked, "Are you the right person to make the presentation?"

Roger answered, "I think so. Everyone else that might do it is away skiing."

Marty then explained, "The President particularly wants a review of the parts of the project classified secret and top secret."

Roger flinched. "I'm afraid all the classified information is locked up in a file, and the only person with access to it is in Vermont."

While Marty took time out to digest that information, Lucille, Roger's operations manager, grabbed his arm and whispered, "The system automatically makes backup copies of every run. We can duplicate and print out in presentation form data from any run you ever made."

Marty came back on the line, and Roger said, "We apparently have an alternate source for the data you want. Thinking about the logistics of getting it ready, we will be hard-pressed to make it at nine thirty."

Marty signed off with, "Do your best. I'll send over a limousine to get you here, and remember, the ten most powerful people in the government will be waiting for you."

Roger first sent Fred back to his office to get together all the background charts they had used in the brainstorming meeting several months earlier. Then he sat down with Lucille, and they agreed on the charts she would pull off the backup files, first the ones that showed the excellent correlation between the five-year runs and the actual weather experience, starting with the year 1920. Last were to be the charts that projected the climate for the next ten years.

Lucille said, "Before Leon shut things down, we were all kind of interested to find out what was going to happen, so we ran ten more years into the future. No one said not to do it. You want that too?"

Grimly Roger asked, "What happens?"

Lucille shivered. "It just gets colder and then stabilizes out."

"OK," Roger nodded. "If you can get it all done in time. By the way, who else knows?"

Lucille said, "All the regular computer operating staff. Everybody ought to know what we are facing."

Roger responded, "I suppose they told their families?"

She shrugged, "I don't know, but if I were married, I'm sure I would have. After all, it isn't every day you get a probable death sentence to be carried out in about three years."

A short while later, with the presentation charts in briefcases, Roger and Fred went out the front lobby and found the limousine waiting that Marty had promised. Meanwhile, at the Oval Office, the group that had met earlier was reconvening. As time passed, they began to exchange nervous glances. Only Ray Carr and the President seemed relaxed and composed. The

President called Marty on his intercom. "When do you estimate they will be here?"

"The limousine driver just called in," she answered. "Right now they are about three minutes away. I'll go down and pass them through security."

When she got down to the side entrance, Roger and Fred were already getting the once-over by a burley guard who, ignoring their NOAA IDs, was insisting that they needed special security documentation for access to the Whitehouse. Marty, who in practical matters was probably the second most powerful person in the government, intervened immediately. "Ron," she said to the guard, "The President is waiting impatiently for these two. Sign them in, and I'll escort them."

Ron, who was quite familiar with the pecking order in the Whitehouse, and had no desire to draw guard duty at some remote military installation, complied immediately. By nine forty, Marty delivered her charges and sat down in the back of the room.

President Morgan said, "I am having Marty record this meeting, and I think she can best integrate the audio with the visual aids by being present." He then turned to Fred, "If you have hard copies, please give Marty one." He then had Roger and Fred introduced themselves, and he also introduced every one else present. "Please proceed, it's your show."

Roger opened with, "If you have any very technical questions related to a particular chart, please ask them when that chart is being projected. If we are going to limit this to an hour, please hold your general questions to the end. Without any questions or discussion, this should take forty-five minutes."

The President then said,

"Roger, before you go into the details of our immediate crisis, could you give us some background on climate variations in general?" Roger was very thankful he was a student of climatology and would be able to talk extensively on the subject without prepared notes.

"Yes, sure, Mr. President. In its long history, the earth has gone through long periods of extended warmth, with no ice at the poles and also periods of extreme cold where the ice at the poles was so extensive that the ocean levels were several hundred feet lower than at present. A big driver was the shapes of the land masses and their relationship to each other.

"Several million years ago, the continents became located in a unique configuration with land at one pole, and not the other, and oriented such as to be nearly balanced between warm and cold. The balance was so close that the earth since then has been switching back and forth between the two conditions about every 100,000 years, with 10,000 years on the warm side and the other 100,000 years on the cold side. The dominant time is called a glacial period, and the shorter time in between is called an inter glacial period, and so far, there have been eleven cycles of this swinging back and forth. A feature of the glacial age is that the North and South American continents have been connected with a land bridge which prevents the exchange of ocean water between the Atlantic Ocean and the Pacific Ocean. The Asian and North American continents have been connected with a land bridge at the middle of a 100,000-year glacial period but open water during interglacial times. Scientists consider the cause of the oscillation to be the geometry of the earth's orbit, which, over a 100,000 years period favors warm or cold conditions largely affecting the Northern Hemisphere where most of the land areas are."

Roger paused at that point, allowing questions, and getting none, continued, "Since the earth is in such a delicate balance between warm and cold, although favoring cold, that apparently a number of things might trigger the climate to the other condition. Because of this delicate balance, there are many theories about what might cause a switch. If the normal end of a period is being approached, the trigger event might to be very slight. Also because of positive feedback factors, once the gulfstream current stops, it is hard to start it again due to momentum, so switching outside the normal periods is not likely.

"It is realistic to be concerned, and why the NOAH program was initiated, because we have been in an interglacial period for eleven thousand years, a thousand years past a normal switch-back time to a glacial period. Factors most related to switching between glacial and interglacial are global temperature, atmospheric carbon dioxide, and ocean salinity in the North Atlantic and how they interact. A random occurrence, such a volcanic eruption or a large comet strike, could of itself trigger a switch if the other factors are favorable.

"The purpose of Project NOAH, of course, was to model the factors in a way that allows a prediction of when the switch is likely to occur sufficiently in advance to allow possible modification of the oncoming climate change or at the least to prepare for it."

Roger next went to the goals of Project NOAH and their early efforts to put together a computer, complex with enough speed and memory to tackle the job of accurately simulating the world climate. He covered some of the breakthroughs they had made in the group handling of weather cells, the variable cell size as a function of rates of change of parameters, and other innovative factors, without which they would have been unsuccessful.

With charts, he illustrated the simulation problems, which led to the brainstorming session. He spent some time on Meriwether's suggestion that the greenhouse effect was largely operative in the tropics, in spite of popular opinion to the contrary. There were questions at that point since President Morgan's staff held the popular view. Roger pointed out that the greenhouse effect would not cause melting of the polar ice caps for more than a short period of time rather more likely the reverse since more heat was absorbed in the tropics where more water was then evaporated and eventually transported in the form of snow to the polar regions.

To demonstrate the validity of the NOAH simulations, Roger next showed the five-year charts, comparing the simulation runs with the actual weather records. The actual records, plotted in red, very closely followed the simulation runs, which were plotted in blue. Roger then explained that each simulation run contained unique random events which accounted for the fact that each one was slightly different from every other one. Turley wanted an explanation of what random events were, and Roger explained that they were mostly volcanic actions.

"You see," Roger said, "we need to know the variability of our predictions due to random events which do occur in nature, mainly the output of dust from volcanoes. We wanted to see the sensitivity of the climate to these things. For example, the chart we are showing now, run two, has a volcanic event of size two inserted at six months into the run. You notice that for this run, the weather is generally colder for two years after the event than the actual weather record."

Basil Harwood then said, "The accuracy of your simulations looks like it would be good enough to tell farmers exactly when to plant, or in some cases, not to plant at all if a very bad drought were coming. I noticed that the simulations predicted the dust-bowl days very well."

"Yes," replied Roger, "it is good enough for that. In fact, the data you have seen is based on no updates in five years. For farming purposes, you would, of course, have yearly updates and get slightly better predictions."

Gil Powers of OMB asked the last question at that point. "Is NOAH good enough to replace our expensive and not-always-reliable weather satellites?"

"No," laughed Roger. "You can't beat predicting that it is going to snow in Detroit on Monday, when it is already snowing hard in Chicago on Sunday and with the weather front moving eastward. That is weather forecasting. What NOAH is all about is climate prediction, something much more long-term."

At that point, Wiley Brooks of the Joint Chiefs brought the meeting back to a more somber tone with, "So far, you haven't told us anything that would have greatly upset the Russians."

The President immediately interjected. "Roger, there is a Russian angle to this which you will be briefed on after this meeting, but for now, please go on with what you have to tell us."

Roger was mystified by the reference to the Russians, but as a good soldier continued, "With no changes to the simulation programs, we next made runs into the future, twenty years altogether, actually. When you run into the future, you can't, of course, do updates, some divergence is inevitable. Based on the historical runs, however, no significant divergence would be expected in twenty years. By significant, I mean, it would be smaller than the effects caused by random events. Random events will hasten or delay trends but generally not eliminate them.

"The runs of the future were very limited because the management put everything on hold and classified the results top secret. Based on the prior close conformance of the simulations to reality, we have very high confidence that these runs are accurate. These next four charts show the climate changes to come in five-year segments. Note the red lines which represent the demarcation zone each summer, north of which the snow cover does not completely melt. There are corresponding green lines for the southern hemisphere. For the next few years, these northern lines shift toward the equator two hundred miles per year. On the five-to-ten-year run, as shown on this next chart, you may note that the rate of movement has slowed. On the next chart, you can see that by the twelfth year, it has stabilized, and the climatic transition to the next glacial period is complete. Of course, it will take thousands of years for a heavy ice cap to build up, but as far as growing crops is concerned, the glacial period will be here."

The President mused out loud, "So we only have a few years to do anything if anything can be done."

Roger responded, "It is really worse than it looks from these charts. On this next set, I have shown what happens agriculturally. What really count are how late your last spring frost is and how early your first fall frost is. Based on that, these next charts show where current crops will no longer be grown. Note, that for practical purposes, most of Canada will not produce viable crops by only a year or two from now. The crop line moves quickly down the United States, so that in seven years, half of the United States will be too cold, and by the twelfth year, when things have stabilized, few existing crops will be grown in the United States."

George Sherwood said, "You are using the term 'existing crops.' Could you define that for us?"

Roger explained, "We used in our simulations crops presently planted in particular areas, such as corn in Iowa, wheat in Kansas, cotton in Texas. By going to crops with a shorter maturation time for a year or two, we might be able to squeeze out a better crop on a temporary basis."

With no more immediate questions, Roger went on. "Well, of course, it is just as bad for much of the rest of the world. As you can see in a few years, most of northern Europe will be unable to feed itself. Russia will be down to 50 percent of their present crop yield in only two years. It takes longer in China, but as you can see, only Southeast Asia is spared, and even there, some rice areas will be reduced to growing less-preferred crops. India is a question mark. The monsoons will definitely be increased, but most of that precipitation will be as snow in the Himalaya Mountains. Whether there will be enough melting in the Himalayas to keep the north-Indian irrigation system going wasn't dealt with in the model."

Cummings asked, "What about the Southern Hemisphere, agriculturally?"

Roger then said as he put up the next sequence of charts. "This is one of the brighter spots in an otherwise pretty grim picture. Because it contains a larger percentage of the world's water and land doesn't get close to the South Pole, the Southern Hemisphere is affected significantly less. This chart shows pretty much an end to the transition by the twelfth year, and you notice that almost all of southern Africa and South America are ice-free. There will be shifts in where the rain falls, however, so some productive areas will become deserts, and other areas will have an excess of moisture. Much of Australia will remain free of ice, and the increased monsoons there will actually increase the area of potential crop lands. Monsoons, however, are a tricky source of precipitation, because you get them irregularly and unevenly spaced."

Finished with his prepared presentation, Roger paused and waited for any more questions. There were none immediately, because his audience was trying to grasp what they had just been told, as well as the implications. Roger decided to volunteer, some of his recent thoughts.

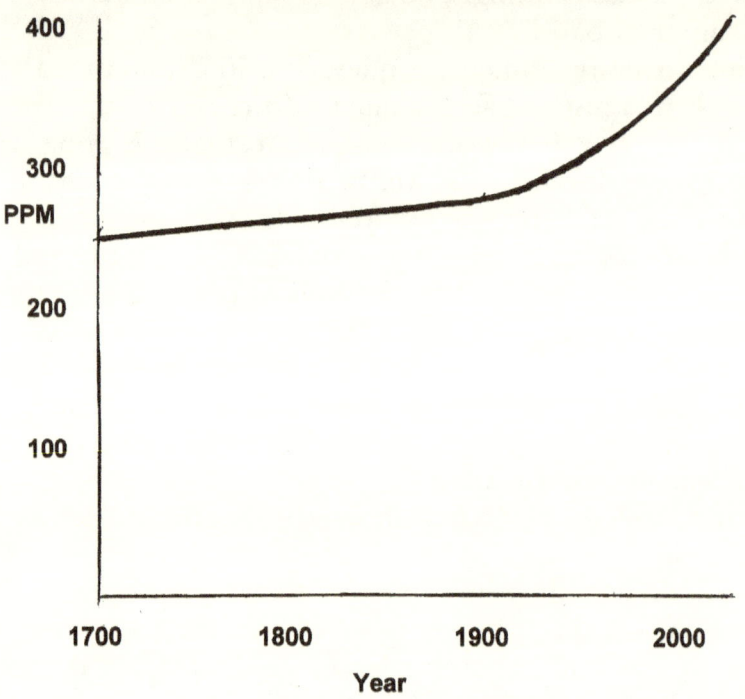

Atmospheric CO$_2$ (ppm) Verses Year

"With rising temperature and CO$_2$ there are three outcomes that the climatologists favor:

1. A complete shift out of the glacial age to a long-term warming age where all the ice melts and the oceans rise several hundred feet to flood all coastal plains.
2. A switch in the glacial age from an interglacial period to a glacial period, initially warming to transfer enough water vapor to coat the polar regions with snow and ice and passing the tipping point, so a reversal takes at least 100,000 years, or so.
3. A start in the switch to a glacial period, but not yet past the tipping point where it is not reversible.

"I personally am convinced we are not going into a long-term warming age because there are no geological changes identified which would indicate a pattern other than the glacial age is changing to its other period. Also NOAH simulations indicate a shift to a glacial period but remaining in the glacial age. At this point it is not clear whether we are past the tipping point or how severe the next glacial period will be."

President Morgan was the first to break the silence when it was apparent Roger was finished. "The implications of this scenario, if they come about, are awesome." Facing the whole group, he said, "I have to excuse myself for an hour. While I am gone, would you as a group try to summarize the major implications so we can formulate what is required to be done by this government. Ray, will you take over until I get back?" Ray nodded.

Ray first looked at Roger and Fred. "You two have been thinking about this for some time. Want to give us anymore of your conclusions?"

Roger picked up the ball first. "Well, the fundamental problem will be the shortage of food. In a worst-case scenario, if nothing is changed, there can be food grown for about 50 percent of the present world population."

Fred chimed in. "Yeah, with so much starvation facing the world, you can expect the have-nots to attack those who are better off, probably with atomic weapons if they have them. I imagine there will be riots and chaos as soon as the general public knows what is coming."

Wayne Turley, who had been looking thoughtful, said, "Under severe weather conditions, if we are to survive at all, we will have to devote a much greater percentage of our resources to the growing of food, in greenhouses, and the like. Obviously, we will have to convert our present wasteful society to one emphasizing survival. Luxury and pleasure activities will have to be curtailed, if not eliminated completely."

General Wiley was next. "What I see as a real problem is that, if some of the world's countries start falling apart, some very frightening weapons may come into the hands of terrorists and war lords. I don't see any easy answer to prevent that." Then he added, "If we can get through that turmoil, a significant portion of the world's population will need to be relocated."

Turley had another observation. "Apparently, there is no answer to preventing a reversion to a cold glacial period unless we can drastically reduce the carbon dioxide in the atmosphere. To even start a reduction, we will have to drastically cut the burning of fossil fuels and replant the trees that humanity is currently cutting at frightful rate." Roger then put up a chart showing atmospheric CO_2 versus year for three hundred years.

Gil Powers had a keen insight. "You are talking about doing things that in the real world of politics and special interests probably are impossible to do, certainly in a short time period. Our present governmental organization is not geared to act quickly, not in the general interests of humanity."

The observations continued on in a similar manner, and at the end of forty-five minutes, Ray called it to a halt. "All right, we are beginning to repeat ourselves. I think I have summarized on paper what we have been saying in five major points. We'll have Marty type them up on a chart for the President to look at when he comes back."

They were just starting to discuss Ray's chart when the President returned.

Implications of the Coming Glacial Cold Period

1. There will be enough food grown for less than 50 percent of the world's present population based on the present system of agriculture. There will be even less for a growing population. There will be major dislocations of major populations.
2. Mankind as a species will survive if the planet is not destroyed in fighting over the remaining food supply.
3. The present wasteful civilization must come to an end to be replaced by one emphasizing survival, probably served by a world government.

4. Democracy will be greatly curtailed. In a survival civilization, everyone will have to do what is required, just to survive. A world-wide totalitarian government has the best prospects of maximizing the carrying capacity of the planet, making sure that those that have, share with those that don't.
5. As present world political institutions fail and areas of the world go into chaos, the tools of war, falling into unscrupulous hands, will pose a frightful risk to the world's population.

The President frowned when he came to point 4. "Curtailing our traditional political and economic freedoms will be very hard for our people to take. It also looks like there will be a lot of sacrifice that we will be asking of the public. Do you really think it will be necessary, Ray? Traditionally, a world government has been hard to sell."

Ray answered. "We talked that over quite thoroughly while you were out. What we are eventually facing is the largest task that humanity has even attempted. Democracies are pretty good at maintaining the status quo, making progress slowly. They are notoriously poor at handling crises and rapid change. I don't suggest that you can sell it. You just have to present the country with an accomplished fact."

Roger sensed that the meeting was coming to a close and mused out loud, "I still hope we will find that somewhere we made a mistake about the coming ice age."

"No, Roger," the President said, "there is no mistake. Russia's Prime Minister has informed us that they too have a Project NOAH which they call ARARAT, and that it confirms all your predictions very closely."

"How could they know about our results? No copy of our data has left NOAA." Roger thought about the copy that was supposed to be locked up in Leon's safe. Leon was ambitious, but it would make no sense for him to give it to the Russians.

President Morgan interrupted Roger's thoughts. "The Russians say that they have had a tap on your computer from the beginning." Roger looked crestfallen.

Lynda Smith of DCA broke in, "Your computer wasn't set up as a secure system either physically or electronically, was it?"

"No," said Roger, "we just wanted the fastest computer possible with the most memory. Nothing was ever classified until recently."

Lynda concluded. "Well, then, for a good KGB operator, it would have been a piece of cake. They could have done it without even compromising anyone on your staff. With just a few minutes' access by an electrician, plumber, or cleaning person, they could have placed the tap, and you wouldn't have suspected a thing. We could probably find it easily, now that we know it is there, but it probably doesn't matter anymore."

Ray Carr had a question at this juncture. "How did it come about that the valid results were classified, and the success of the project was not announced to key elements of the government, particularly in view of the gravity of the conclusions?"

Roger felt uncomfortable answering, since it put Leon in a bad light, but he really had no choice. "Leon Strongfellow, our manager, did the classifying of the data and took what, at the time, I thought was all the data and kept them in his safe. If he ever mentioned anything to anyone above him, I am not aware of it. He said to me that he wanted to be sure of the results before going forward with them and also that he wanted to think about where in the government would be the right place to go. He would, of course, have been here today if he weren't skiing in Vermont."

President Morgan turned to Ray. "If there is no more to it than that, when Leon gets back, maybe we should offer him the option of early retirement." Ray made a note to talk to Leon.

The one-hour presentation had stretched to over two hours, and President Morgan turned to Roger and said, "Thank you for an excellent presentation. I've decided to create an ad hoc coordinating task force to direct the country's efforts during this crisis. Ray will be the chairman. Would you be willing to serve under Ray, representing the specialty of climatology?"

"Yes, certainly," Roger answered.

"And, Fred," the President continued, "can you keep the computers of Project NOAH running while Roger is up here?"

"You can bet on it," Fred answered.

"Very well," the President addressed the whole group, "we will locate the task force in the offices here in the Whitehouse that were vacated the last time we went through a 'lean and mean' operation. I want each department and agency that was represented in this meeting to designate a full-time member to serve on the coordination task force. You better pick carefully, because that person is hereby authorized to commit your organization. Ray, in the case of departments not represented today that will still be key players, such as Energy and Agriculture, will you contact the appropriate people and get a representative designated?"

Ray nodded.

The President continued, "I suggest that the task force convene at two-thirty this afternoon with the first agenda item being a replay of Roger's presentation. Next, each member should be given a copy of Prime Minister Petrovich's message. I suggest that the first output of the task force be a recommendation for a reply to the message, which is now due back in two days. The third task is to prepare options for me to take to the summit, which is scheduled one week from today in Naples. You also should probably think of precautionary measures the government should take in case word of any of this goes public. We can't sit on this very long. We ought to plan on a public announcement two days after the summit, hopefully including anything on which Prime Minister Petrovich and I agree. Let's make that a press conference here in Washington. Is there anything else? Oh, yes. Keep all of this very close to the chest until after the news conference. Whatever we do, we have to keep the public from panicking." The historic meeting suddenly came to its end.

CHAPTER 5

The Response

The letdown after the frantic morning didn't make itself felt on Roger until after Marty had arranged for him to have permanent access to the Whitehouse. Alone, looking for the office area President Morgan had mentioned, the enormity of what lay ahead began to creep over him. Was there really anything that could be done, and even if there were, how could humanity be motivated to do it?

Before he got very far with that line of thought, Ray came across him in the hall near the offices. "Roger, I've been looking for you. I held the limousine that is taking Fred back to NOAA so that you could go back with him. You won't have much to do here until midafternoon, but after that, I don't know when you'll get a break. Why don't you use the next couple of hours to move those things in your office that you will need over here so you will be able to operate efficiently. I'm sure we are not done looking at the climate simulations, and even though the computer complex is at NOAA, we will want to ask the questions from here. You might want to ask your people to see if they can put in a terminal for you here at the Whitehouse."

Looking ahead, Roger thought to ask Ray about utilizing Meriwether. "There is a climatologist who I think could help us a lot, the one that gave us the ideas that led to our breakthrough, Dr. Jim Meriwether. I think it would be very valuable to bring him aboard."

"Oh yes," Ray injected before Roger quite finished. "I've met him socially around Washington. If you think he can help, get hold of him right away, and if he's agreeable, get him set up in the office next to you. I won't know for a couple of days how and by whom everybody who is not already in the government is going to get paid, but with the urgency of the situation, that should be a small problem."

When Fred and Roger got back to NOAA, the limousine driver offered to take Roger back to the Whitehouse, but Roger told him he would need his own car and sent the driver back alone. As Roger and Fred got to their offices, all of the staff crowded around and wanted to know about their Whitehouse caper. Roger briefly said that they had just told it like it was, that for the time being he was moving over to the Whitehouse, and that Fred would temporarily be in charge of the project here at NOAA.

Roger took Lucille aside and made arrangements for her to get some of her technicians to set him up with a Project NOAH computer terminal in the Whitehouse. As they talked, Roger sensed that Lucille seemed to have changed in some undefined, subtle way. On a hunch, he suggested that they go to lunch at the cafeteria together. It would be about his last chance for lunch anywhere that day.

As they descended the stairs to the basement cafeteria, Roger was acutely aware of Lucille in a warm, personal way, not as just an associate. They had worked together for years, but he had never before wondered how he felt about her as a woman. While she worked for him, he had deliberately stayed away from the possibilities of a personal relationship. He had always had a strong code against dating in the office, particularly between boss and subordinate. He rationalized that now that she worked for Fred, he could think about her without his previously, self-imposed limitation.

As it occurred to Roger that maybe Lucille was thinking the same thoughts, Lucille said, "What do you think you will be doing now over at the Whitehouse?"

"Well, for starters," he said, "there are a lot of VIPs that need to be educated about the climate if they are going to make any rational decisions in the near future."

"I know," she responded, "but what real work are you going to do? I mean, is there anything we can do to change what the project has predicted will happen?"

They were selecting items from the salad bar, and Roger hoped that Lucille was a health-food nut like himself. He put his attention back on answering her question. "It is too early to tell. Leon shut us down before we could try varying single parameters at a time, things we might be able to control. I am looking for Meriwether to help there, and if we can get him aboard, we should have some things to try out on NOAH."

Most of the rest of the lunch was finished in silence, Roger thinking that is was very comfortable just to be with Lucille, not talking.

Back in the office, Roger called Dr. Meriwether and was gratified to find him in his office. Since Meriwether was to be brought into the task force, there was no point in continuing withholding information from him. "Dr. Meriwether, we made a presentation to President Morgan and his staff this morning on the climate predictions from the project, with the main conclusion that we are already in a transition to the next glacial period. The President has established a special task force to provide planning and recommend policy. You have met Ray Carr whom the President has named to lead this group. Ray would like to have you serve on the task force and, of course, so would I."

Meriwether said, "Before I agree, I would like to know what year your project says we will be in trouble."

"We are right at the point of trouble already," Roger said. "The simulations predict that we have probably already seen the last good crop that will be grown in Canada for a 100,000 years. Before twelve years, we will have trouble growing things in the United States. Convinced?"

"That soon?" was Meriwether's rejoinder. "Well, if it's that bad, there isn't much else I might do that's very important. Where to and when should I come over?"

"The first meeting of the task force is at two-thirty today at the Whitehouse in the office area. If you have any problems getting in, just ask for Marty, the President's secretary. She seems to run things. I'll tell her you are coming over." Roger hung up the phone.

Before saying hurried good-byes at NOAA, Roger spent a little time with Fred, talking about setting up the remote terminal in the Whitehouse and getting a dedicated voice line established so that they could have regular conferencing on a reliable basis. Roger also suggested to Fred that he have the project ready to make any special runs that Meriwether might suggest. With that, Roger hurried off to the Whitehouse where he was pleasantly surprised to find that a reserved parking spot went with his new assignment.

Ray had not been idle while Roger was away. He had already made arrangements for the task force to have the full-time use of one of the briefing rooms. Ray was already convening the task-force members who, with a few exceptions, were new faces who had not been present in the morning. Roger returned to the office area to drop off the things he had brought over from NOAA and pick up his briefing charts for the meeting. Dr. Meriwether was waiting for him, and they went off to the meeting together.

Ray called the meeting to order, and next he made sure that everyone was introduced. "How many of you," he asked, "have been told why you are here?" A show of hands indicated about 50 percent.

"Very well," he continued, "first, I want you to know that this is a highest possible priority task force, reporting directly to the President. For the foreseeable future, this is your only assignment. If you haven't already done so, turn over everything you have been doing to someone else in your department. I have directions from the President, and agreement with each of your bosses, that you will speak for your organizations and, when required, will make binding commitments on your organizations. If you don't feel this is already in place as of now, be sure it is by tomorrow morning. Any questions so far?"

Julia Warrens of CIA spoke up, "What about security?"

Ray said, "I was coming to that next. The really tight security period will be for the next ten days. We don't have time to set up a formal security program, and it would slow us down too much. You all have clearances from your parent organizations, and that will have to do. Don't say anything about the task force's business except to those you see in this room and any others I or the President may bring into these proceedings. You will, of course, need to talk to people in your parent organizations and direct them to act as required, but critical information should flow only in our direction. Work with individuals you have known to be discrete in the past."

"Now down to the real business of this group. We will be generating planning and policy material for use by President Morgan in dealing with the greatest challenge this country, any country, literally the whole planet, has ever faced. It is our plan to be working in close cooperation with the other great atomic power, Russia. To be successful, we must work more closely with the Russians than we have ever done with a present or past ally." Ray wanted the attention of the group, and with this last statement, he certainly had it.

Ray continued, "At this point, each of you will receive a copy of a communication we received from the Russian Prime Minister early this morning. Please take five minutes right after the copies are passed out to read the message. As a task force, our first goal will be to make recommendations regarding the response our government should make." As the copies were passed out, he added, "As you can see, as you read the message, you will need to know about Project NOAH, and that is the next item on our agenda. Roger, would you take five minutes and get set up for the presentation you gave the President this morning?"

Roger took out his charts and moved to the projector. Waiting for the five minutes to be up, he looked over the rest of the members of the task force. They looked like an aggressive, productive bunch. In almost all cases, they were the number two person from their organization. In the case of the Department of Defense, Paul Cummings had turned over the department to his number two man and appointed himself to the task force.

Being more familiar with the material, Roger found his presentation went much smoother than it had in the morning. He was, in fact, able to observe his audience for their reactions as he talked. There were fewer reactions than there had been at the prior meeting, which Roger attributed to the present group being career professionals, while the morning's group had been largely appointed politicians. There were, however, many and varied responses when he put up the charts projecting the climate for the next twenty years, ending in arctic conditions in Washington, DC.

The bulk of the questioning dealt with establishing the validity of the predictions, and rationalization and discussion at that point very closely followed the morning's meeting. One solid argument was that the Russians had independently arrived at the same conclusions. As the briefing came to an end, a new question came from Julia of the CIA that had not been asked in the morning session. "What do we know about the Russian Project ARARAT? I am sure we have not heard about it over at the agency. We have just their word that they have a project like ours."

"Good point, Julia," Ray commented. "We should ask them for proof." Then he continued, still addressing Julia, "There is something you've got over at Langley that we need right away. Julia, do you think that you can get the CIA to bring over a terminal to their 'What If' simulator, the super computer that predicts the future, and hook it up in this room?"

Julia showed surprise. Whether real or feigned, Ray could not tell. She responded with, "I didn't know What If was known outside the agency, but yes, we can do that. There are secure, fiber optics data links between here and Langley, so it should work just fine."

Ray said, "OK, if there aren't any more serious questions, let's break this up so you can finish shedding your old job responsibilities today and be back over here tomorrow at eight thirty. I want us to get right on working up the President's response to the Russians."

Back at his new office, Roger felt at loose ends and thought to call Lucille back at NOAA but then realized that she would have already left for the day. Meriwether came in and suggested that they have dinner together, which seemed like a good idea. Roger agreed as long as they went to a favorite place of his, which was near his apartment in Georgetown, but more important, served his kind of food.

At the restaurant, Roger ordered mostly raw, vegetarian food. It looked to Roger that Meriwether didn't seem to particularly care what he ate, since he ordered the first thing listed on the menu. With the food ordered, they got down to business.

Meriwether laid it on the line up front. "If we can't do anything about the climate, this whole exercise is a waste of time, and we could find more pleasant ways to spend the next few years."

"You're right," Roger responded. "I don't find the bureaucratic meat grinder my favorite place, but there might be some things we could try. With a massive change in the world's lifestyle, we could reduce the amount of carbon dioxide going into the atmosphere. We could stop cutting down the forests and plant new ones, drastically reduce our burning of fossil fuels . . ." From Meriwether's look, Roger knew they were thinking the same thing, which Meriwether voiced.

"It will take too long, doing just those things, to make a difference now. The system has so much inertia. Of course, those things have to be done for the long-term. From the data you showed today, however, we are in a transition into the next glacial period. The only things that will make any difference now are to reduce the water being evaporated in the tropics and to warm the Polar Regions. If we are now past the tipping point, even those changes may make little difference."

Roger responded, "I suppose artificial clouds in the tropics would reduce the evaporation, but I don't see how you can heat the Polar Regions enough to make any difference."

Meriwether explained, "There is a great deal of thermal energy locked up in the ocean currents, much more than in the atmosphere. You can't do anything at the South Pole, but that is not where the problem is. It's conceivable that the narrow channels of the Arctic regions could be opened up enough to make a difference."

Roger was awed by the concept. "The effort would be immense."

"Yes," Meriwether agreed, "but if we have no other choices for world survival, I expect we will have to do it. A few million years ago, when the Bering Strait was wider, the warm currents flowed easily to the Arctic, there were few ice ages."

Roger suddenly recalled a comment of Meriwether's, made several months back. "You had these ideas in mind when we first met, and you said we would eventually be making differential analyses. That's what we need to do now, isn't it? Repeat the climate computer runs again, but with changes to blockage of the sunlight and increased warm ocean currents to the Arctic?"

"You've got the idea, Roger. Specifically, the Kuroshio current is coupled into the Oyashio current and brings water through the Bering Strait into the Arctic Ocean. It's giving up heat all the time, moving around a number of islands. It eventually comes out on the west side of Greenland. We will need the computer simulations to find out accurately, but I imagine it would take a few hundred large atomic explosions to increase the current flows significantly. There is the risk of triggering volcanic events with unpredictable consequences."

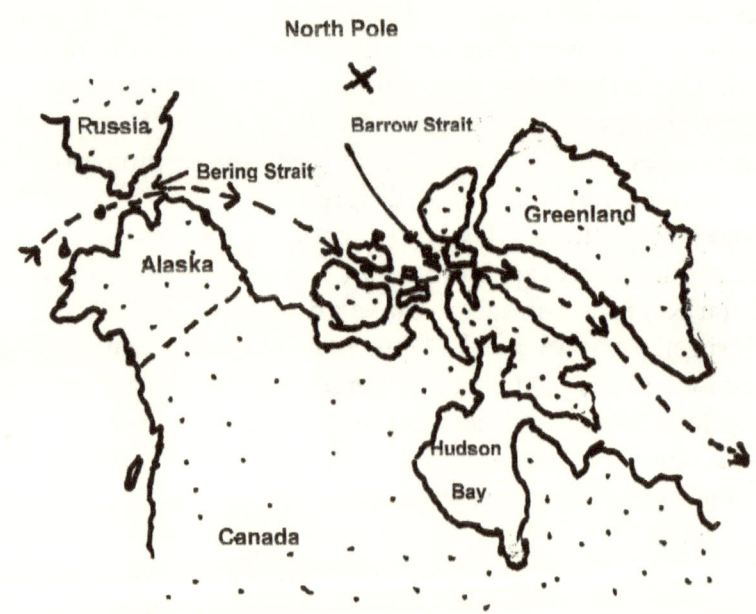

Arctic Warm Water Current

Roger thought that one would take lots of study.

After leaving the restaurant, Meriwether, on impulse, asked Roger to stop by his townhouse, which was not far away, and Roger accepted with anticipation.

As a widower, Meriwether lived alone, but once inside his home, Roger had the impression of walking into a museum, not a bachelor's home.

What most got Roger's attention was the collection of paintings and large photographic prints around the walls, depicting all varieties of landscapes, with special emphasis on the sky. The landscapes showed all varieties of deserts, mountains, oceans, and rain forests. The skies in the pictures included the bright, white, puffy clouds of the tropics, the bright blue skies of the deserts, the black, ragged storm clouds of the Midwestern tornadoes, and the less dramatic grey of the northern winters. The showpiece of them all, however, was a large, back-lighted transparency over the mantel, depicting a hurricane over the Gulf of Mexico, photographed from space. Roger didn't miss a small computer connected by a modem to Meriwether's office to give him access, even from his home, to his large office computers devoted to weather and climatology research. Obviously, Meriwether lived, breathed, and talked weather twenty-four hours a day.

As they sat down to relax, Roger asked the obvious question, "When did you first get interested in the weather?"

Meriwether settled down comfortably to what Roger could see might be a long story. "When I was fifteen years old, I traveled back to the United States from Beirut to New York which was to become a five-month trip. This was during Rommel's drive on Egypt. There were a lot of other refugees also trying to leave that part of the world. We were in Jerusalem for a month waiting for visas to enter Egypt, and we were another month in Cairo waiting for a ship to the United States. With the Mediterranean blocked, the options were to go by way of Australia or around Africa. The first boat left to go around Africa, so that is how I came by a deluxe tramp steamer."

After a pause, he continued, "As trips go today, it was a very long trip with not much to do except when we stopped in one of four ports along the way, Mombasa, Cape Town, Pernambuco, and Trinidad. I spent a lot of time stretched out on my back on a hatch cover looking up at the sky and wondering what was behind the ever-changing wonder of the clouds and weather. By crossing the equator twice on the trip, we experienced the full range of summer, winter, and fall in a short period. I think my real interest started then."

Roger felt Meriwether was waiting for him to say something, "Were you traveling alone?"

Meriwether smiled. "No and yes. That means that there was no family with me, except my younger sister. Our parents stayed on in Beirut to continue teaching at the American University there. There were other kids with us, also going back as a group. It was a bit of a scary time. We had a close encounter with what appeared to be a German armed merchant ship, and of course, other ships were being sunk in the south Atlantic by submarines."

Meriwether lapsed off into his own thoughts, then continued, "The other lasting impression this voyage made on me was regarding Shakespeare. One of the girls my age was a student of Shakespeare, and naturally I had to become interested, an interest that has stayed with me ever since."

"But back to weather and climatology. Having observed a wide variety of weather and climates, on settling down in the United States, I became interested in following the weather forecasts. It was strange to observe that in the foremost scientific country of the world, the weather forecasts were frequently wrong. In fact, the long-term forecasts were poorer than the several almanacs. As I pursued my formal education, this lack was always a nagging question at the back of my mind, and with that, I just seemed to move in the direction of the weather professionally."

He paused and Roger asked, "When did you shift to climatology?"

"In our earlier attempts to predict the short-term weather, it was not much more than saying weather moves from west to east. Going beyond this kind of prediction, even though in those days we didn't have the computer models, we knew we had to understand the basic thermodynamic forces of nature that drive the weather. Pretty soon, we were looking at long time-constant parameters such as ocean currents, ocean heating and cooling, atmospheric gases, snow cover, and before we knew it, we were dealing with climatology."

Then Roger asked, "You said you were expecting a glacial period before you knew that NOAH was predicting one. What led you to believe that?"

Meriwether replied, "I ran across a video, 'Stopping the Coming Ice Age,' distributed by 'People for a Future.' It summarizes the life work of John Hamaker who ties up the loose ends of ice age cycles. Here, I'll lend you my copy. You can watch it tonight when you get home."

During the evening, they discussed several other things of mutual interest and ended up looking at Meriwether's collection of early and rare volumes of Shakespeare. It was interesting to both of them that weather played an important part in many of Shakespeare's plots. Roger felt it had been one of the most relaxing evenings in a long time.

When Roger got back to his apartment, he made a note to himself to call Fred first thing in the morning and to get him started on the differential analyses, both for increased sun blockage and for increased warm water current flows to the Arctic. Then he watched the ice age video.

The next morning, Ray started off the meeting of his task force as soon as the participants had settled down with coffee and sweet rolls. Roger wondered if it would do any good to talk to the caterer about possibly providing some fruit and maybe hot water for brewing his herbal tea. The water in the bathroom wasn't really hot enough, and besides, it reeked of chlorine.

Ray quickly got deep into the topic of how the return message should be sent to the Russian Prime Minister. "There is probably a good reason he sent his message through our Ambassador. Speed, of course, but probably more important, it would give him privacy on his end. He probably is afraid to tip his hand to the rest of the Russian government while it could be reversed. Julia, what does the CIA assume in this case?"

Julia looked up, glad to perform in a largely male arena. "Well, yes, we agree that the use of the Ambassador implied a desire for privacy. Also the text in English was analyzed by our computer file on Petrovich, and it uses a vocabulary entirely consistent with its having been drafted by him in English. It was definitely not first drafted in Russian and then translated into English."

"Good work," Ray responded. "Unless there are other reasons not surfaced so far, we should respond in English through the same channel." There seemed to be general agreement. "In fact," Ray added, "I feel, tentatively, that we ought to propose that the summit meeting itself should be conducted in English with President Morgan and the Russian Prime Minister having a one-on-one with no translators or secretaries. The Russian is very proficient in English. Each side should, of course, have recorders."

With questioning glances from around the room, Ray added, "If the agenda for this summit meeting develops like I think it will, neither side will want to take the slightest chance of a premature leak. OK, let's continue to go down the Russian message point by point. We have already covered point one. Is there anything we should respond to in the second point?" No one said anything.

"What about the third point about the Russian Project ARARAT?"

Nathan King, the representative for state, spoke up. "When we go public with the Project NOAH story, we will need all the credibility we can get. So far, all we have from the Russians is their statement that they have the same results. We ought to have in our possession a detailed copy of their full program at least one day before the summit."

Ray said, "Good point," made a note, and continued, "what about the fourth point where he concedes everything on the arms reduction scenario?" Here, Ray looked to Ulysses Gonzalez, who usually went by Uly.

Uly knew he would be expected to comment in his own area and so was prepared. "It looks to me like the Russian Prime Minister is out by himself. I can't imagine his military agreeing to all those concessions. I can see that by making the concessions, he can be assured that the summit doesn't get hung up on things that he now considers secondary. I'm sure we feel the same way, but he doesn't know it yet."

Paul Cummings spoke up, "Why don't we take all we can get?"

Nathan King of State reacted strongly. "Actually we have already reviewed all their proposals in the last NSC meeting and decided that we could concede them if we get our proposals. I think it is important to strengthen the Russian Prime Minister's hand with his own people, and so I would recommend we concede all their earlier proposals even though that is no longer necessary."

Uly concurred with that position. Ray noticed that Cummings was grumbling under his breath but decided that at least in this matter that Nathan and Uly were more perceptive. "Let's go with conceding the original Russian proposals for now. Of course, the final say is up to President Morgan. I will note for him that Defense is in disagreement."

"Now," he continued, "we are down to the last and toughest point. What should we recommend as joint actions for President Morgan to propose that the United States and the Russians should take in face of the return to a glacial period threat? I think we need to generate a written list of specifics, and that the Russian Prime Minister should bring his own written list so that the two could be exchanged. We have a few days to work up the specifics, but we ought to indicate the topics in our response."

At the end of the day, a suggested response to the Russians had been drafted and typed by Marty. President Morgan approved it without any changes and had it transmitted to Ambassador Will Commons in Moscow. The following morning, Will delivered it to the Russian Prime Minister, who read it in Will's presence.

To Ivan Petrovich:

1. I am replying to your message by the same channels for reasons of security.
2. A detailed description of your Project ARARAT is needed in my hands one day before the start of the summit.

3. Even though you no longer require them, as a good faith gesture, I am conceding all of the original Russian proposals regarding the arms control agreements. I concur that you and I need not concern ourselves with this further at the summit, except for the public signing ceremonies.

4. For the meeting on joint actions, I suggest that it be conducted in English and that no others are present. Each of us should have a personal recorder.

5. I plan to bring a written list of proposed joint actions to be taken by our respective governments and hope that you will do the same. My list will cover at least the following: a. Creation of a supreme world government to direct the planet's efforts regarding the challenge with which we are all faced b. World-wide food production, conservation, and distribution c. World-wide energy management d. Potential climate-modification programs e. Resettlement of threatened populations f. Population control g. Manpower mobilization h. Economic and monetary reform i. Transition to a sustainable civilization

6. I am planning a press conference to take place forty-eight hours after our meeting ends, and I would assume that you would want to make your announcements at the same time. May we both have good insights for our coming meeting.

Your friend, Robert Morgan

Ivan Petrovich read the message twice and then turned back to the Ambassador. "Tell your President that I agree fully. Also, it would expedite our meeting if each point for the proposed joint action be on a separate sheet of paper, make it two copies." He winked at the Ambassador as the Ambassador left.

One day later the Ambassador had delivered to him a copy of the Russian Project ARARAT with appropriate commentary. This was forwarded promptly to the special task force in Washington where, after examination, it was declared valid.

CHAPTER 6

Playing Chess

The Naples summit unfolded almost exactly as it had been planned, which was also quite different from what the press had been led to believe. After an hour and a half on Thursday morning, the two leaders of the great atomic powers broke for lunch and issued a joint communiqué which was handed out to the press. It read,

> "The United States of America and the Russian Republic have agreed on all points on the agenda for the Arms Reductions and Limitation Talks. The previously thorny problems of American and Russian troops have been resolved. All troops will return to their own countries. With no further outstanding differences remaining, the two world leaders for the next two days will discuss items of mutual interest, while their staffs work out the detailed wording of the agreements. The signing ceremony will take place during the late afternoon of the second day."

When the two leaders got back together, again without aids, interpreters, or other staff, President Morgan got out a sheaf of papers. "We can probably get on with this the quickest if we start by exchanging papers." He was conscious of needing to stay within the vocabulary the CIA had briefed him on that was known to the Russian.

"Certainly," was the reply. "Here is my list. While I have had a month more to prepare for this than you have, I have only a very small staff whom I can trust, and only one of them can type. The rest of my government leaders, as you may have surmised, know nothing of these proposals, and they must not know until they are announced to the world. That is the only way to be sure of their eventual cooperation and of my personal survival. I assume you too are working this problem with a small and discrete staff?"

President Morgan nodded and, as he went over the Russian's list, began to chuckle. "This list is almost the same as the one I gave you, except that it is worded differently. You must have a mole at the top levels of the Whitehouse."

"No," the Russian Prime Minister insisted, "I think that when it comes to surviving under the present circumstances, logic dictates, and that there are certain obvious things that must be done from whatever the place you are looking." He paused and then continued, "My friend, may I call you Robert?" When President Morgan nodded he continued, "That is good. We must become better friends. You must call me Ivan." Again President Morgan nodded.

"Robert," he said, "it is known to me that you play chess quite well. I have found that when I play chess, the answers to other problems also come to me." Taking out a small chess board from his briefcase, he went on. "As we talk of these problems concerning which we must decide, let us play a game or two. The world need not know."

Robert was surprised, but agreed, and they set up the pieces. As they did so, he laughed at the innocent deception of the world that they were about to embark upon. Ivan said, "I will give you white, since I believe chess is taken more seriously in Russia, and you may need the advantage of the first move."

Robert didn't know how good a player the Russian was, so he had no idea what style of game he favored. He decided to play cautiously and hoped for a game he was familiar with. He opened with, pawn to king's four.

"So," said the Russian, "would you like to play 'Ray Lopez'? One of my favorites." He responded with pawn to king's four.

"You know," Ivan said while Robert was pondering his next move, "I am not entirely in favor of a Supreme World Government. There will be many problems, particularly because the member states are so diverse. It will not be practical in a short time to change all the countries becoming member states to quickly adopt similar state governments."

Moving his knight to king's bishop three, Robert replied, "I agree, so initially the state governments will have to remain what they are at present. In the future, they can be changed to become more in conformance with our future needs. The Supreme World Government must be set up right from the beginning so that between our two countries we control it, at least in the beginning. The rest of the world will just have to accept it that way."

Ivan moved his knight to queen's bishop three. "I assume that you do not favor maintaining the United Nations?"

"No," Robert said strongly. "Our two countries as the organizing states must be in strong control, and there must be no veto. I cannot see the United Nations accepting such conditions." He moved his bishop to knight's five.

"Very well," Ivan said, choosing the Berlin Defense, "it shall be a Supreme World Government. We must be sure that the key positions are filled by individuals you and I agree on from our two countries."

Robert smiled. "I would suggest that security and food be staffed by your people. We have good candidates for climatology, communications, and the overall coordination of the Supreme World Government."

Ivan laughed. "You strike a hard bargain, but then, you are in the stronger position. We are already out of food. Why only five leadership posts for the two of us?"

Robert frowned. "The ones we will staff between us are the key ones for maintaining control of the key issues. We must have other countries participating if we are to get their cooperation."

Ivan responded, "I yield to your greater experience in soliciting voluntary cooperation."

Robert had a last point on that subject. "Something you and I must both give up. Once our people go into the Supreme World

Government, we must give up control of them. They must be free to do what seems best from their new perspective. I propose that those serving in the New Supreme Government have a special federal citizenship, and that all their close personal family members go with them. The rest of the world will not accept it if there are still strings on these people. Thinking of the long-term future, this is the best way."

Ivan sighed. "I had suspected you would propose something like this, and perhaps you are right. For those of us brought up in Mother Russia, it will be very difficult. We do not have the melting-pot traditions of the United States. However, there will be many changes in the world, and I know it is time to begin thinking of it as one world."

Both players played well with Robert leading an attack and Ivan avoiding the traps laid for him. Eventually, they agreed they had a draw. The Russian put the game away, and they chatted about their two countries, soon to become states in a larger entity, before adjourning for the planned banquet.

The next day, they played two games. In the first game, Prime Minister Petrovich opened as President Morgan had the previous day with pawn to king's four. President Morgan responded with the Sicilian Defense.

As the game progressed, they discussed the issues confronting them. At first, President Morgan felt it would be impossible for the world to immediately cut its energy consumption in half, but eventually agreed with Prime Minister Petrovich that is was necessary, whatever sacrifices were required. Prime Minister Petrovich, on the other hand, felt much of the world was just coming to democracy with market-driven economics and would resist a tightly controlled economy as a step backward. In the end, he had to agree that the market economy approach could not be tightly focused on the problems of survival that they faced. They both agreed without argument that population control, economics and monetary reform, and resettlement of large populations were problems that they recognized but ones that the Supreme World Government would have to solve after some study.

The game they were playing developed along the lines of the Dragon Variation with the Russian getting the upper hand and eventually winning. Their last game was a Queen's Gambit Declined. President Morgan, early on, managed to get a piece ahead of the Russian, which eventually made the difference in the end game.

Having used up the scheduled time enjoying themselves, they called in their aids and proceeded to the signing ceremony. Thus ended the most momentous summit in history where the important decisions were yet known only to the two leaders.

There were, of course, loose ends to tidy up back home. As soon as President Morgan got back, he called Ray to his office and gave him his copy of the agreements reached with the Russian President. "Get enough copies of this made for the task force and also to hand out to the press the day after tomorrow. We agreed to do it in the morning, Washington time. That way, we can catch most of the world awake. Also, I would like a meeting with the task force tomorrow afternoon. I hope by then you can get an output from the What If on the world's reaction to this announcement. Do you think that Julia will have time to work the What If on the CIA computers?"

Ray responded, "She is waiting in the task-force area right now for a copy of this. We assumed you would want a What If done right away. She has already made runs using the proposals you took with you, so unless there are some major changes, it shouldn't take too long.

"No," said the President. "I was surprised at how similar to us their thinking on all this has been. In several cases, we used our own proposals without changes and some of theirs also exactly as proposed."

A few minutes later, Ray gave Julia a copy of the joint action agreements and left her alone at the CIA What If terminal. Julia quickly entered the changed conditions that the President of the United States and Prime Minister of Russia would announce to a surprised world that would only be expecting routine announcements about arms reductions. Instead, they would be providing copies of their announcement about the coming cold glacial period and their decision to create a Supreme World

Government, whether the world wanted it or not. The text of the agreement, as Julia entered it, read

Joint Communiqué
From the Naples Summit

This communiqué is being released simultaneously by the United States and the Russian governments in Washington, DC, and Moscow. It will be available also to diplomats from all US and Russian embassies worldwide in the local language.

Our two governments, having examined the latest scientific data, are convinced without a doubt, that the world is faced with a return to a cold glacial period climate in less than a decade. The problems of saving humanity from anarchy, panic, starvation, and war will be stupendous and can only be successfully accomplished by a strong, Supreme World Government.

We, therefore, jointly declare that, at the time of the issuance of this document to the world, that a Supreme World Government is hereby created, with the United States and the Russia as the first two member states. Any country wishing to do so is welcome to join simply by agreeing to the principles further outlined in this communiqué. Two weeks from this day, an organizational meeting of the Supreme World Government (SWG) will take place at the United Nations' headquarters, and countries wishing to join should send representatives. Representation (voting) will be related to population and the assets each member state contributes to the SWG. The United States and Russia have at this point transferred their Armed Forces to the control of the SWG. All other joining states will be required to do so as well.

To be a Supreme World Government in fact will require that the SWG be capable of protecting the persons of its staff and enforcing its decisions, by force, if necessary. For the interim, until a safer society can be created, the strategic armed forces coming under the control of the SWG will be the ultimate means of enforcement.

The problems that the SWG faces are global, and whether countries join or do not join, they will all be required to cooperate in the decisions reached by the SWG.

Initially, the SWG will take over the facilities of the United Nations, which at this point are redundant. The scope of the SWG will, of course, be immensely greater than the UN and will require the creation of new facilities.

To aid in the decision process to join SWG, scientific briefings will be given during the next week by the scientists who have made the climatology investigations. Any governments that wish to do so may learn first-hand of the great challenges facing the planet. These briefings will be open to accredited representatives of all countries and will be given in Washington, DC, Moscow, and Geneva.

After organizing itself and selecting individuals to serve in the SWG, the SWG will immediately address at least the following areas for action.

1. Worldwide Food Production, Conservation, and Distribution.

    All world food production, conservation, and distribution will be directed by the SWG World Food Authority and implemented by its member states. Wasteful practices of cropland destruction, and the feeding of human edible grains to food animals will be discontinued.

    It is intended that as soon as possible, every human being will be provided with a minimum diet sufficient to sustain good health. Should insufficient food be available on the planet, priority in providing a minimum diet will go to 1) personal of the SWG and others providing essential services, 2) general populations of SWG member states, and 3) populations of non-member states.

    Depending on food stocks and the rate of onset of the cold global period, food rationing may be required. Food hoarding will be considered a serious crime.

    A long-term goal of the SWG World Food Authority will be the growing of needed food on a permanently sustainable basis without contamination or destruction of the environment.

A major share of the world's construction capabilities will be directed toward the building of solar greenhouses, solar algae farms, and desalination and irrigation projects in parts of the world that will not be adversely affected by the cold climate.

2. Worldwide Energy Management

Major contributing factors to the onset of a glacial period are the widespread burning of fossil fuels and the destruction of the world's forests. The SWG will create a World Energy Authority which will direct through member states all policies involving energy production, distribution, and consumption. Fossil fuels will be restricted to essential uses only and be phased out eventually. Consumption will be decreased 50 percent immediately and fossil fuels will be phased out entirely in ten years. Tight rationing will be required until alternate, non fossil energy sources can be developed.

Clear-cutting of forests, particularly the tropical rain forests, will be discontinued immediately. Selected harvesting to assure permanently sustained forests will be instituted and massive replanting of the depleted forests will be initiated.

3. Climate Modification

The SWG will greatly enlarge existing scientific programs that are looking at climate-modification techniques which might reduce the severity or slow the onset of the impending glacial period.

4. Resettlement of Threatened Populations

The SWG will plan and implement the resettlement of populations from those areas of the world that will become uninhabitable. Existing housing facilities in non threatened areas may be requisitioned, causing some crowding and personal hardships. Whole new communities may be created and, if appropriate, in states that have not joined the SWG.

At this time, it is anticipated that all of Canada, the Northern United States, and Northern Europe will be vacated, as well as some areas of northern Asia. Those persons refusing resettlement will have their food rations withdrawn as an inducement, because the SWG does not intend to support populations that require significantly more than their share of world resources.

5. Population Control

With a limited world food supply, the continued growth of the world population cannot be tolerated. Regional and local governments, whether they are part of SWG or not, will be held responsible for achieving zero growth populations within nine months in their geographical areas. Those that do not will have their food supplies progressively reduced until they comply. The SWG will devote significant resources to family planning, both educational and material.

As time progresses, and the full extent of the impending glacial period on the ability of mankind to produce sufficient food is determined, it may be necessary to establish lower birth rates, worldwide, to reduce the world population to a level where is can be supported.

6. Manpower Mobilization

All able-bodied persons will be expected to contribute to the welfare of the planet in exchange for their basic food ration and simple necessities of life. The bulk of the world's armed forces' manpower will quickly be funneled into the agriculture, energy, and reforestation projects. It is anticipated that a large manpower pool will become available as nonessential activities are phased down, and this surplus will also be applied to those areas that will aid in mankind's survival, food growing, alternate renewable fuels, wind energy, solar energy, algae farms, and additional housing for resettled persons.

7. Economic and Monetary Reform

During the climate transition, a worldwide controlled economy will be implemented with one monetary unit to be called the Credo. One single planetary bank will take over all existing banks, national or private. The primary economic factor will be that everyone who is capable must work to receive his or her basic necessities of life. The ratio of the basic wage to the highest paid will be no greater than one to four, based on skill, its associated scarcity, and the contributions of the individual.

Except for personal property, private property will no longer exist. Control of businesses will be in the hands of the workers of the businesses, who, in large concerns, may employ professional managers. Those businesses not contributing to the common good under the present emergency will be liquidated or converted to needed activities.

All money and paper assets will be exchanged for the new world currency that will be issued shortly. In the exchange, no one individual will be issued more that the equivalent of one thousand dollars of the new currency.

Initially, all individuals are to continue to occupy their present dwellings, which will become the property of the member states, who will establish equitable rents. Where dwellings are larger than the basic needs of the current occupants, it can be expected that others will be assigned to share the dwellings.

Both of us hope sincerely that all of mankind will join with us in this greatest challenge, and that we can show that mankind deserves to live on earth, our only home.

The leaders of the United States and the Russian Republic
Pres. Robert Morgan   PM Ivan Petrovich

While Julia was exercising the What If, George Kelly was sitting on his front porch several hundred miles away. For the tenth time, he aimed his hunting rifle at the center of a pine tree at the end of his driveway and squeezed off a shot. Each time, he imagined he was aiming at a government troublemaker. Yes, he thought, the government was always behind his troubles, making him pay taxes, causing bad times, and restricting his hunting. The latest was just too much. Talk about everyone having to turn in their guns. They wouldn't get his guns unless it was over his dead body.

George was waiting for five of his hunting buddies. They had a plan to drive into Washington with their guns to demonstrate the right to have them. It wasn't very clear in George's mind exactly how they would demonstrate, but he thought they ought to start at Arlington National Cemetery. Just about everyone buried there had been a good American with a gun. He would show them that they couldn't push George Kelly around.

CHAPTER 7

What If

While the happenings of the past week seemed unreal to Julia, the outputs of the What If for the immediate future really got her attention.

As she began to query the What If for what was in store after the President made his planned announcements, the possible scenarios that unfolded looked quite unpleasant. Her past encounters with the What If had been almost like a game, where the eventual results did not have an immediate effect on her personal life. As she moved ahead, looking at likely world reactions, Julia was further struck that this was not a game and that the ugly probabilities out there could very well threaten her and all she held dear in a very real way. She even thought at one point during the night that maybe she should just leave Washington and the government service for some place safer. Her higher self, however, quickly brought her to the realization that being in the center of things was better, because she at least would know what to expect. Out in the general world, she would just be an unsuspecting victim. Knowing had always given the knower power and that was not going to change. Late that night, when she had finished running the What If through its paces, she knew the President and his special task force would have a lot to think about and act on after she finished briefing them the next day.

At two thirty the next day, President Morgan joined the task force in what had now become the crises-management center of the government. Ray called the meeting to order and then promptly sat down, nodding to Julia. "Julia, this is your meeting.

Why don't you summarize what you have learned from the What If, and after that we can talk about it."

Julia quickly moved to the end of the table around which the group was seated and took out her charts. The What If terminal had also been moved into the crises room and placed so that all could see the screen. Since no one there had seen the What If in operation before, except for Ray, President Morgan, and herself, Julia decided to begin with some history. "Many years ago, the government realized that it had a very good intelligence system, but that it almost never took timely action in response to fast-developing situations. Also, when the government took some initiatives, the reactions of both friends and potential enemies were often surprising. The conclusions reached by some perceptive staff members in the agency were that no human mind had the capacity or the speed to hold enough facts together along with their interrelatedness. The obvious conclusion was to reach timely decisions, forecast developments accurately, and determine trends or changes in trends that would likely result from new initiatives, computer use was mandatory and so the What If was a logical development.

"Here is a past example. On the terminal, I have just selected Cuba. As a new initiative, I have just keyed in that the price that the United States will pay for sugar be dropped ten cents per pound. What If predicts immediate, angry rhetoric from Havana, a blockade of our base at Guantanamo, and one week later, a note from the Russian Ambassador, suggesting that if we return to the old price for sugar, he might be able to get OPEC to hold off on their planned increase in crude oil by offering more Russian oil on the international market. Sometimes we introduce deliberate initiatives just to see how well our model represents reality. Any questions about how What If works so far?"

Roger spoke, "How well can you model a closed society like China which is so secretive and about which little is known with assurance?"

"Actually, sometimes the totalitarian societies are the easiest to model since only a few people control the whole society, and so all you need is to model the thinking of a few people if you can ascertain it. Sometimes a leadership is so rigid, you can model it as if it were one person."

As there seemed to be no more questions, Julia shifted to the meat of the meeting. "Since last evening, I have been running the What If to predict the reactions of the countries of the world against the text of the announcement that President Morgan and the Russian PM plan to make public tomorrow morning. I believe Ray already gave all of you copies. Not surprisingly, the universal reaction during the first twenty-four hours is disbelief and shock. As the information is confirmed through multiple channels, there will be a quick building of resentment, turning to hate against the major atomic powers. Our usual friends and allies will feel betrayed and let down that they were not made a part of the decision process. The third world countries will look at the announcement as further proof that the Russians will try to bully them and that the United States is out to squeeze more blood from them. With the lack of sophistication in the third world countries, it may take some time for them to consider a shift to a cold glacial period seriously.

"One area of exception to what I have outlined is the eastern European block. They are in such immediate, desperate shape, particularly for food stocks, that a cold period a few years down the road will not seem that important. The minimum food standards that the Supreme World Government will provide will look like a significant improvement, certainly on the short-term.

"In about a week after their scientists have examined our data and that of the Russians, our normal friends and allies, whose geographical locations are such that they would be very adversely challenged by the cold glacial period, will do an about face when they realize they are at maximum risk. The Australians are an exception to this in that they will see themselves as a logical candidate to host a few hundred million refugees. The What If says that they would resist with armed force unless atomic weapons are threatened against them.

"An early joiner of SWG will be Japan. They are already importing most of their energy and significant amounts of food and will always want to ally themselves with the world powers controlling both of these vital resources.

"In spite of what I said about totalitarian regimes earlier, What If is not able to make a prediction with a high degree of probability about China. The old guard, who is in charge, has not shown sensitivity for the welfare of its own people, which is the big issue in this case. Even if half of China starved, the leaders might not cooperate with the SWG, because they would not be affected personally. China has a two-thousand-year history of the masses mostly obeying the government even while starving. Except for extremely corrupt governments, overthrow has generally been from without.

"As a conclusion," Julia said, "a basic pattern seems to apply generally. Those countries that will perceive that they will have enough food in the face of the cold period will resist the planned actions of the SWG. Those without sufficient food will cooperate. The key for the SWG will be in controlling the food supply and, where the food supply cannot be controlled, controlling the energy which is needed to grow food and distribute it."

Ray asked, "What happens in Russia itself?"

Julia responded, "Even though Russia will be a joint architect of the SWG, What If predicts they will be very fragmented. Their immediate neighbors, the previous republics of the old Soviet Union, the Ukraine, and others, will perceive that they are better off distancing themselves from Russia, fearful of being swallowed up again. The key in these republics are the local commanders who have gained some control over significant elements of the Strategic Rocket Forces. What If has flagged this as the most dangerous aspect of the initiative. In fact, What If predicts that at least two previous Soviet republics may use the threat of their atomic weapons to further distance themselves from Russia, and if they desperately needed food or energy resources, they might use blackmail on more fortunate neighboring countries. Russia would certainly not interfere unilaterally for fear of attack by nuclear weapons on the homeland itself."

Julia finished her presentation by projecting a map of the world, showing in green those countries that would cooperate and join the SWG, those in yellow that would cooperate under duress, and finally those in red that likely would put up armed resistance, even against the threat of atomic weapons.

President Morgan noted that the countries in red included China, North Korea, Australia, Cuba, Brazil, Libya, India, and South Africa.

Julia added a postscript, "As a secondary point of interest, What If predicts that within a week of the announcement, quite a few existing governments will fall, the majority being replaced with military dictatorships."

Ray thanked Julia for an excellent presentation and asked if there were any more questions.

Nathan King asked, "Is there anything that could be done differently in the announcement to improve its reception by the world?"

"Yes," Julia said, "I only had a little time to vary the scenario and look for different results, but the one with the most leverage is to emphasize that most people will end up with more food than is available to them presently."

President Morgan made a note to work that into his press conference and pass the idea on to the Russian leader.

Ray noticed that Julia was looking around nervously and asked her, "Is there anything else?"

"Well," she said hesitatingly, "I know that the CIA is prohibited from operating domestically, so it is a well-kept secret that we do 'What If' runs on the United States also. The rationale is that making computer runs is not technically the same as mounting an operation. I'm sure that the results of these runs are given to the administration to aid in taking domestic initiatives. Anyway, the domestic runs don't look at all good."

President Morgan said, "Julia, I know about the domestic side of the What If. It has been very valuable to me in the past and, I must say, amazingly accurate. What does it say now?"

Convinced she was still among friends, Julia continued, "Concluding that the agreements made with the Russians are beyond the authority of the President, as well as unconstitutional, the Congress will by midday tomorrow declare the President's actions null and void and by evening will be close to impeachment. They will be well supported by the press and the media, who will suggest that the President has become unbalanced. At this point, there will not yet be any independent opinions publicized and supporting the claim of an emminent shift to a cold glacial period. The 'moral majority' will combine with other conservatives to urge an armed overthrow of the administration. Some major money centers of power will see in the economic agreements an end to their ascendency and will recruit drug lords and some other criminal elements in assassination attempts on high officials, especially the President. Some elements of the armed forces may be persuaded to take sides against the administration." Julia fell silent.

President Morgan said, "I expected opposition, but the What If indicates that it will develop much faster than I had thought. Well, that brings us to the second part of this meeting, what we should do to preempt the opposition." The meeting went on for several more hours, with the FBI, the Department of Defense, and the Joint Chiefs of Staff taking most of the action items. President Morgan decided he would have to adjourn Congress in the morning.

Ray Carr said at the end of the meeting. "We need to get on with the preparations for the climate presentations. I want Meriwether to take the lead on those to be given in Washington. Roger has agreed to fly to Geneva and take some of the Project NOAH staff along for the meetings we will be promising to have there. State is already making arrangements in Geneva through our embassy."

As the meeting broke up, Roger thought he would ask George Noble and Lucille Van Brunt to go with him and needed to call both of them right away so that they would have time to make arrangements and pack for the trip. He also made sure he had Hamaker's book, *The Survival of Civilization* that was mentioned in the video Meriwether had lent him. It had not been hard to get a copy sent over from NOAA's technical library.

CHAPTER 8

Wolves at the Door

When President Morgan arrived at the press room the following morning, he noticed it was packed more heavily than usual. Perhaps the earlier-than-usual time had alerted the news hounds that something different was afoot.

"Gentlemen and ladies of the press and media," he began, looking at the large wall clock, "at this very moment in Moscow, the Russian Prime Minister is giving his report of our summit meeting to his people and, as I am doing, also to the whole world. As you already know from the press releases from Naples, our two countries have agreed to the most comprehensive arms reduction in history, including both nuclear and conventional weapons, not to mention large reductions in service personnel. We also agreed to something the experts said would never happen: we and they will remove all our troops from all foreign countries. The agreements meet all the guidelines I have talked over with the Senate leaders, so there should be no problem of Senate ratification."

So far, there was a ho-hum response from those gathered there since all of this was two-day-old news at best. The President went on, "As has been reported by some of you, the Russian Prime Minister, Ivan Petrovich, and I met for another day and a half, which we exclusively devoted to the greatest problem ever to face civilized humanity, how to survive the coming cold glacial period. I don't mean a problem someday in the distant future. I mean one which will affect each and every one of us in the next several years."

After a moment's silence, an angry buzz of conversation broke out, and only after calls for quiet was some semblance of order restored. The President continued, "I have a lot to tell you, the American people, and the world, and I can't do so with rude interruptions. You may notice that security is thorough today." The President paused to allow those gathered to look around the room and notice the large number of young, strong men in grey blazers standing around. "Those unable to control themselves will promptly be helped to leave. To continue, the Russian government and this administration have examined recent, unpublished scientific evidence that demonstrates, without doubt, that the world is already in the transition stage back to a cold glacial period. It is unlikely that crops will be successfully grown in Canada next year, and within two years, the same will be true of the northern United States and northern Europe. Within a decade, this spot, Washington, DC, will have a near arctic climate." The President paused to allow what he had said to be assimilated.

"Obviously," he then continued, "the biggest problem for the whole world will be the growing and distribution of enough food to prevent wholesale starvation and the subsequent disintegration of civilization as we know it. I don't intend to give a full briefing on the expected changes in the climate and the scientific reasoning behind it. That briefing will be given at NOAA headquarters twice a day for the next week, starting this afternoon. All accredited scientists and selected press and media representatives are welcome to attend. What I want to tell you now is what the Russian Prime Minister and I have agreed to do in facing this most awesome threat to humanity."

The President took out another set of notes and began to read, "The Russian Prime Minister and I concur that there is no time for debates and the usual rounds of discussions and further studies, and hopefully, downstream sometime, the reaching of a consensus. The Russians normally go through this process; it's just not as out in the open as ours. We decided two days ago that it is already very late for humanity, and so we agreed on a joint set of actions. Since these actions are worldwide in scope, we have concluded that the only hope for success is through the formation of a Supreme World Government. So that there is no misunderstanding in the world, the Russian Prime Minister and I agreed to give out identical, written statements. Will the ushers please do that at this time? I will give you ten minutes to look over the joint agreements and then I will return for questions." The President left the press room while the text of the agreements was being passed out.

Ray Carr, who had stayed after the President left, noticed that in contrast to ten minutes earlier, there was a hush in the room, broken only by the noise of the turning of pages. Toward the end of the ten minutes, whispering began between neighbors, which ended as soon as the President returned.

"All right," he said, "we are ready for questions."

The first person recognized was the head of the AP, Washington, DC news office. "How can you be sure that the climate projections that NOAA is predicting are accurate? Most of us know that the long-range weather forecasts can't be relied on." This drew a short laugh from the press and media and tended to relieve the tensions that had been building.

The President responded, "These projections are based on our new system at NOAA and have been thoroughly checked. They have also been independently confirmed by the Russian climatic scientists. I can't go into the details here, but you will be able to do that with our NOAA scientists this afternoon and for the next week, as I already announced."

The next question was from the NBC news team. "What coordination has there been with the Congress, and what is their reaction to this crisis? It seems that many of your planned actions are unconstitutional on the face of it."

The President paused before answering. "No one except those on my immediate staff has been informed of anything until now. The graveness of the situation requires immediate, authoritative action that cannot await normal due process. A simple announcement of the coming cold glacial period with a gradual and drawn-out decision process would result in the breakdown of law and order and the disintegration into chaos of civilization as we know it. Therefore, as of this morning, I have declared a state of national emergency and rule by martial law until such time as it appears no longer necessary. The Congress has been recessed for the time being. Appropriate units of the armed forces and the National Guard have been alerted. The Delta Force and certain units of the Marines are already moving into the Washington area to ensure that the government will continue to function."

The President paused to allow the press and media time to realize the utter seriousness of the situation and then continued, "The whole country, in fact the whole world, must be geared to an emergency basis more severe than any previously faced. Ladies and gentlemen, I am talking about the survival of each and every one of you. If we do nothing and somehow survive the likely wars that would follow inaction, in ten years, there would only be enough food grown to feed less than one-half of the world's population. It is very difficult to visualize the kind of world that would be. As the leader of the world's most powerful country, I must take whatever action seems necessary."

As those present began to visualize a world as the President was describing it, a hush fell over the press room. Then the representative from the *Times of London* was given the floor. "Some of the conditions in your agreement with the Russians seem overly harsh and surely could be put off a few years."

The President patiently answered, "I originally thought as you say. However, as we analyzed the projections, we realized that the time we have to do anything is very short for what has to be done, and that the only way we even have a chance is to start at full steam. Also there are the possibilities of random events not taken into the predictions, which could bring on the cold glacial period sooner than the standard projection. There is really so much to do. For example, we anticipate the conversion of millions of acres of the Sahara Desert to the growing of food. This will require the building of new cities, the creation of fresh water from salt water in vast quantities, and the establishment of large power-generating plants where none exist today. This does not even address the actual relocation of possibly hundreds of millions of people. The transportation facilities as well as the new housing needed, of course, do not at present exist. In normal times, such monumental tasks such as I have just described would take literally decades, time we don't have."

An unidentified individual asked, "What are random events?"

The President was happy to be able to show his new knowledge and change the subject. "A random event that significantly affects the climate is either a volcanic eruption that adds a lot of dust to the atmosphere or a large meteor strike that does the same thing. The latter are very rare."

The last question came from the lady representative for the *Los Angeles Times.* "Mr. President, how do you see this Supreme World Government being implemented, and what would be the relationship to it of existing governments?"

The President had expected this question and had a ready answer. "During a transition period, existing governments will continue in their present roles, except as they join the SWG, their armed forces will come under control of the SWG. Eventually, more and more of the critical functions will be transferred to the SWG, such as the issuance of money, control of food and energy policies, and the relocation of populations. The present governments essentially become states of the SWG. We have to be prepared, of course, in some cases, for existing governments to disintegrate, in which case, the SWG will have to step in and establish a stable state government. To be sovereign, the SWG will have to have the means to enforce its decisions and protect its government personnel and therefore will have to give this first priority."

The same lady had a follow-up question. "Historically, it takes quite a while to get agreement, the UN took years and it isn't even a government. How will this problem be solved?"

The President smiled, "I think we have read the same history. The Russian Prime Minister and I recognized this problem from the beginning. Each country joining and becoming a state of the SWG will get a voting representation related to its population and the value of the assets it transfers to the SWG. The United States and Russia have already transferred their armed forces, except for the regional militias. The combined voting strength of the two will assure, at least in the formative period, that when our two countries agree on some issue, it will be resolved to our satisfaction. During the transition to a glacial period, which is projected to be for the next ten or twelve years, our interests will coincide since both our two countries are threatened in a similar manner. We do intend to deal fairly with everyone that joins SWG as is indicated in our joint statement. It is also planned to recruit appropriate administrative personnel from all countries joining. Naturally key positions can be expected to be filled from our country and Russia. As the widest known language, English has been agreed on as the official language of the SWG."

The press and media had few other questions. With the story of a lifetime, they were all anxious to get it out and departed in a near panic.

Chapter 9

Flight to Geneva

After the news conference was over, Roger decided he had barely enough time to collect George and Lucille and make it in time for a leisurely boarding of the Swissair flight leaving from Dulles Airport.

Roger called George at NOAA who told him that, after talking it over with his wife, he had decided that this was not the time to be away from his wife and new baby. Things were just too uncertain. Maybe he would get stuck over in Geneva. On the other hand, Lucille was enthusiastic about going, so Roger headed over to NOAA to pick her up. He noticed, as he arrived at the entrance, a squad of soldiers who looked just as tough as the ones who had reinforced the Whitehouse guards. They gave him a wary eye until he showed them his federal ID.

Lucille came out quickly, threw her bag on the backseat next to his, and jumped into the front passenger's seat. As they pulled away, she said, "Have you seen the TV since the President's news conference?"

"No," he answered. "I have been too busy pulling together the briefing materials we will need in Geneva. What are they saying about it? Mostly bad I suppose."

"Well, I certainly wouldn't call it good. I know that President Morgan needed to do something drastic, but he surprised both me and the rest of the world by recessing the Congress. Being left out, the Congress is as mad as a nest of hornets. The network news anchor men got together on a panel, and they were all for Congress impeaching the President or getting the Supreme

Court to set aside his actions. Most of them halfway don't believe that there is even going to be a climate change. Roger, what do you think about all that?"

Roger looked thoughtful. "It all justifies the President's actions. Democracies, particularly ours, have a great difficulty facing up to crises. Historically, we shut our eyes to what was happening in Europe in the early parts of the two world wars. In recent times, we have ruined our economy because we have been unable to face up to taxing ourselves for what we want to spend. Individual members of the government know better. They are some of the brightest people in the country, but they have learned what you have to do to stay in power: you keep the people happy even if the people don't know what is good for them."

"Well," said Lucille, ready to change the subject, "I hope the President can keep things under control. The enormity of the climate change doesn't seem to have made much of an impression on the public. On TV, they are talking as if it would be over in a week, like the invasion of Panama. It seems to me that the media is trying to push Congress into impeaching the President or at least, getting a ruling from the Supreme Court to set aside all the actions he has taken. Someone was even suggesting swearing in the Speaker of the House as the President."

Roger interrupted with, "Look at those marines around those armed personnel carriers. I expected them around the government buildings, but those guys must be prepared to throw up a roadblock. I didn't think much of it a few minutes ago when we passed through the last circle, but there was a group of soldiers back there, also with armed personnel carriers."

Their route took them to the Arlington Circle, which seemed to be blocked by stalled cars in the exit they needed to take toward Roselyn and the parkway along the Potomac, to Langley and then to Dulles. There was a small crowd on the grass on one side, and Roger and Lucille stopped and got out. A lone soldier was down on the grass and several passers-by were trying to stop bleeding from a wound in his shoulder. It seemed that some armed civilians were approaching from the cemetery woods and, seeing the soldier on guard, had shot him. The soldier was saying that his unit had dropped him off a half hour ago, telling him to keep the road open. He had been expecting some reinforcements, but Arlington was a big place and, the reinforcements must have become lost.

Roger looked up and saw that the armed civilians who had shot the soldier were coming closer, pointing their guns at the group helping the soldier on the ground. Before he could think to do anything, Lucille picked up the soldier's rifle and dropped to a prone position, facing the ragged line of armed civilians who were approaching across a brown field. The civilians carried an assortment of small bore rifles and shotguns. Lucille set the rifle on semiautomatic fire and started with the man on the left. Before they knew what was happening, the first three of the six were down. There was no cover for the others, even though they went to the ground, and Lucille finished off the last one about twenty seconds after she had started. She never learned that she had ended George Kelly's demonstration against the government before it had had a chance to cause serious loss of innocent lives.

The gunfire attracted the attention of some soldiers down the road who got into their armed personnel carrier and started toward the circle to investigate. Roger grabbed Lucille's arm and pushed her toward their car. "We have to get going or we might get involved and not make our plane to Geneva."

Lucille had kept hold of the rifle and had it between her legs as they drove off toward the parkway, managing to get around the stalled cars. "Where did you learn to do that?" Roger wanted to know in awe of the performance he had just witnessed.

"My dad taught me early," she said. "He wanted me to be able to protect myself, whatever the circumstances. He taught me to shoot when I was twelve. I haven't had any practice since I visited my folks last summer when my dad and I went out to the local rifle range."

Roger thought about what Lucille had done and decided she had reached the correct conclusion regarding the threat of the armed civilians and had acted properly in next to zero time in self-defense of the group. He thought, any armed civilians who shot a soldier without provocation were outside the law and deserved to be shot, the same as dangerous, mad dogs.

The rest of the way to Dulles was uneventful, although the military presence was noticeable at strategic locations. They were stopped at a roadblock near the entrance to the airport, and the soldiers eyed the rifle Lucille had between her legs with suspicion. Roger quickly flashed his credentials and said, "We are on a very important mission to Europe for the President and had the rifle along just in case we had trouble getting here."

"Well, you won't need the rifle here," the soldier said. "We have the airport well guarded." With that, he took the rifle away from Lucille and passed them on into the airport.

As they entered the terminal building, they could hear their Swissair flight being called which was a surprise, since it was still two hours to departure time. They hurried through security and on to the departure gate where the Swissair agent told them the flight was leaving early. He explained that, due to the very unsettled conditions in the United States, Swissair was anxious to get all its planes out of the country. While the plane had just arrived, they were turning it around immediately with what passengers they could assemble. Along with the others waiting, they were rushed aboard a gate transporter and moved out to the airplane. As soon as fueling was completed, the flight attendants hurried preparations for an immediate departure, actually leaving one and a-half hours early.

Because Roger's and Lucille's reservations had been made only that morning, Swissair had been unable to offer tourist class. They were then in first class, very unusual for government employees. Roger had requested a vegetarian meal, but because of the short notice, it had not made it. However, the flight attendants had been able to put together an acceptable substitute. Lucille had the choice of steak or fish and elected fish.

"Why don't you eat regular food?" Lucille asked. "I noticed in the NOAA cafeteria you seem to eat mostly raw vegetables, never meat, fish, chicken, or even eggs."

"Well," he started, knowing it could lead to a long story. "Some years ago, I wanted to take up a particular meditation practice, and the diet I follow is one of the requirements. I can eat dairy products if I want to, but I minimize them because they are not all that good for health reasons."

She was puzzled. "Why would it matter what you ate to follow a particular meditation practice?"

Roger moved into an explanation he had given on occasions before, "I guess it's an aspect of self-discipline, mainly, but there are several reasons. The animal products agitate the body cells after they are absorbed in digestion, so that relaxation, followed by meditation, is not as easily done. There is also a spiritual aspect of not causing pain to any living thing."

Lucille had a sharp mind and said, "But vegetables are living also. I suppose it causes them pain to be picked and eaten."

"True," Roger agreed, "but the consciousness of a vegetable is very low compared to that of an animal, so the pain caused to the vegetable would be very small. One does have to kill to live, but it is better to kill only the lowest life forms."

Lucille wanted to get on a more personal basis with Roger and so she changed the subject. "What was the happiest time in your life?"

"By 'time' I am assuming that you mean 'period' rather than a particular moment?"

She nodded, and he continued, "When I was very small, we lived near a dairy farm. I think I was about four years old. I used to go off by myself to the windmill on the dairy farm and climb to the top. It was about forty feet high above the ground, and the stronger the wind blew the more I liked it. From the top of the windmill, I used to imagine I was a bird, soaring high over everything. This used to remind me of a favorite dream I used to have a lot when I was small, of being a human but with functional wings and soaring over a beautiful landscape. Life was much simpler and lots of fun when I was young. What about you?"

"In my happiest period, which I think was several years later than yours, just before I started to school, we were living in Ohio and had a big garden. Since we had just moved, and there were no children near my age in the neighborhood, I played by myself quite a lot. When I was out in our garden, I would imagine a playmate my own age. I gave him the name of 'Johnny.' He became so real for me, that I could even see him and talk to him. Johnny was much more fun than real kids because he always did just what I wanted him to. Eventually, I made the mistake of telling my parents about Johnny, and they so discouraged me in believing in Johnny that pretty soon I couldn't see or hear him anymore. That was reinforced by my parents making sure then that real live children came to play with me."

After a pause she said, "What was your worst period?"

"I think it was about when I was ten," he said. "I was having some teeth out with surgery and had recently had to start wearing glasses. I only had sisters to play with, and at ten, they aren't much fun. So my parents came up with a 'wonderful' idea, to send me to spend the summer with my uncle's family, who lived about forty miles away. Well, that was even worse, because the only boy in their family was a year older than I, and he bullied me. He had two sisters who, at the time, I thought were worse than mine. I used to just close my eyes and think that by wishing hard enough, I would find myself at home. Of course, it didn't work that way: wishing never changes reality."

After a pause, she volunteered, "My worst probably came in my late teens when I just couldn't decide what I was going to do with my life. My parents were forcing me to face the issue because we had to decide if I was going on to college and, if so, where? I went into computer sciences, more as a holding action to allow me to decide later. In the end, things more or less got decided for me by events for which I never planned."

Roger, who had traveled abroad to international conferences many times, suddenly remembered the time changes coming. "We better try to get some sleep if we can, morning will come six hours early." Roger got the flight attendant to take out their seat separator to give them more room. With pillows and blankets, they lay back to rest. Lucille's hand was on the seat between them, and Roger covered it with his. She smiled, turned toward him, and leaned her forehead against his shoulder. Under the blanket, his hand came to rest on her right breast and she snuggled closer.

Sunrise and breakfast came all too soon, and before they knew it, they were landing at Geneva. After brief stops at immigration and customs, they were met by a Joe Ballard of the American Mission, who whisked them into town in a large limousine. After a few minutes of small talk, which sufficed to get them acquainted, Joe said, "The first briefing is scheduled for just after lunch. Are you up to it?"

"Sure," Roger answered. "I've given this pitch a few times now. I could probably give it in my sleep if I had to. I've got viewgraph slides. What equipment will be available?"

Joe laughed. "There are so many people who want to hear your briefing that it has been decided to do it in the Palace of Nations. This is the pitch capital of the world. They have every type of projector imaginable."

Lucille, who had been quiet for the last few minutes, said, "Where are we staying?"

"The Holiday Inn," Joe responded. "When Ray Carr called, I booked you right away. The Holiday Inn is close to the Palace of Nations, so it should be quite convenient. By the way, the Russians are sending a climate expert to support you. He will not be making any part of the formal briefing but will support any questions that are appropriate, particularly about the Russian simulations."

Roger picked up on that quickly. "We ought to get with the Russian expert before the briefing, just to make sure things will go smoothly."

"Sure," Joe responded. "I thought you might want to. He is staying at the Holiday Inn also. He got in last night and is waiting for us at the hotel. His name is Boris Kosygin."

At the registration desk, the clerk was apologetic, saying, "We have been getting phone threats against the hotel because most people identify the Holiday Inn with the United States, even though this one is Swiss owned. As a precaution, we are not renting our outside, lower-floor rooms, so we must ask our guests to double up where possible."

Roger and Lucille looked at each other, and Lucille spoke up first. "It's OK by me as long as we have separate beds." Roger nodded his agreement, and the clerk thanked them for their cooperation.

Joe left them with, "Ask the phone operator to put you in touch with Boris. I'll pick you up for lunch at eleven thirty, and afterward, we will go over to the Palace of Nations. We need to allow a little extra time to get checked in with security." Roger and Lucille headed for their shared room.

CHAPTER 10

Media

Marty had standing instructions that whenever Ray Carr called the President, to put him through right away, and that is just what she did. Ray had indicated that he had a priority message for the President.

"Bob, this is Ray. I'm down in the task force area. We have a situation that needs your immediate attention. If you could come over in ten minutes, I would like to show you the current prediction on the domestic scene that the What If is projecting. I'll have the members of the task force present to give us support on planning some actions."

When the President arrived, the task force was convened around the What If terminal. Ray asked Julia to brief the President on the latest domestic predictions.

Julia started by filling in some background. "The validity of the What If is based on having a current, accurate database. Obviously, when we went public with the glacial period crisis three days ago, it produced a major perturbation to the database. We sample reactions and update the database accordingly, a process that in this case took almost two days before we could get valid outputs on the domestic scene. The media has taken a much more hostile position to the administration than we had projected originally. We had expected a neutral attitude.

"What you see on the terminal right now is the What If's prediction, if the administration takes no more actions for the time being. As you can see, the enmity of the media will so poison society against the administration that, in about five days, large segments of the military can be expected to refuse to take orders, and some elements of the military may attempt a coup. This government will, shortly after that, cease to control events, and the country will move toward anarchy, guaranteeing a military coup. The opposition is so fragmented that no stable or effective leadership will emerge from them."

President Morgan asked, "Have you queried the What If on what happens if we place the media under direct government control?"

"Yes," she said, "it is too late to do that now. It would have worked two days ago. To do it now will speed up the disaffection of the armed forces. There are too many independent radio stations. It is not feasible to take control of enough of them in time."

"Does What If indicate that our NOAH briefings are not going over?" the President asked next.

"What If says that they are going over well with scientifically trained people," Julia responded. "The media people, by and large, are a very cynical bunch, and those making the policy decisions are largely not scientifically trained, certainly not in climatology. They are probably not convinced that what we face is all that serious. We don't think that they are listening to their scientific staffs."

Ray commented out loud, "I suppose the central problem is that as a people we have been used to the democratic process for so long that to turn to totalitarianism, even as the only answer for survival, runs against the very grain of our people. It is certainly easier to accept tough measures when you are in on the decision process. Suppose we bring in the media chiefs and let them see where they are taking the country with their present hostility. Let them use the What If to search for a better answer, and if they can't find one, maybe they will give their voluntary cooperation."

Julie picked up on Ray's idea. "I think it would go over best if we could do that on neutral ground, or even in their territory. How about the National Press Club? I think we should be able to patch in a broad band-pass line to the CIA headquarters at Langley where the What If is located."

The President was not known for dragging out decisions. "OK, Ray, let's do it. Work out the various questions they would be likely to ask the What If and run them ahead of time along with varying degrees of media cooperation. Get me the names of all the key people we ought to have at the Press Club, and I will call them personally. Let's try for 2:00 p.m. tomorrow so that when we win them over, they will have time to begin to work for our side on the evening news. We ought to have some of our climatologists there just in case there are still lingering doubts about the climate change."

As the President was leaving, Ray commented, "It is beginning to get ugly on the streets. I'll arrange for an armed guard for anyone who will be going over to the Press Club." He turned to the Whitehouse security representative and suggested that he make the arrangements for the Press Club as well as for security there.

The next day, the President, followed by his task force and a handful of climatologists, filed into the Press Club auditorium, where a place of honor for the President on the stage had been prepared. Some leaders of Congress, the vice President, the Speaker of the House, and the majority and minority leaders had been invited and were there also. The President's entourage took seats in the first two rows which had been reserved for them. Four officers of the Press Club were on stage with the President, when the Secretary of the Press Club took his stand at the rostrum.

"Mr. President, members of the Congress, and members of the press, I am glad that the Press Club can be of service at this time of great crisis for our country and, for that matter, for the world. At the request of President Morgan, the facilities of the Press Club have been made available, although I am as much in the dark as to the purpose as the rest of you. I therefore, without further delay, turn the meeting over to the President."

The President stood and took his place at the rostrum. "Ladies and gentlemen of the press and media, as I told you at my last press conference, the country and the world face the greatest crisis in our history. We are drifting into chaos and disintegration of our society, a trend which can only be reversed with your positive assistance.

"Today I would like to do two things. First, if you have any second thoughts about the seriousness of the climate crisis, we have the experts here who can answer any of your questions. Second, I will show you where our country will be shortly if you continue your present anti-administration slant in your editorials and news broadcasting. Will the climatologists present please join me on the stage?"

As they trooped up onto the stage, the President continued, "We have with us nine of the leading independent climatologists in the country who were able to join us on short notice." The climatologists sat down behind name placards, identifying their organizations. "These experts have all been given the data the government has on the coming changes in the climate. I would like to have you feel free to ask them any questions you still have at this time."

The first question was from the chief of the world's largest wire news service. "I would like the gentleman representing the University of Maryland to comment on the thoroughness of the NOAA's climatology simulations."

The senior climatologist from the University of Maryland took the portable microphone, "I have reviewed the NOAA simulations and have concluded that they are at least an order of magnitude more sophisticated than any previous known effort, in other words, the best in the world. The significant certification for the NOAA simulations is that they track very closely the known weather for nearly a century, demonstrating that all important factors are properly modeled. There is no doubt in my mind that their forward projections are accurate."

The next questioner recognized was the NBC vice President for news who asked, "I would like a comment by the appropriate expert on the validity of the government's projections on crop losses and the southward rate of movement of the line of year-round snow cover. What do you call that, the perennial snow line?"

The gentleman from the National Weather Institute offered to answer. "Yes, perennial is the right term. Actually, the perennial snow line had been moving southward for the past five years. So far it has not moved far enough to affect the growing of crops. The customers of our institute are largely agriculture, and this trend has had us worried for a number of years. Now that NOAA has pointed it out, we have to agree that this trend follows the classical transition into a glacial period. The NOAA simulations which we have examined appear completely valid and indicate that the severity of the coming cold glacial period will be approximately the same as the last. We agree with the NOAA projection that the perennial snow line, when it stabilizes, will start in central New Jersey and run more or less west until it reaches the Rockies which will be permanently covered with snow and ice. From the Rockies, the snow line will run pretty much west along the Oregon-California border to the Pacific. In passing, I might add, that there will be a band approximately 150 miles wide south of the perennial snow line, where the deeper ground will be frozen year-round, a situation common at the present time in parts of Alaska, Canada, and Siberia. This band would be classed agriculturally as tundra, where the upper few feet would thaw in the summer. South of this tundra band for hundreds of miles, the land would not be suitable for normal agriculture, because late spring and early autumn frosts and freezes would make for too short a growing season for anything but hardy grasses. The southern United States, where crops could still grow, will be greatly challenged because changed precipitation patterns will prevail."

The secretary of the Press Club asked the next question. "Would the same gentleman comment on whether he agrees with NOAA's projected timing, that the alleged coming cold glacial period will be in place in only twelve years."

The Weather Institute man responded, "Yes, twelve years seems about right since all the evidence indicates we have been in a transition for some time. Studies of lake-bottom sediments done many years ago for transitions into previous cold periods indicate that the transitions, when they occur, can be very rapid. The twelve years assumes no random events occur to speed the transition up, such as a major volcanic eruption. Such an event might reduce the twelve years to nine years."

The questions and answers continued for about an hour, covering much the same ground but allowing all the climatologists to be heard. They were all largely in agreement with the government's position, with none actually in disagreement. Some did feel there should be more research into temperature and CO_2 history in prior times. Several said that they wished there were more independent confirmations besides that of the Russian studies but agreed that the magnitude of the task was such that it could only be taken on by governments with large funding availability.

As the questions died down and began to cover old ground, the President moved back to the rostrum. "Well, then, based on what we have heard, I am sure you will agree with me that the administration's view that we face the greatest challenge in our history is a correct one. With that established, I would like to move on to our second subject. I know it is unenforceable, but I request that the remainder of the meeting be off the record, for reasons that will soon become apparent.

"What I plan to do now is share with you the various options that we considered when the coming climate change was first thrust upon us, and the projected results for each.

"For this discussion to be meaningful to you, I am declassifying a major project of the CIA called What If. What If is a sophisticated simulation of the social-economic-political scene of all the countries of the world, including the United States. The known and likely actions of those with which the What If is concerned are continually entered into the What If database as they are identified. The What If predicts expected changes in the given country or countries in question. As a tool for generating policy, the What If is particularly useful in showing the results to be expected if a new change is deliberately initiated by us. Examples might be the reduction in interest rates, the disappearance of some political figure, or the use of force in some international dispute. Because others will be taking actions which are not publicized and, on occasion, may not be anticipated by the What If, the predictions do diverge with time. The What If is most accurate in the near term, less accurate in long-range trends.

"Two weeks ago, this administration became aware of the projections of Project NOAH and at the same time was presented with a firm decision by the Russians to go public with the coming climate change. All reasonable What If scenarios were exercised, and the only scenario yielding a favorable outcome, by which I mean survival of what we call civilization, was some version in which we and the Russians took joint and immediate action to be backed up by our armed forces, if necessary. The best framework for this was in the garb of a Supreme World Government, in which the other countries could participate.

"In any of the scenarios in which we allowed due process, that is informing Congress, allowing for extended debates, abiding by majority decision, etc., resulted in an inability of this country to act. The greed and special interests in the Congress are so strong that they are shown to block any timely action that would be required. Obviously, while we deal with this crisis, great sacrifices will be required, and the game of making money will have to be put on hold. To get back to the due process scenarios, in all cases, by the time the public could be educated and aroused to put pressure on the Congress to act, conditions in other countries became extremely chaotic and unstable, including Russia. Atomic weapons were brought into play in the conflict over diminishing food supplies. What If demonstrates conclusively that only immediate action, highly visible to the rest of the world, and taken while there is still reasonable order and cooperation, has a good chance of succeeding.

"In order to get you a feel for what we were and are still facing, we have hooked up a What If terminal, here in your Press Club, to the What If computer in Langley. Julia, will you please set the terminal up here on the rostrum so everyone can see it?" As Julia did so, the President continued. "I would like to have the chiefs of the four major media networks come up on stage and, with Julia's help, ask the What If to predict the outcomes of actions the government might have taken. For this exercise, we have set the What If back two weeks in time as the situation was after we had absorbed the impact of the NOAH predictions but had not yet formulated any actions."

As three gentlemen and one lady came on stage, President Morgan said to them, "As you query the What If, please state your question orally, and Julia will input your question on the terminal. The results will be displayed on the terminal, projected on the large wall screen, and printed for a permanent record.

For this exercise, only strategic results will the shown. The What If normally includes much more detail than we can cope with today."

In about five minutes, Julia was ready for the first question, which was, "What if the administration took no action other than making an announcement of the Project NOAH results, with recommendations to Congress regarding food and energy conservation, planning for eventual population shifts, and the development of new technology?"

In about one minute after Julia's entry on the terminal, the results started to be projected on the wall screen for all to see:

1. 1 week   Food hoarding in the United States. Fall of three western European governments to be replaced by military dictatorships.

                     Move of the Russian armed forces toward the Indian Ocean warm water ports and oilfields.

2. 4 weeks   Financial collapse of US financial markets due to uncertainty of future businesses, particularly in the agricultural areas.

                     Starvation in Russia proper with its breaking up into several autonomous areas under local military warlords.

                     Ethnic riots in India and China, resulting in millions of deaths. Tripling of oil prices due to the threat to Mid-eastern oilfields from Russian armed forces.

3. 3 months   Worldwide depression and disruption of trade causing widespread starvation.

                     Threats of atomic bombing of neighbors by Russian warlord states to extract scarce food stocks.

Unsuccessful attempt by US forces to protect oilfields, United States backs down under atomic threats from Russian warlords.

Disintegration of governments of thirty developing countries.

4. 6 months   Crop failures in Canada due to July freezes.
Armed insurrection in the United States countered with the rule by martial law.

Atomic weapon usage in the Middle East. Russian warlord states enforce their demands on neighbors.

Julia pushed the stop button on the terminal and the displays froze without anymore activity. Julia explained, "With such radical departures from what we call 'normal,' the accuracy of the projections diverge so that it is not useful to go beyond the six month's projection. Shall we go on to the next What If?"

The next question stated was, "What If the President forcefully presented his full program to the Congress, including the recommendation to join in a Supreme World Government?" Julia broke the question down to include more specifically the details of the President's program and inserted it on the terminal.

In one minute the What If was again ready with its findings, which turned out to be almost the same as the previous projections, with the addition at each time interval of the statement:

President's program not enacted by Congress,
Obstructed by special interests.

Try as they could, the media chiefs were unable to come up with a scenario with a favorable outcome, and in some of their scenarios, there were atomic exchanges as early as three months into the projections. They even asked what would have happened if no climate change announcement had been made and the results were that Russia, knowing about the coming climate change militarily improved her position in preparation for it. Without an announcement, the United States could not rally opposition.

Finally, one of the media chiefs had Julia input the conditions that represented the actions that had been taken by the administration, including the formation of the SWG. In contrast to all the previous runs, the new results showed world stability and general, if forced, cooperation in facing a reduced world food supply and major relocations of large populations. The media chief asking the question turned to the President and said, "Mr. President, what is your problem?"

The President replied, "The What If projections are, as I should have explained in the beginning, no better than the correctness of the inputs. What you have been seeing so far are the outputs of the What If, based on what we had expected a neutral, objective media attitude of wait and see. We have, instead, been experiencing an openly hostile media and press, which have shown a strong bias against the administration, including frequent questioning of its motives and veracity regarding the coming climate changes. The media and the press may not realize their power in today's open society, and neither did we until we ran this exercise with the What If. Julia, will you repeat the last run, but change the assumption regarding the attitude of the media and the press?"

Julia proceeded to do so. The What If output repeated what it had done the day before, showing a breakdown in military control now only four days away and a loss of the ability to govern, going into chaos and anarchy in a week.

"My problem," the President said, "is that the media and press are using their monopoly in communicating with the public effectively to destroy the course on which the administration has committed itself and, unknowingly, most assuredly, to destroy the country in the process. We have looked at, with the help of the What If, the taking over of the media and the press, but that only delays the disintegration of our society and is not a solution. The damage is done, and the What If predicts that only the media and the press themselves can undo it. At this time, I can only appeal to you for your positive support and cooperation. It cannot be forced. You have seen where we are headed if you are to continue on your present course. Is there anything else we can say or any further information we can give you to help you understand the gravity of the situation?"

One of the network chiefs said, "It might help to be able to quote some of what has happened here today. Would that be possible?"

The President, with all eyes on him, paused and then answered, "All runs we have made with the What If indicate that if the public begins to panic, conditions will snowball out of control. We have already put a lot of stress on the public, so use your discretion as to how the public will react."

A very somber mood had come over the whole group, and there were no more questions or comments. The President and his entourage filed out to be escorted back to the Whitehouse under unusually strong security.

After an early supper, the task force settled down to watch the evening news. There was no mention of any significant political news on the local newscasts that came on before the network news. Ray divided his team into four groups so that between them they would get a full exposure to all four of the major networks.

The national news channel Ray was watching opened the news with the announcement that the President had held a special meeting with the press and media at the National Press Club but the reporting was very vague on details. It depicted the President as very open in making available all the government's data on the coming climate changes. The modifier "alleged" had been dropped. It was reported that all the independent climatologists present had supported the administration's views, which now appeared to be on solid ground. The news announcer went on to report that the President had presented convincing evidence that the course of action that the government was pursuing in conjunction with the Russians was in the best interests of the United States and the world at large. The report ended with a commentary that in the next few days, it was expected that there would be more information available on the implementation of the Supreme World Government, the creation of which should help bring stability to the world in these trying times.

When the news turned to other matters, Ray got the whole group together to compare notes. While the details varied and were given in different sequences, the four networks had all projected a similar story, similar enough to suggest that there had probably been some prior coordination. It seemed that the administration had finally gained the confidence of the media and, hopefully, the press, in the directions it had taken.

Julia came up to Ray and asked, "You have been in politics a long time. What finally convinced them? What changed their minds?"

"You know," Ray answered, "the media and press people are about the smartest people around when it comes to politics. Part of their attitude was a way of trying to smoke out what was really going on. When the President really leveled with them, all the pieces fell into place, and they could see without a doubt that what he had told them was the only possible explanation for what otherwise looked like a President gone mad. I hope they can convince the rest of the country."

"Don't worry," laughed Julia. "These are the people who can sell anything from soap to cars to people who have no intention of buying, and then without even believing in what they are selling. The way they have turned around, you can bet they will support President Morgan 100 percent. Too bad he had to lie about those runs we never made."

Ray smiled slyly. "He didn't lie. Many runs were made secretly over at Langley. We weren't told at the time because he wanted us to give him an independent input based on common sense. We must be a good team to have come up with the same answers as the What If."

CHAPTER 11

Moscow Center

Will Commons, the American Ambassador in Moscow, was really wondering what the Russians were up to because of the unusual things that were in process. It was unprecedented that he had been requested to attend a meeting of the Russian equivalent of Ray Carr's special task force. He had started to make arrangements to bring his personal translator but had been told it would not be necessary.

The last person to enter the meeting room was Ivan Petrovich, the Russian Prime Minister, who stopped in front of Will's chair and thanked him for coming. The Russian started the meeting, speaking in English. "Since the new world language is destined to be English, it is important that we all become proficient in it and practice it at every opportunity. We will speak English, always, in these meetings in the future. Each of you did not know it at the time, but one of the qualifications to be a member of this special group is to speak English well. I have asked Mr. Will Commons, our very good friend, to join us today, since much of what we must discuss involves the United States, and it would be better for him to know at firsthand with what we are dealing.

"First, I will speak of the good news. We have been concerned for the past few days that things were not going well for President Morgan. There are disadvantages to the democratic system, the people must be kept happy. The American television has now changed from giving President Morgan what in America they call a 'bad time,' to giving him praise. This is good, because making a Supreme World Government would not be possible without President Morgan being in a strong position. Our computer projections now show a general acceptance of President Morgan's commitments to us that he made at the summit and even his Congress will be cooperative in time. So, we should now turn to look at our own immediate problems." He turned to Olav Kerensky, "Would you please summarize in order of importance? Remember Mr. Commons is hearing this for the first time, so do not leave out important things you have told us before."

Olav took the floor. "We have problems that the special group has classed from major to urgent and have been grouped into categories:

1. "In some parts of Russia, food stocks are near ending. Where there is food, it is not a good nutritional mix. To avoid rebellions that would probably be successful, we must have food arriving from outside Russia in one month's time. We will need the equivalent of ten million metric tons of wheat by the fifteenth of April. While it is not required to survive and, in fact, is not always the most nutritional food, meat is very short, which is causing much grumbling. Because the northern ports are closed this time of year, the food will have to be brought in through the Ukraine. We are sure we can exert sufficient pressure on the Ukraine to allow this, particularly if some percentage of the food is given to them.

2. The harsh winter has interfered with our energy production, with much reduction in coal and oil. This has greatly hurt our ability to distribute food. Without hard money, I mean currency, OPEC will not sell us additional oil. Several of our major refineries have been out of production, so we are particularly short of motor fuels, automotive grade diesel, and gasoline for the food trucks. It is estimated that we need twenty tankers of refined products, evenly spaced between now and June 1. Again the early deliveries would have to be through Odessa.

3. Our rail-rolling cars have been going out of service faster than the workers can replace or renovate them. This

problem cannot be helped from abroad, because Russia uses a unique, wide track, originally chosen to slow down invaders who would not be able to use their own trains on Russian tracks. A short-term solution is to support our rail system with long-haul road trucks, what I think are called semi's in America. We will need one thousand such vehicles in the next two months.

4. Many of our key industrial personnel, particularly in Siberia, are without adequate clothing to perform their duties. This is particularly true of the coal miners, who are expected to strike if clothing is not found. For the rest of the winter, we need five million sets of warm work clothes with boots.

5. A serious problem is with atomic weapons. Our atomic weapons under the Soviet Union were deliberately dispersed, and with the breakup of the Soviet Union, some weapons ended up in several of the republics besides Russia, as you know. We have stated publicly that all tactical weapons have been returned to Russia, but this is not quite the case. The tactical atomic weapons can be armed and launched by the local commanders. We have had safeguards to prevent the launching of strategic weapons without command from Moscow Center, but over time, we are sure competent technicians could bypass such safeguards. We are concerned that several of the republics with these weapons might use them as blackmail on their neighbors to obtain food and other resources. Since we have joined with the United States in the Supreme World Government, this independent capability of atomic weapons is not good and must be neutralized."

As Olav fell silent, the Russian Prime Minister turned to Will and said, "So you see that, while your country is preparing the fight with the ice coming in a few years, we have problems that must be solved in the next months if the world is to live to fight the ice coming. These are problems that will not wait for the Supreme World Government to become in place and are beyond what we can do ourselves. I think now that the help for us must come from America, and I wish you to talk to my good friend, your President Morgan, and make sure he understands the urgency. We ourselves must work on the last problem, but if you clever Americans have some ideas about these atomic weapons, please tell us." Petrovich fell silent, and it was apparent the meeting was over. Will bowed out and returned to the embassy.

Will immediately got Ray on the phone at his home in Washington, at an hour much earlier than Ray would have liked. Ray joked, "It must be pretty bad to have to get me out of bed." Will repeated the five points that Olav had made in the meeting, which Ray made notes of so he would have an accurate account to present to the task force and the President.

At the end of the phone conversation, Ray commented on the Russian needs. "It doesn't sound as bad as the What If has been projecting. They must have already done more belt-tightening than we thought possible. When the task force gets together this morning, we'll kick it around and let you know what the President approves. With the belt-tightening we are doing ourselves, we ought to be able to handle most of what they want. It is the last one that really worries me, though."

Back in the Kremlin, the Russian Prime Minister had reconvened his special group, this time, of course, without Will Commons. He addressed Olav. "I consider the fifth problem you listed as the most urgent and potentially the most dangerous."

"Yes, Mr. Petrovich," said Olav, "You are right. The situation in some of the republics can quickly become very unstable, particularly Kazakhstan, which is a net food exporter and will wish to keep all their food for themselves. They will see us as weak, and, with the Supreme World Government not yet functioning, maybe consider a good time to cause trouble. This is what our computers predict. We have also received intelligence reports that General Zellov has ambitious plans for the area that will not be good for us. I did not wish to overly disturb the Americans. This is our own problem to solve at this point."

"Yes," said the Prime Minister. "What action do you have to recommend for Moscow Center to take?"

Olav replied, "We must eventually remove all the atomic warheads or destroy them by hostile action if necessary. We have agreed that only the Supreme World Government is to have control over atomic weapons. But this will take time to implement. The distant republics have heard the same announcements as the rest of the world, and they have not rushed to join the Supreme World Government and place their forces under its command. I think most will eventually come around if we pressure them. They may then feel less afraid of us because they can look to the Supreme World Government for protection. But General Zellov will be difficult. He is playing for high stakes and will not be easily pressured."

"Yes," the Russian leader said, "we have talked of Zellov before, but now it is more urgent. Let us take this up in a meeting devoted just to this problem. Olav, you will please prepare such a meeting soon. Try to get the latest intelligence from Kazakhstan to work into a plan on how to deal with Zellov."

* * *

Meanwhile in Kazakhstan, the general in question and his security chief were again in conference. Andrei spoke, "There is the unresolved problem we have discussed before. Our counter-intelligence teams continue to report that there is an unidentified radar beacon in our vicinity that triggers irregularly. We think it happens when particular Russian surveillance aircraft based in Russia proper are overhead. The beacon seems to be moved frequently, so no progress has been made in finding it. If we shoot down the aircraft, that would really aggravate Moscow."

"No," the general said. "We are not ready to be the side to take the first action. But this beacon may be a serious threat. Double the teams that are looking for it."

"Very well," responded Andrei.

CHAPTER 12

The Witch's Wind

After a few days in Geneva, Roger and Lucille were over the jet lag and felt that they had fairly well settled into their routine. Roger at first was surprised at how slow the presentations went compared to making presentations to an all-English speaking audience. The so-called real-time translating going on in many languages simultaneously still required that he go slowly. He also needed to explain nearly every point on all the charts so that they could also be translated.

When it came to questions, he found that he needed to be sure that he understood the translated question clearly before answering them. Also he was more than usually careful to avoid ambiguous language in his own answers. He noticed from their questions that the third world country representatives were often not very conversant with computers, a circumstance which made for some difficulty in communication. From informal conversations when making social contacts in the evenings, Roger felt that in general his message was being understood. Because of a sense of inferiority which they would try to cover, many that he contacted at first tended to dwell more on their own accomplishments rather than the serious business at hand. It was a slow process at which he had to work hard.

He vividly remembered the question the Norwegian representative had asked on the third day and the quiet that had settled on the hall when the answer was understood. The Norwegian had asked, "Where do you project the permanent snow line to cross Europe, ten years or more from now, when the transition has settled out?"

Roger had displayed the appropriate chart and answered the question, "In the west, the line starts here on the Irish coast and moves across central Britain. On the mainland, it picks up around Antwerp and heads across central Germany and Poland into the Urals. While Siberia will be colder, there will not be much snow accumulation because of the large land masses between it and sources of moisture. Manchuria, which is close to the western Pacific warm water currents, will pick up significant snow cover. In central Siberia, the tundra line will move south at least a few hundred miles."

The representative from Turkey next asked, "Then south of this line, there will generally not be much change caused by the cold coming?"

"No," Roger said. "You must have missed the significance of these two charts." He put them up in sequence again. "Here you see another line which varies from one hundred to three hundred miles south of the snow line which represents the probable points where the ground will be frozen solid almost the whole year. The top few feet may thaw briefly in the middle of summer as they do in Siberia and other northern areas. This last chart shows a line even farther south where there are predicted to be ninety or more days each summer that are free of frost or freezing conditions. The important point is that ninety frost-free days are required to bring most modern crops to harvest."

Roger had felt he should expand on the answer and continued to do so. "You note that the ninety-day frost-free line eliminates most of Europe and Asia Minor except for small pockets around the Mediterranean Sea. Going east through Asia, you note that little food will be grown until you come to India. Even here, there will be problems because changing wind patterns may make some areas, like the Punjab, which are now quite fertile, more arid. Other locations may, of course, receive more moisture. For example, the Sahara Desert has in the past been moving south, and we see this trend continuing. In compensation, northern Africa along the Mediterranean Sea should see significantly more rain."

Every day the most popular question had been, "How do you see the climate changing in my country?" Roger would first have to get the country identified before he tried to answer the question. Often, however, he would not have the detailed data at hand and would simply say, "My assistant, Lucille Van Brunt, who is in the back, has specific material for most countries. Please see her when you leave or during one of the breaks."

Roger did give them a general rule to apply regarding changes in expected moisture patterns. "Expect about the same precipitation from the equator to latitude 10° north or south. There should be less moisture from there to latitude 40°, and then more moisture, much of which will be in the form of snow. Areas fed by the monsoons have their own special rules."

There were certain political questions Roger would not answer, like the one from the Danish representative. "Could you provide more information on the conditions to join the Supreme World Government?"

Roger had commented, "Your question is outside the agenda for this meeting. However, I believe it was announced earlier that the United States and Russia are hosting a separate meeting in this building to deal with such questions."

One of the evenings, when Roger and Lucille had been relaxing at the Holiday Inn, Joe Ballard had introduced them to some of the visiting climatologists whom they had not yet met. They were pleasantly surprised by Sir William Suitland of the United Kingdom who said, "You put on a really good show today. Your Project NOAH is something we talked about doing for years but never had the money to get around to do. I personally am not surprised at the results. The signs of transition to a cold glacier time have been around us for years. We just haven't paid attention. You know during the last cold period half of my country was under ice, and we have a great many geological records showing it."

Lucille then said, "What sort of records do you mean?"

Sir Suitland had responded, "Well, the best records are probably the pollen deposits in the bottoms of lakes. They show, for instance, that changes from interglacial to glacial climates take place with declining forest growth as we have been experiencing. There must be some feedback mechanism because, as your simulations show also, the transition time can be very short. During the transition times, there are wide variations in the weather, heat to cold, drought to deluge. Other records of carbon dioxide samples from ice cores from existing glacier ice show an increasing level, something man has been contributing to. The carbon dioxide content of the atmosphere actually began increasing before man was making a significant contribution, probably mostly due to the dying of the forests. You know North Africa used to be largely forested."

Lucille asked again, "What makes the forests die back if it started before man did so much polluting, like with acid rain?"

This time it was Roger who answered her, "Well, the answer to that is still being debated, but a mechanical engineer by the name of Hamaker probably has the best explanation. It's documented in his book, *The Survival of Civilization.* He said years ago that the forests die back because they eventually use up most of the trace minerals in the soil and no longer have proper nutrition. They give up their carbon dioxide which results in a greenhouse effect. Hamaker believed, and Project NOAH has proved, that a greenhouse effect in the tropics provides the necessary additional energy needed to move the huge quantities of moisture from the tropics to the northern and southern regions which results in a glacial period. It was an Englishman, I believe, Sir George Simpson, many years before the time of Hamaker, who saw that enormous amounts of additional heat would be needed to bring on a glacial period, not cold as has usually been thought." It takes heat to vaporize water before it can move from equator to the poles.

Lucille was still puzzled. "All right, even if Hamaker is right on how glacial period starts, how does it stop?"

Suitland laughed. "I've heard Hamaker's answer to that one. The glaciers act like gigantic rock crushers and make stupendous amounts of rock dust that gets blown all over the world. Finally, the soil regains its nutritional value for the forests, and they come back, reabsorbing the carbon dioxide in the atmosphere. This reduces the greenhouse effect and hence the heat source that drives the cold period. Why the ice melts is still a puzzle."

Suitland then asked a question himself. "I have always wondered what a mechanical engineer was doing as a climatologist."

Roger laughed. "Too bad there are not more like him. Climatology is largely a case of thermodynamics applied on a very large scale. Thermodynamics is one of the core disciplines of mechanical engineering. Most of our climatologists come out of geology where things are much more static."

Suitland wandered over to another table, and both Roger and Lucille began to think about something much closer to home, each other. Lucille decided to change to a lighter topic. "Roger, I notice you are drinking orange juice again, even though it isn't nearly as good as the fresh juice we get back home. Don't you ever have a drink?"

"No," Roger responded without an explanation.

Lucille persisted, "Why not? This champagne is the best I have ever tasted."

Roger didn't answer right away, groping for the right words that would make sense to Lucille. "It's sort of like not eating meat that we talked about on the airplane coming over. When you take alcohol, or other drugs that effect your mind into your body, their vibrations change how you think, and you really aren't in control of yourself as well and might even do things that you would regret later."

"I see," said Lucille, not quite sure that she did. She was really enjoying the rosy glow from the champagne and didn't see what was wrong with it.

Roger broke into her thoughts. "It is beginning to get late. We really ought to find some supper and get to bed. I notice that morning still seems to come very early over here."

When they got back to their shared room, Roger found his ionizer and plugged it in. Located more or less in the center of the room, it did a good job of countering the excess positive ions that were prone to flood Geneva during the winter. Geneva had a reputation for a host of winter ailments that were attributed to the wind off the nearby glacier. The wind was known locally as the witch's wind. Roger had encountered it before and had made sure to bring an ionizer.

As they were sitting on the couch, Lucille thought about their present experience, sharing a hotel room. So far it had been platonic, each one dressing in the bathroom and avoiding embarrassing the other in their personal grooming. It had seemed natural at first when they were both tired from the trip, but Lucille thought it was time for a change. She turned to Roger and snuggled up to him, remembering how nice it had been on the airplane. In a little while, Lucille turned her face up to Roger so he could kiss her, but he just kept looking out toward the center of the room.

"What's the matter," she whispered, "Don't you want to kiss me?"

"Of course I do," he responded. "I also feel very much like taking you to bed right now." But Roger made no move in that direction.

"What's wrong with that?" Lucille asked, squeezing his hand.

"At some point, there will be no stopping," he said softly. "Then after a while you will come up with twins. I know it sounds old-fashioned, but I believe in not having sex except in marriage, when you have made a permanent commitment to each other and taken on all the responsibilities that go with a sexual relationship."

"Have you ever gone to bed with a girl?" she asked.

"Sure," he responded, "enough to know that promiscuous sleeping around, or even having sex with a steady partner, is not what I am looking for. What about you?"

"Well, a girl would be really weird today if she hadn't had some experiences. It's one way to handle the loneliness of life today."

Roger still made no move to increase the tempo of their embrace. Lucille broke the impasse with a low laugh. "Well, kissing isn't sex, and I promise not to vamp you."

Roger gave her a long, hard kiss, to which she enthusiastically responded by hugging him with both arms around his neck and pulling herself hard against his chest. Reluctantly, Lucille let go, and Roger said, "You can have the bathroom first."

As Lucille took her bath, occasionally breaking into song, Roger wondered if he was falling in love and if his resolve to limit sex to marriage would last long. He had noticed that sharing a room with Lucille really set his blood pounding. Lucille, humming to herself, came out of the bathroom, got into her bed, and was very soon asleep. It was a long time before Roger got any sleep that night.

CHAPTER 13

Onto Greater Things

It was ten days after the President's news conference, and Ray had just convened a meeting of the President's task force. To Roger, who was just back from Geneva, the country seemed relatively calm under the soothing influence of the media and the press. They were reporting President Morgan to have reached an all-time high in public popularity. There were exceptions. Members of the ultra right had participated in a few armed demonstrations to show their displeasure with the government for placing its power under a higher authority, the SWG. Several small communities in the remote west had declared their separation from the rest of the United States, but no one seemed to notice the difference. The only discontent Roger had sensed in the general population was that now that the world's greatest crisis had been declared, why wasn't something happening? Roger reflected that even in trying times, the wheels of government grind rather slowly, particularly when seen from the outside.

Roger was pulled away from his thoughts by Ray's voice, and he realized that the meeting was in progress. Ray was saying, "We have a lot to cover today as you can see by the topics on the agenda that each of you has received."

1. Countries currently asking to join SWG
2. Initial SWG organization and staffing
3. Implementation of items agreed to at the summit
4. Candidate projects for climate modification

5. Response to the Russian President's appeal for assistance.
6. Reassignment of task force team members.

From the quizzical looks on many of the faces, Ray could tell that most were wondering what was going to happen when they came to the last item on the agenda. He had deliberately put it at the end so that the other items would be out of the way when they came to it.

Ray began, "Between ourselves and Russia, we have so far heard from twenty-nine countries that want to participate as charter member states in the SWG. These are Sweden, Norway, Denmark, Finland, Belgium, The Netherlands, Switzerland, Germany, Poland, Austria, Hungary, Romania, Czechoslovakia, Turkey, Israel, Saudi Arabia, The United Kingdom, Ireland, Iceland, Greenland, Costa Rica, Sri Lanka, Oman, Muscat, Peru, Chile, Honduras, New Zealand, and the Baltic countries as one state. The Baltic countries have been in the process of negotiating a combined political organization, and have requested to join as a single state. I am sure that there will be a lot more who will join right away when they see how many already have. The charter members fell in line with the What If predictions that those most adversely affected will join immediately. It is unfortunate that France, China, North Korea, and several of the old Soviet Republics have not seen fit to join because some of these countries have a significant nuclear capability, and if they decide to resist SWG's plans, things could get very dangerous. We will just have to work around them initially."

Nathan King of the State Department interjected, "We understand some African countries are interested but want clarification on voting and how much influence they might have on decisions of the SWG."

"That touches on our second agenda point," Ray said. "President Morgan and the Russian Prime Minister in their joint agreement made it clear that, at least initially, might makes right, and they intend that the United States and Russia together will dominate the SWG. This is particularly important in the structuring of the organization, as well as the establishing of the goals and objectives. What is planned to be announced as of today is an organization similar to the United Nations without the veto, except that each delegation will have a vote equal to its country's population, multiplied by the value of the resources it has turned over to the SWG. This group of delegates will act as a legislative branch which will select individuals from the member states to head up each of the major administrative departments. The department heads will form an administrative council which will be headed by a chief administrator. Even using conservative estimates for the values of the armed forces that we and the Russians have committed, between us we will have a large majority."

"Wow," said Julia, "Looks like President Morgan and the Russian Prime Minister between them have stacked the deck."

"Well," continued Ray, "this is not set in concrete until it is announced later today in both Washington and Moscow. We can still suggest and get changes made, providing that the Russian Prime Minister agrees. Any suggestions?"

Wiley Brooks spoke up. "Let's face it. We are about to embark on the greatest human endeavor ever attempted and under very difficult conditions. History shows that only a strong, central government has a chance to succeed. Even democracies in the past, when faced with great challenges, have had to curb their freedoms and revert toward totalitarian forms. We will be entrusting the people that are selected for positions of leadership with a great deal of power. There can always be a rotten apple in every barrel, and we need some kind of check for just such a contingency. I suggest that there be some kind of judiciary."

"Good point," Ray agreed. "We'll recommend that to President Morgan and the Russian Prime Minister as well. So far, he has been very agreeable, and when we get to agenda item number five, you will see that he will be getting even more so. The Russian system is not based on an independent judiciary, but a good case can be made that having one should also help attract other undecided countries to join the SWG."

"What individuals make up a country's delegation is really up to the country, and some countries may wish to continue the personnel they now have at the UN. The main difference is that the SWG will be capable of enforcing its decisions. There will be no vetoes. There should also be no stalemates, at least in the immediate future, as long as the United States and Russians agree. Naturally, the scope of the SWG is much broader than what was ever considered for the UN, and so it will require a much greater staff with much broader skills. To focus the initial direction to be taken by the SWG, it is intended that the department heads selected are committed to the stated goals of the SWG as enumerated in the joint statement from the summit. Since English will be the language of the SWG, all staff members will need to be proficient in it. Obviously they should also have appropriate governmental experience. I am dwelling on this topic because I believe that some of you are good candidates, but we will come to that later.

"One problem, for the SWG to be really sovereign, is that it must be physically secure, which is not possible when it is hosted by a member state. That was the reason for the creation of Washington, DC, for the United States. I anticipate that the SWG will quickly decide to locate its headquarters on an island which would really provide physical security. In fact, from a point of view of dispersal, several islands would be a good idea. To my mind, Puerto Rico, Hawaii, New Zealand, and Sri Lanka are viable candidates."

Julia spoke up again, "For a government that so far only exists on paper, it seems to me that a lot of decisions are already being made."

Ray laughed. "Well, some of us who expect to be part of the SWG naturally can't help thinking ahead.

"Getting to the next agenda item," he continued, "as far as the implementation of the items agreed to at the summit, where applicable, the various departments of the United States Government should move out and start implementation. As you will see later, that is not intended to be a responsibility of this task force. The various departments of the administration already have the machinery in place, and there is no point in duplicating it.

"In this implementation, the Department of Agriculture should start initiating for the United States the plan for food production, storage, and distribution. A standby rationing system should be put into place.

"The Department of Defense is in the process of being combined with the other armed forces that are being transferred to the SWG. Some of its forces will not be required, and they will need to be disbanded. It is likely to take a month or so to effect the transfer. At this time, it is anticipated that land-based strategic forces will be eliminated. I would expect that most of the sea-going forces will be retained, as well as most of the military satellites.

"The Department of Interior will take over the management of the forests and has the immediate task of stopping the cutting of the trees and the initiation of the planting of vast quantities of new trees both in public forests as well as on what used to be private lands.

"The President has decided that he wants the Department of Health Education, and Welfare to take on our commitment of zero population growth. When the time comes, HEW will also have the responsibility for population relocation from our northern states as well as from Canada.

"HUD will be responsible for generating new housing and working out the doubling up in existing housing. HUD will also take on the building of the large number of greenhouses that will be needed.

"The Department of Energy has the responsibility of transitioning our society to the use of one-half the energy we currently use within three months' time. A major thrust of the department, in cooperation with the Department of Science and Technology, will be to bring on stream renewable energy sources and fuels that produce little CO_2 in their utilization."

Ray paused and looked around the room. Then he said, "Moving the economics of this country from one of personal and group greed to one of mutual survival may be the most difficult task facing us. It certainly will be the responsibility of all of us, not just one department. It means completely changing everyone's value system drastically. Our lifestyles, which have been oriented around luxury and pleasure, will have to be changed to ones of work and sacrifice. This will be harder for us than the developing countries where people are largely just struggling to survive anyway. Public or group ownership of the majority of our civilization's assets will have to replace private ownership and exploitation.

"A first step of the SWG will be the issuance of a new, universal currency. The Treasury Department will have the responsibility of the conversion of our dollars working through the banks which will be nationalized. The new currency will be backed by the gold reserves of all the member states.

"A pillar of our changed world will be universal work for everyone who is capable. The Department of Labor is charged with implementing this drastic change in our society. They will match up talent with job needs. Where there is no fit, people will have to take jobs that need to be done anyway, like planting trees. In essence, if you won't work, you won't eat. Those that steal will be dealt with harshly; we can't afford a large prison population.

"An even greater challenge is how to manage the existing businesses we will need and how to create quickly enough the new ones we will create for our survival. There is no department in the administration for which this task is appropriate, so a new department is being created, the Department of Economic Activity, broader than the War Production Board organized during WWII. Besides those things already mentioned, this department will also be responsible for converting or liquidating those businesses that are not essential. Business activity will be for the survival of the people rather than for profit. Generally then, any business will be managed by those participating in it, more or less along the lines of a cooperative. Large businesses will still need professional managers, but they will not be the robber barons of the past, rather they will be responsible to the people."

Ray then turned to Dr. Meriwether and Roger. "On the next agenda item, do you have any promising possibilities for minimizing climate change?"

"Yes," Meriwether said. "We have two approaches that look very good. The first is to use atomic explosives to widen certain channels in the Arctic which would allow more warm water currents to flow there, reducing the snowfall in the northern regions. The effect on the climate looks promising. The

Department of Defense is looking at the best warheads to adapt to minimize radioactive fallout. That study should be done in a week, and our schedule requires that existing warheads be utilized. The second project would be to inject clouds of particulate matter into orbits near the equator to reduce the absorbed radiation from the sun in the tropics and hence the amount of moisture evaporated, in other words, to balance out the greenhouse effect. We have NASA doing a study for us which should be complete in two weeks. This second approach is not a permanent fix because the particulate matter will eventually fall back to the earth's atmosphere, but it will buy us time while we work on getting the carbon dioxide level in the atmosphere down. The Russians are looking at moving icebergs to the tropics to cool things down and reduce moisture evaporation, but that is really a long shot."

"OK," Ray said, "keep up the good work at NOAA. Get these ideas developed more fully and plan on a comprehensive review in about three weeks."

Going to the next agenda item, Ray said, "Since we received the recent request from the Russians for substantial immediate aid, it has been under study by the CIA to coordinate a recommendation. Julia, do you have something for us yet?"

Julia responded, "Yes, we have a pretty thorough response. The What If has been of considerable help in reaching the conclusion that it is feasible to meet most of their needs.

"First, regarding food. If we get all the meat animals that are in feed lots and the open ranges to market, there will be a temporary surplus of meat, even if we send the Russians a substantial amount. The human edible grain saved by not feeding these animals is enough to feed six hundred million people a year, so we can meet the Russian grain requirements and put aside a very sizable surplus. In fact, before our capability to grow grain is reduced, we should have a year's harvest in surplus of wheat, corn, and soybeans. Getting all that meat to market in such a short time will require reopening some closed packing houses. Availability of food is not so much of a problem as getting it to the Russians. Fortunately, an amazing number of ships in the world are of Russian registry. I'm sure the Russians will know how to arrange priorities when we tell them where the food is.

"With regard to the needs for gasoline and diesel fuels, the Middle East OPEC countries have more than adequate surpluses, as well as the tankers to transport them. Up to now, they haven't been accepting anything but hard currency payments for oil products. With two of the big producers already asking to join the SWG, it looks like leverage could be applied there." Ray made a note to himself to see action done.

Julia went on, "The rail-rolling stock problem has a short-range and a long-range solution. For the short-term solution, the What If concurs with providing the Russians with semi-trailers. As the luxury market in this country dries up, there will be a large surplus of long-haul carriers, a trend which is already apparent in long-haul carrier bankruptcies. Also energy rationing will force a great deal of freight now carried by the trucking system back to the railroads, which can haul a ton of whatever for about one-tenth the energy cost of road vehicles. Approximately 75 percent of the current long-haul trucks will be idle, the remainder will be pressed into short haul use. One thousand of these types of carriers won't put a dent into the surplus. There will obviously be widespread unemployment of drivers and mechanics who might find it a good idea to drive in Russia if that is where the only driving jobs are. The long-term solution, so that the Russians don't waste energy, is to get them using the rails more. Fortunately, we located an idle factory in Poland which is capable of turning out the needed wide-track rail cars, and we should make sure that facility is reopened. With Western technology, in this case from Germany, we estimate that the existing Russian rail car capacity can be doubled in four months." Ray made some more notes.

Julia went on to the next Russian need. "There is more than enough clothing of the type the Soviets have requested in the current stocks of our various discount chains in the United States and a lot more in the pipelines from the Asian countries where most of this clothing is made. There are also a few million service uniforms in government stocks that now will never be issued. It shouldn't be a problem to have all the semi-trailers that we are going to send them pick up the clothes before heading for the ports at which they would be loaded. Of course, the private stores need to understand that it is in their interests to cooperate." Ray made his last note of the meeting.

Julia concluded with, "So far no one has come up with any good ideas about what to do with the Russian's fifth problem, the possible use of atomic weapons in their old republics who still have atomic weapons. The Departments of Defense and Energy are continuing to study the problem. Personally, I don't think the Russians have told us everything they know. I suspect that they already have a problem republic in the process of causing trouble."

Ray concurred with the last point by nodding his head and said, "From the beginning on that one, we knew it was basically a Russian problem. We should know more about it, however. I'll suggest to the President that on the next opportunity to probe the Russians."

After a pause, Ray said, almost to himself,

"We haven't made a decision on whether to continue our efforts in manned Space flight; has anyone done any serious thinking on it? We really have two major programs that require significant resources, the space stations, and our initial colony on the moon where we currently have four personnel, two who are Americans, I believe."

Gil Powers of OMB was the first to comment. "Cancelling either of these two programs or both will not save as much real resources as it might appear on paper. The people would have to be supported somewhere. It would also be very expensive to restart them if we wanted to, assuming we come through the climate change with some kind of civilization intact. At the very least, we should evaluate their potential value to our climate change efforts."

Meriwether took the floor next. "If we find inserting particulate matter into orbital space to be viable, we would want to make tests in free fall before committing to a particular design and the space stations would be the ideal place for that."

Paul Cummings was next. "We have been counting on doing basic materials research on the moon's surface with materials found naturally there in an un-oxidized state. That program has just got underway at our Perry Crater base at the North Pole."

Ray then summed up what he thought to be the consensus position, "Very well, then leave the manned space flight programs as they are, but consider reducing the Perry Base personnel to two if the right mix of talents can be achieved to still do the material research work."

"Very good," Ray said, "Thanks all of you for the hard work. Now we are up to the item which I am sure you have been waiting impatiently for since it involves each of us personally. The President has decided that the purpose for which this task force was created is nearly finished, and I would like to pass on to all of you that he has been very pleased with your performance. Now that a direction for the future has been settled on, it is best discharged in the United States by the bureaucracies that are already in being or the several new ones being created. We personally have the opportunity to move on to greater things. I will be transferring to the United States delegation to the SWG as of tomorrow. The President and I both would like each of you to join me with the expectation that we will all become key members of the SWG staff. The challenges there will be great and, of course, the future uncertain, but certainly it will not be boring. Those of you who do not wish to do so may return to the jobs you had before the task force was established. I would like your firm decisions in the morning so that if your decision is negative, I can arrange alternates in a timely manner. If there is nothing else, I again thank you for a job well done and hope you will join me in the SWG."

As they walked away from the meeting, Meriwether commented to Roger that he planned to accept Ray's offer since that was where the action was going to be. Fred was now acting in Leon's old position, now that Leon had taken early retirement and figured that would be a good deal for him as long as Roger didn't return to NOAA. Naturally interested in what Roger was going to do, Fred said, "Roger, what are you going to do, join the SWG?"

"I haven't decided," Roger said as they separated in the hall. Roger very much wanted the challenging and what he expected would be exciting work at the SWG, but Lucille had been very much on his mind. He knew that if he moved, first to New York, and later to who knew where, that he might be seeing a lot less of her.

With that on his mind, Roger called Lucille at NOAA and got her just before she was about to leave for the day. "Say, Lucille, a lot has happened over here today. Can we get together for supper and talk about it?"

"Sure," she replied, and they agreed to meet at the Purple Onion in Georgetown.

Over dinner, Roger told her what had happened and about the offer to join the SWG.

"Sounds great," Lucille smiled, "You won't get an opportunity like that again. Why are you waiting?"

"Well," he said, as he put his hand over hers, "I was hoping from now on for us to really get to know each other better. You know, to decide if we want to make this between us permanent. My being in New York almost immediately won't help."

Lucille asked, "Just what do you mean by 'making this permanent'? Do you mean getting married?"

"Yes, exactly," he answered.

"Most people," Lucille said, "would just get married, and if it didn't work out, well, even in New York, these days, it isn't hard to get divorced."

"I don't feel like most people" was Roger's response. "I want to be sure it is right for us and, if it is, get married for keeps. Right now, I feel that I love you and want to be with you and get married, and even have children when they let us have them again. But I haven't ever felt this way about anyone before, and I don't know how to be sure."

Lucille smiled. "I know a way that ought to help you to be sure."

Roger wouldn't be diverted and continued his thoughts out loud. "I know about the passion side. I'm sure we will be great together in bed. But for me, there must be so much more to a good marriage. I want to be sure that we are also good friends, that we will enjoy doing a lot of the same things, that we respect each other, and also that we allow each other space to be ourselves. You know we have only known each other on a personal basis for two weeks! Maybe the way I eat bothers you."

"Roger," she said softly, "it seems to me that I have known you all my life or maybe all of some other life. Anyway, I don't need to wait to be sure. But I want you to be sure. Why don't you take the SWG job, and I'll see if I can get something in New York?"

Roger had a brilliant idea. "SWG will certainly need many computer experts, if they take on half of what they are planning. When I talk to Ray tomorrow, why don't I con him into taking you on too as part of the deal?"

After having shared a hotel room for over a week, it didn't seem unnatural for Roger to spend the night in Lucille's apartment. Her apartment mate was away, so there was a spare bedroom for him.

That evening Roger held Lucille in his arms, tenderly, for a long time. They lay on her couch as they talked about the things new lovers talk about. While neither one said anything about it, Roger felt as though they were engaged. They kissed frequently, wanting to prolong the magic moment. Without discussing it, neither one felt that this was an occasion for engaging in wild passion.

CHAPTER 14

Moscow Center Revisited

Russian Prime Minister Petrovich had convened his special group. He seemed to be in a more positive mood than the last time they had met. He spoke first. "We have received good news from the American Ambassador. He has told me that the United States can provide everything we asked them to send us. Perhaps we should have asked for more. Regarding the immediate need for food, there is a problem with sea transport, and they have suggested the use of Russian ships. Comrade Sopolov, have your department establish priorities and route the needed ships to the United States' ports without delay. You should have our Ambassador in Washington coordinate these shipments with their Secretary of Commerce. This time of year we will have to use the Black Sea ports and the ports on the Baltic. The latter should not be difficult, since the Baltic Republics have felt indebted to us for letting them become independent." He laughed at the irony of the word: independent one year and then under the SWG a year later.

Olav felt it proper to comment. "We are planning to increase our dock-handling capabilities at all these ports where the food will be delivered. Odessa particularly needs an increased capacity. Since they will be getting a share of the food, they have agreed to cooperate and let our shipments come in through there. However, special Russian security forces will be attached to the ports to make sure there are no diversions. The long-haul trucks should arrive soon with their drivers and mechanics to be available to start food distribution immediately."

"Yes," said the Prime Minister, "this is as we discussed this morning. Also we must be sure that the petrol facilities are ready to receive the diesel fuel and gasoline. They will arrive first since they have only to come from the Persian Gulf. We must anticipate every possible problem to make sure all is handled properly. We must concentrate our snow-removal machinery along the highways that the trucks will use.

"Now let us discuss the main reason for our meeting. Olav, you have a report on the problem of the atomic weapons previously controlled by us."

Olav turned to a slide projector and projected a map of Russia and its neighbors that had been specially prepared the previous day. Contrasting colors were used to depict the various republics and the locations of the atomic weapons. "As you can see, the major land atomic weapons in Russia are deployed in areas that are generally accessible from the Trans-Siberian Railway. These are of intercontinental range, capable of targeting nearly any location on the earth. Our rail-deployed forces can be anywhere on the rail system that we want them to be and are currently widely dispersed. We also have deployed some land-transportable rockets of lesser range, some of which carry only single warheads. These latter are in the border areas. As called for in our agreements with the United States, we no longer deploy tactical atomic weapons. We still have a considerable number of atomic weapons on long-range bombers and aboard nuclear submarines. All these forces will soon be transferred to the Supreme World Government Command."

Olav paused to allow for any questions. When there were none, he continued, "Both the Ukraine and Belorussia, which, between them, have some weapons have indicated their intent to join the SWG, so those weapons also will pass to the control of the SWG command."

Olav paused again, then continued, "The problem is Kazakhstan, the only other republic of the previous Soviet Union known to have atomic weapons. Some of you already know General Zellov's intentions from other briefings, but for the benefit of others, I will repeat them. Based on the latest intelligence from our operator in General Zellov's headquarters, the general has no intention of joining the SWG. His military district covers the western half of Kazakhstan, and although there is a nominal civilian government, by means of the military forces under his control, General Zellov is the virtual dictator of that part of Kazakhstan. He has a strong internal security system in place which will be effective for some time in preventing any challenge to his leadership.

"Based on secret monitoring of several of his most recent staff meetings, we know that he intends to establish an area he controls from western Kazakhstan, south through Turkmenistan, to include all of Iran. Besides the ground forces under his command, General Zellov plans to use his atomic weapons to blackmail to get cooperation from his neighbors. Turkmenistan has apparently already agreed to allow him uncontested passage thorough its country to his primary goal, which is Iran. We know that there are approximately fifty SS-18 ICBMs in the area under the general's control. Again, based on our secret monitoring, we must assume that many of these missiles, each with ten warheads, have been modified to be targeted, armed, and launched by the local missile crews. Also there is good evidence that the propulsion systems on some of these SS-18 missiles have been altered so as to allow them to be used in an intermediate range mode which would allow their use against Russia if we were to oppose his actions. There is partial evidence that some reserve SS-18 warheads are being modified so that they could be airdropped from aircraft that are under the general's command. Lastly, General Zellov apparently has in his possession 150 tactical missiles with atomic warheads which were missed when all such weapons were recalled to Russia. These were in some type of reserve capacity and were not counted when the return occurred. As you know, the tactical missiles have always been locally controlled, so no modifications are needed to them for General Zellov to use them if he sees fit." Olav had come to the end of his planned presentation.

The Russian leader turned to General Boris Metchnikoff, his senior military staff present. "I had asked you to study the problem of neutralizing Zellov's atomic forces. Do you yet have a conclusion?"

"Yes," the general replied. "Of course, we can neutralize the atomic forces under General Zellov, but we could expect he would be able to successfully destroy a number of Russian cities in the process. It would be suicide for him to attack us first, so we can assume we will have the advantage of the first attack. However, with the weapons available to us, we would not have a complete surprise. I suggest we coordinate this with the United States, and with the help of their stealth aircraft, we should be able to destroy Zellov's atomic forces without retaliation."

The Prime Minister turned back to Olav. "What is your evaluation of the likely success of a surgical team to eliminate Zellov himself?"

Olav shook his head. "The projection is that Zellov will be on the move more or less continuously for the near future. This would be an almost impossible target for any team we were to send from here or from any other republics that would be sympathetic, such as the Ukraine. I think a better option for taking Zellov out is to rely on the beacon that we are now sure our operator was able to plant in his command car. The beacon seems to have been in the vicinity of wherever Zellov has been for the past few weeks. At the appropriate time, we could launch a homing missile tuned to the beacon's transmission."

"Very well," the Russian leader said, "let us make contact with our counterparts in the United States and plan the mission to remove Zellov's atomic forces. It must be done before Zellov gets in firm control of Iran because at that time we understand he plans to make an alliance with the Chinese."

Then he seemed to clear his thoughts for other matters. "We have heard from the United States, confirming the timetable for the organization of the SWG. Our delegation needs to arrive in New York on the day after tomorrow in time for the opening meeting in the afternoon. The SWG will become the most powerful force on earth, compared to the weak UN that was just a convenient forum for propaganda. We must send the very best people we have. Olav, I wish you to be the head of our delegation, and I know that you will become very important in the SWG. Will you do this for me?"

"Of course," Olav answered, somewhat surprised at the sudden turn in his projected future.

"Thank you, Olav," the Prime Minister said, "You will then need to move all of your present duties to your second-in-command. You may stay a Russian at heart, but you will be SWG first from now on. So that your loyalties to SWG will not be questioned, it is required that you take all your immediate family with you. If you never see Russia again, may you still have as happy a life as these times permit you."

Ivan Petrovich leaned back in his chair and closed his eyes. It was a sign that the meeting was over and that he wished to be left alone. The others left quietly. It was a sad time for him. He had never had a son of his own, but often thought that if he had had a son, he would like to have had him be like Olav Kerensky. It was too bad that Kerensky had lost his wife after she had given him a son and a daughter. The musings of a man getting old, he thought. He had never asked Olav why he had never remarried and now he probably would never know.

CHAPTER 15

The Big Sticks

The first meeting of the SWG Congress was scheduled for an afternoon early on a cold winter day at the old UN headquarters. Those UN delegations whose countries had not yet joined SWG had moved out of their quarters, making the building seem relatively vacant. Only thirty-five were to be the charter members by last count. Most of the support staff of the now defunct UN had been very happy at the opportunity to stay on, so the SWG had at least a minimum staff of secretaries, translators, clerks, and general administrators. The old UN Secretary-General had agreed to stay on for the first meetings in the role of chairman, at least until such time as the SWG got organized. It was he who lowered the gavel and called the meeting to order.

The thirty-five delegations were arranged alphabetically by the countries, now called states that they represented. As required by the agreement that had been made between the leaders of the United States and Russia, all business would be transacted in English. Those delegations not fluent in English were assigned translators. As he pounded the gavel, Hamar Arundel was pleased to notice that many of the faces were familiar as old standbys from the UN. The American and Russian faces were largely new, and Hamar recognized the significance of that. They knew they were playing for real this time and had sent in their first teams.

Hamar began in a slow, but well-ordered English, "Ladies and Gentlemen of the Supreme World Government, I am pleased to be of assistance to you in this, your beginning, and I hope you will have more success in the affairs of men than did your predecessor organization, the United Nations. As has been agreed upon by the majority of the delegations, the first order of business is to announce the voting strength of each delegation. The voting formula all of you agreed to in joining the SWG is that each delegation's vote is in proportion to its population times the value of its contribution to the SWG. So far each country has contributed its armed forces. The value of each state's armed forces in United States dollars has been estimated by Jane's of London. Each country's own most recent census has been used for the purpose of establishing population. For each member state, these two factors have been combined and normalized for a total of one hundred for the combined thirty-five states. These are then the various delegation strengths in voting and will be projected on the screen on your right."

The screen came to life, showing the United States at 39.1, Russia at 37.2, the next largest at 4.3, and so on down to a fraction of a percent.

The spokesman for Switzerland rose to be recognized and spoke, "The system of voting strengths is patently unfair since a large country will normally spend more on its armed forces, and hence the voting strength will tend to follow the square of the country's population rather than be proportional to the population."

Hamar Arundel answered, "The system may seem unfair to some. I will not express my personal opinion, but I must remind you, however, that it was the system described and widely publicized by which all who wished to join the SWG would abide. Also you should remember that the armed forces are not the only assets that can be transferred to the SWG. When such other assets are transferred, the voting ratios will certainly change."

The gentleman from Switzerland sat down, and Hamar continued, "For the time being, until this body sees fit to organize itself differently, I will chair this meeting along the lines of Robert's Rules of Order but simplified in those areas which might otherwise allow undue delaying tactics. This group meeting today has been referred to by some as the 'World

Congress,' the legislative body of the SWG. Until some other term is designated, I will refer to it by that name."

Then he said, "The business at hand today is to implement the body called for which is to be the executive body of the SWG. The agreement calls for the election of directors of major departments of activity of the SWG who, together with a coordinating director, will be the executive body of the SWG. I suggest now is the time for motions which designate the departments that the SWG should create. After that, you will elect persons to fill those positions."

At that point, a number of delegation spokesmen rose, and Hamar recognized the spokesman from the United Kingdom, who said, "I yield the floor to the delegation from the United States."

Ray Carr rose to speak, "Fellow members of the Supreme World Government, we and the Russian government have, of course, had considerably more time to think of the various aspects in which the SWG should get involved, and how the responsibilities involved might be divided into directorates." He held up a piece of paper and continued, "I move that the directorates listed herein be created to discharge the obligations of the SWG. I request that the chairman read the list to this august body. This list represents the joint desires of our delegation and that of the Russians." As the paper was passed to the chairman, Olav Kerensky of the Soviet delegation nodded his agreement.

Chairman Hamar Arundel took the paper and said, "I will read the list, and we will then see if there is to be a second." After reading the list to the assemblage, he added, "The motion includes that the terms for directors will be for six years, except that the term for the chief coordinating director is only for two years. There appears to be no prohibition on serving more than one term. Is there a second to the motion?"

The Russian spokesman, Orlov Kerensky, stood and said, "I second the motion."

The UN electronics method of vote tallying was in use but had been modified to take into account the voting strength of each delegation. Five minutes after the voting began, it was complete, and Chairman Hamar Arundel announced from the rostrum, "The motion is carried by a majority of 82.6 for, 16.1

against, and 1.3 abstaining." The results were also displayed on a voting screen. He then continued, "The next order of business is to elect individuals to fill these positions that you have just created. I have been informed that the Russian delegation and the delegation from the United States suggest, in the interest of saving time, that a complete slate be elected at one time. This has been coordinated between these two delegations, and the Russian delegation is prepared to make such a motion."

The spokesman for Israel rose and announced a point of order.

Hamar Arundel said, "Please state your point of order."

Benjamin Klein, the Israeli spokesman said, "Since there is no precedent for this, should we not vote first on whether to elect a whole slate or to vote on each director individually?"

Hamar said with a chuckle, "If you insist, we will do so. However, since the United States and Russia have agreed on a whole slate and their combined vote is a majority, in practice, it will make no difference." Benjamin did not insist on his point of order and sat down.

Chairman Hamar Arundel then said, "I recognize the gentleman from the Russian delegation."

Olav Kerensky rose, walked to the rostrum, and handed the chairman a piece of paper on which was a written list. Olav returned to the area of his delegation and said, "I move the election of the persons on the list I gave to the chairman as directors of the SWG. I request that he read the list of names."

"Security	General Boris Metchnikoff	Russia
Food	Olav Kerensky	Russia
Energy	Akmed Hamid Saudi	Arabia
Population	Benjamin Klein	Israel
Economics	Robert Schuman	Switzerland
Science and Technology	Greta Schmidt	Germany
Climatology	Jim Meriwether	USA
Reforestation	Lars Berg	Sweden
Facilities and Personnel	George Henson	United Kingdom
Communications and computation	Julia Warrens	USA
Transportation and Logistics	Bani Shinto	Japan
Chief Coordination	Ray Carr	USA"

As the chairman finished reading the list, Ray Carr rose, and after being recognized, said, "I second the motion."

On the second vote of the day, there were 92.7 for, 6.0 against, and again, 1.3 abstaining.

Chairman Hamar Arundel then announced, "This has been a busy afternoon, and many of you must still be tired from your recent travels to be here. Unless I hear a dissent, this meeting will be adjourned until tomorrow at nine in the morning. Tomorrow the business will be to establish the broad policies that SWG should pursue in the years ahead, which will provide direction to the executive body you have just elected. You must be aware of the broad goals desired by the United States and the Russians, which they announced after their summit. With time that has passed since then and with more time for reflection, perhaps some refinement of these desires may be in order. I have, for instance, heard some talk of a judiciary branch to provide some checks and balances in the SWG." With that, he banged the gavel and the delegations adjourned for the night.

Roger, who was temporarily part of the American delegation, returned to the old UN quarters to which he had been assigned. When he had given Ray his commitment to join the SWG, Ray had agreed that there should be a place for Lucille but suggested waiting until the SWG began to take form. As he walked down the hall, Ray was coming from the opposite direction and stopped to talk. "Roger," he said, "the way things are going, I will need a number of personal assistants, and I would like you to be the first, to watch over the climate projects for me and some of the other high technology efforts into which we will be getting. How does that sound?"

"Great" was all Roger managed to get out on short notice.

Knowing that Roger would have Lucille's future on his mind, Ray went on, "Most of the computing will be set up in Julia's directorate, and she has already said she would like to have Lucille in her department. One of the first projects will be to set up a SWG version of the What If."

"That's wonderful" was what Roger said this time.

After a hasty dinner, Roger called Lucille in Washington, and he brought her up to date on the day's affairs, including the prospect of a job for her with Julia. Lucille was excited that Ray had been chosen as the director of coordination, in effect the head of the SWG, because she had been greatly impressed with his performance in the President's task force. She was more excited at the near prospect of moving to New York and being with Roger. Roger said he would try to contact Julia in the morning and call her back with specific plans. He then drifted off to bed and sleep.

The next morning, Roger found most of the American delegation at the UN having the usual coffee and doughnuts. Julia confirmed her desire for Lucille to join her department as soon as it could be arranged. Roger also ran into Meriwether who said, "I understand that Julia is out trying to recruit Lucille into her department. You know the SWG is going to build a Project Son of NOAH, and I really need Lucille for that because of her invaluable experience with NOAH. I'm sure Julia will be able to find people over at the CIA to put her in business with the SWG What If. If you are in touch with Lucille soon, please tell her for me."

"I'll call her right now," Roger said and found a quiet spot where he could use his cell phone. He knew Lucille would be thrilled with the choice of two jobs. Personally, he hoped she would take Meriwether's offer because that way, they would see more of each other.

The day's business of the World Congress got under way promptly at nine, as had been promised the day before by Hamar Arundel. Its first business was to ask Hamar to be the permanent chairman of the Congress, which he accepted.

Benjamin Klein asked for a ruling regarding the status of an individual who was a delegation member and was then elected as a director. Hamar ruled that no individual could be both in the legislative body and at the same time be in the executive. Those joining the executive would have to resign their positions in the delegations in the Congress.

The spokesman for the Polish delegation made a motion, which was seconded, to the effect that a SWG judicial body be established with two primary responsibilities: first, to be sure that the executive faithfully carried out the mandates given to it by the Congress, with the powers of impeachment if required, and, second, to be a forum for the settling of disputes between member states of the SWG. The motion carried by a small majority, with the American delegation voting for it and the Soviets voting against it. It was decided to elect judges the following month to serve in the judiciary.

The bulk of the day's business was devoted to the establishment of policies in the various areas that the SWG intended to make itself felt in the world. The motions were generally made either by the American delegation or the Russians. Roger noticed that the mandates being passed for the executive to carry out followed very closely the initial agreements announced jointly by the President of United States and the Russian Prime Minister after their summit meeting. There was more detail, as could be expected upon reflection, but the main thrusts were the same.

All through the deliberations, there was a recognition that the solutions implemented needed to be sustainable on an indefinite basis. Pollution and destruction of world resources would no longer be acceptable. The motto finally adopted to express this concept was, "May the world become a better place to live in for my having been here."

One item related to the future location of the SWG headquarters. Recognizing that the personnel of a government must be secure in their persons if a government is to be really sovereign, it was moved, seconded, and approved to give the coordinating director the authority to move the SWG and acquire facilities as necessary to carry out the mission of the SWG.

At the end of the day, Roger thought that more had been accomplished than anyone could have imagined. He then began to wonder what he would be doing, even though Ray had already given him a general idea. He didn't have long to wait as Ray looked him up the next morning at the start of the World Congress wrap-up session.

"Roger, we didn't have enough time to talk yesterday, but I want you to get on with your work right away. You know the general technical areas that SWG is going to be getting into, and I'd like you to become familiar with all those with which you feel you have some competence. Let me know which ones you don't, such as microbiology, so that I can arrange for some additional technical staff. I want to have an independent technical opinion on all the proposals that will be brought up for approval. I expect you to spend much of your time keeping up with Meriwether, but I'd like you to follow the solar and wind energy work and its related projects as well. I am particularly interested in opinions on adverse consequences of doing anything. You know the principle, 'You can't change just one thing.'"

Roger was gratified for the greater explanation of what Ray wanted from him and said, "That's fine. Do we have office space assigned yet?"

Ray responded, "We certainly do. Why don't we walk over there right now so you'll know where it is?" As they walked along the old UN building halls, Ray continued, "Meriwether is planning to present the options Fred has been looking at for climate modification in a couple of weeks to the directors. Of course, I want you to sit in on it and give me your opinion. In fact, it would probably be best if you sat in on their dry run so if they have missed something important, you can tell them before they do it here. Is Lucille coming up here to join you?"

"Yes," Roger answered, "as soon as Meriwether's presentation is over. They are working hard back at NOAA, looking at the three options. Between Julia's and Meriwether's operations, it looks like she is going to stick with climatology and help set up Son of NOAH."

Roger then felt bold enough to ask, "Ray, if I am going to work for you directly, I need to know something about your basic philosophy of life so that when I make recommendations, I know what generally is needed. So far, in all the meetings, I haven't been able to figure out anything about you except that you did exceedingly well at everything President Morgan wanted you to do. Now that you are your own man, that is something else."

Ray laughed. "Well, it's really quite simple. From your personnel file, I know that you are deeply committed to eastern mysticism. In that frame of reference, you might say that my orientation is one of karma yoga, the path of discharging my duty to the best and greatest extent possible. I see my ultimate duty as serving humanity in the best way my background and training allow. While doing my duty, I try to enjoy the world, but not to the extent of getting attached to it. You know the famous saying. 'Be in the world but not of it.'" Roger nodded.

Ray then said, almost to himself, "The key is to be always in the present in your awareness, the *now*. Don't live in the past or the future. Accept what *is* rather than living in the world as you imagine it should be."

Roger was glad to have asked Ray about his philosophy of life. It was good to be working for someone who had such similar viewpoints.

*   *   *

Meanwhile, nearby in New Jersey, Sam Trevor's report on the newly discovered fault near the Bering Straits arrived at Alaska Oil's headquarters. With the changed energy policies, no one was interested in new drilling, and the report was filed without being reviewed. No copies were forwarded to organizations in the government that would have been interested in the discovery of a major new fault area. Sam Trevor was caught in the massive layoff and joined the ranks of the tree planters.

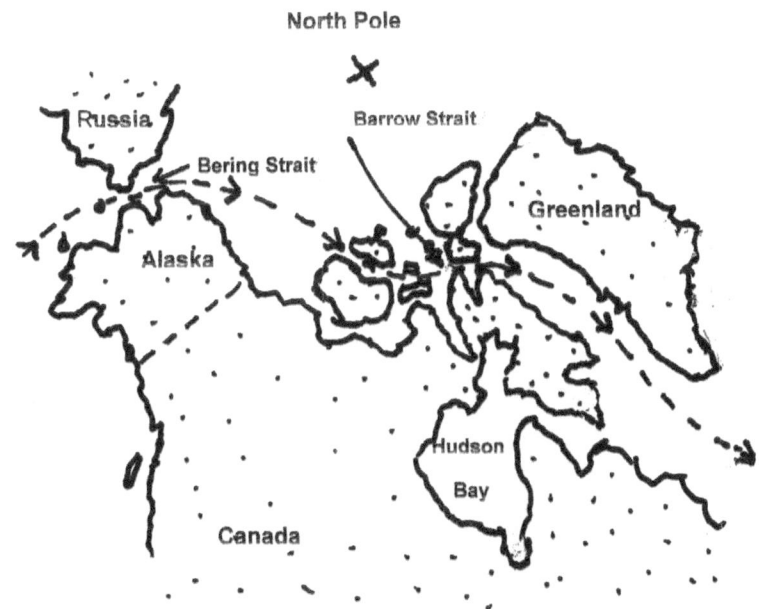

Arctic Warm Water Current

CHAPTER 16

Playing God

It was mid-February when Meriwether convened the climate modification presentation for the review by the full director membership of the executive of the SWG. Meriwether had been intensely busy for the past two weeks, staffing his new organization, initiating the orders to put together the new project, Son of NOAH, and keeping in touch with Fred. Fred had been running the differential analyses that would be the basis for the presentation to the directors. Fred and Lucille had come up that morning from Washington with a senior NOAA climatic scientist and Roger, who had been back at NOAA, to sit in on the dry run. They had arrived on time in spite of the fact that a record cold spell was playing havoc with travel.

Meriwether made introductions, explained what the purpose of the meeting was, including the objective of reaching agreement on the direction to precede on possible approaches to modifying the climate, and then turned the meeting over to Fred.

Fred, who was anxious to get started to show off his expertise in front of the world body, began, "We have had discussions with the scientists who have come up with three-candidate climate change possibilities. We proceeded to model them on the Project NOAH computer system. The three candidates are: ocean current modification, sun screening, and the moving of icebergs." The last candidate mentioned drew a small laugh as Fred went on to say that he would discuss them in that order.

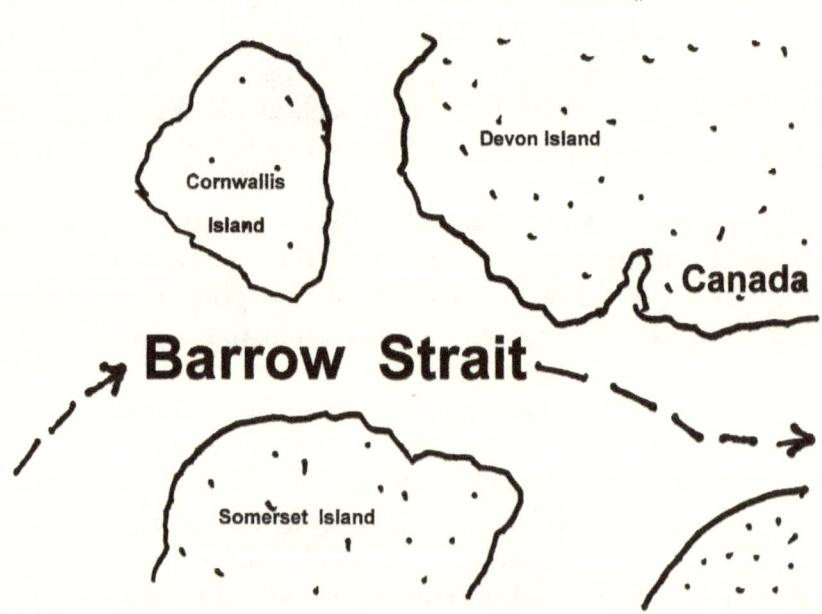

Projecting a map of the world, Fred pointed to the ocean currents, emphasizing those in the Arctic regions. "Here at the Bering Strait we have a small current of moderately warm water that moves north into the Chukchi Sea, the Beaufort Sea, and then between these northern Canadian islands, through this narrow channel, the Barrow Strait. From there, it continues into Baffin Bay, west of Greenland, and then south along the Newfoundland coast. By then, of course, it has become a cold current. In our simulations, we assumed that by widening the channels at both the Bering Strait and Barrow Strait, the two main choke points for the current, we would significantly increase the warm water flow in the Arctic region, raising its temperature."

Fred got his first question at that point. The director for energy Akmed Hamid, asked, "What is the benefit of raising the temperature of the Arctic region?"

Fred answered patiently, realizing that most of the directors had not been exposed to much of the science of climatology before. "The differential temperature between the tropics and the polar regions is the thermodynamic engine that moves the weather. Raise the temperature of the Arctic and the severity of the storms moving north is reduced. The important thing is that the total moisture being moved by the storms is reduced, resulting in a reduction in the snow and ice buildup. Too much moisture makes the seawater of the North Atlantic less salty which slows the gulf current, also reducing the heat transferred."

Seeing that his answer was understood, Fred continued, "We obtained information from the United States Department of Energy and the equivalent Russian agency, on the candidate atomic warheads to use for the earth-moving process. We limited our choice to existing warheads, the easiest being five hundred, ten-megaton warheads. The next chart shows where we placed the warheads. It was assumed in our study that all of these shots could be deployed in a year's time and would require the use of nuclear submarines for their placement."

The prospect of detonating five hundred large, atomic warheads put a damper on the audience, and there were no more questions at that point. Fred went on, "The increased current flow in the Arctic was next used as an input to a fifteen-year forward projection on the climate. The end result is that the transition to a cold glacial period is slowed, and the final, permanent snow line lies 250 miles farther to the north than the situation if we do nothing. The line north of which it would not be practical to grow crops also moves by the same amount."

Since the details of the perennial snow line and crop limit line were new to some of the directors, there were many questions at this point. Fred had expected that and was prepared with many of the charts that had been used in prior presentations.

The last question came from Ray Carr who asked a key question, which Fred was again prepared for. "What is the radioactivity resulting, and what does it do to the various populations?"

Fred responded, "We made some special simulations of the Arctic air current patterns, and where they would deposit the radioactive fallout. By limiting the time of setting off the shots to times during favorable air-current patterns, most of the radioactive fallout can be contained in the Arctic areas. Of course, it would be prudent to evacuate all the people living there currently. Most of the radioactive fallout would remain trapped in the Arctic snow and ice and largely decay before it melts. Enough radioactive fallout will get into the lower latitude atmosphere so as to cause an increase over a twenty-year period of about 5 percent in the current cancer rate. This could be reduced by monitoring the most affected food source, which is ocean fish. While a 5 percent increase in the cancer rate might be unacceptable by past standards, it is a very small number compared with the number of lives saved by significantly increasing the food capability of the planet.

At this point, there was a long, unstructured discussion on the pros and cons of increasing the cancer risk. Ray asked that the project look at possible ways to reduce the radioactive fallout.

The director of security, Boris Metchnikoff, wanted to know about the method of placement of the atomic explosive devices. Fred answered, "The Bering Strait which is only fifty meters deep on average is generally accessible in the summer by surface ships, while the Barrow Strait is inaccessible most of the time due to thick sea ice. Submarines would be essential in the Barrow Strait. If just one system of deployment is used, then we prefer submarines."

Boris Metchnikoff commented, "I think that no existing warhead could be used exactly as is since what we are talking about is a time-delayed atomic mine, moored to the bottom. It should, however, be feasible to fabricate a suitable case for existing warheads in a short time period. They could be carried piggy-back and remotely deployed. I would recommend the availability of divers to be able to make a manual deployment in the event of complications or problems we haven't anticipated."

Fred then went on with his presentation. "There is an option that can be added to the basic plan already presented. There is a large pool of frigid, bottom water trapped in the Norwegian Sea." Again he referred to his charts. "This water spills over high sills in the Denmark Strait, between Iceland and the Faroe Islands and also between the Faeroe Islands and Scotland. If these sills were lowered, again with atomic warheads, the cold water spilling over into the Atlantic would push more warm water back into the Greenland and Barents Seas. It should be noted that this is a one-time effect because in five years, the top of the cold-water pool will reach the new levels of the sills, and we will be back where we are now. It will, however, buy some time and slow down the transition time to a glacial period."

Julia asked the first question. "What type of atomic explosives would be used on the sills, and what is the radioactivity situation?"

Fred had expected someone to ask that and was ready with an answer. "It takes about 250 ten-megaton warheads or their equivalent. Since we would be mostly using the ten-megaton warheads up on the Arctic straits, for the sills we would use an assortment of both larger and smaller warheads. The sills are open to navigation year round, but are pretty nasty on the surface in the winter. As a precaution against radioactive fallout, Iceland, Scotland, and, of course, the Faeroe Islands would need to be evacuated. They will be evacuated eventually anyway as the Arctic weather moves south in a few years."

Again Boris Metchnikoff asked about the method of deployment of the atomic explosives.

Fred answered, "The study, supported by the United States Armed Forces, now a part of your organization, showed that it was feasible by either submarine or surface ship. I expect that the Security Department would get the job, and it would probably be up to your experts to decide the method." Boris nodded his agreement.

With no more questions, Fred went on to his second topic. "The next candidate project we call 'sunscreening.' The purpose here is to block some of the sun's energy from reaching the tropical oceans. Our specific goal was to reduce the amount of heat received from the sun by the same value as that gained by the tropical greenhouse effect. This way, there would be no excessive heat to evaporate more than the usual amount of water vapor, hence world precipitation would be more normal."

Everyone seemed to understand the basic principle, so Fred went to the details. "Smoke or other particulate matter in the lower atmosphere won't reach up high enough or stay there long enough to be practical for the amount of matter we could put up. The tropical rains would keep washing it out of the atmosphere anyway. We can get around this problem if we put the material in low earth orbit, where it would reflect the sun's energy before it ever gets into the atmosphere. If we choose low inclination orbits, we can keep the effect limited to the tropics; we certainly don't want cooling in the temperate zones because that would accelerate the ice-age transition. Another reason for not using smoke in the lower atmosphere is that the smoke would migrate to the higher latitudes, with undesirable results again."

Lars Berg asked, "Can you put enough material into orbit to make a difference?"

"Yes," Fred responded, "we can get enough material in orbit if we use all our large rocket boosters without their present warheads but with special dispensers. The most efficient scenario seems to be to have dispensers which blow bubbles with microscopically thin walls. With the right material, the bubble-wall's thickness can be close to one wavelength of light. The advantage of a bubble over flat film is that bubbles will block the same amount of energy from any direction, and they still work OK if they tend to clump. Very fine particles or flat films might stick together and reduce their effectiveness. The bottom line is that with about two thousand of the largest US and USSR rockets, we could compensate for the carbon dioxide greenhouse effect for about five years, delaying the onset of the glacial period. Like the sill effect I talked about before this, we don't get a permanent climatic change because the bubbles will eventually fall into the earth's atmosphere. An adverse consequence, by the way, is that, for that time period, we will be dirtying up the low earth orbits, particularly the low inclination ones. All low earth orbits will be affected somewhat because the high inclination orbits cross the equator twice per revolution."

Fred continued, "Again with the assistance of the scientists in the United States and Russia, we have estimated that the first of these rockets could be launched in eight months and that all two thousand or so could be completed in less than two years. We will need to design and fabricate the dispensers and a new nose cone. We first assumed that existing military launch facilities would be used but sea launch has some advantages." Boris nodded his agreement again.

There were no controversial questions this time, probably because there were no apparent dangerous possibilities, such as radioactivity, as had been the case with the warm current enhancement project.

"The third candidate project," Fred went on, "is the cooling of the tropics by means of moving icebergs from Arctic and Antarctic seas by towing them. Most of the currents in the tropics are deep-sea bottom ones, so the icebergs won't go where we want them to on their own. This study was done largely by the Russians, but we concur with their general conclusions. There is no existing towing system available that will get an iceberg to the tropics before it has melted. The big ones will melt slower, but the towing speed is very slow. The small ones tow faster but melt faster. There might be some means to insulate the icebergs so that they would melt slower, but it is not in the technology available to us now or in the immediate future. Unless something comes up that we have missed, there is no further work planned with this last approach."

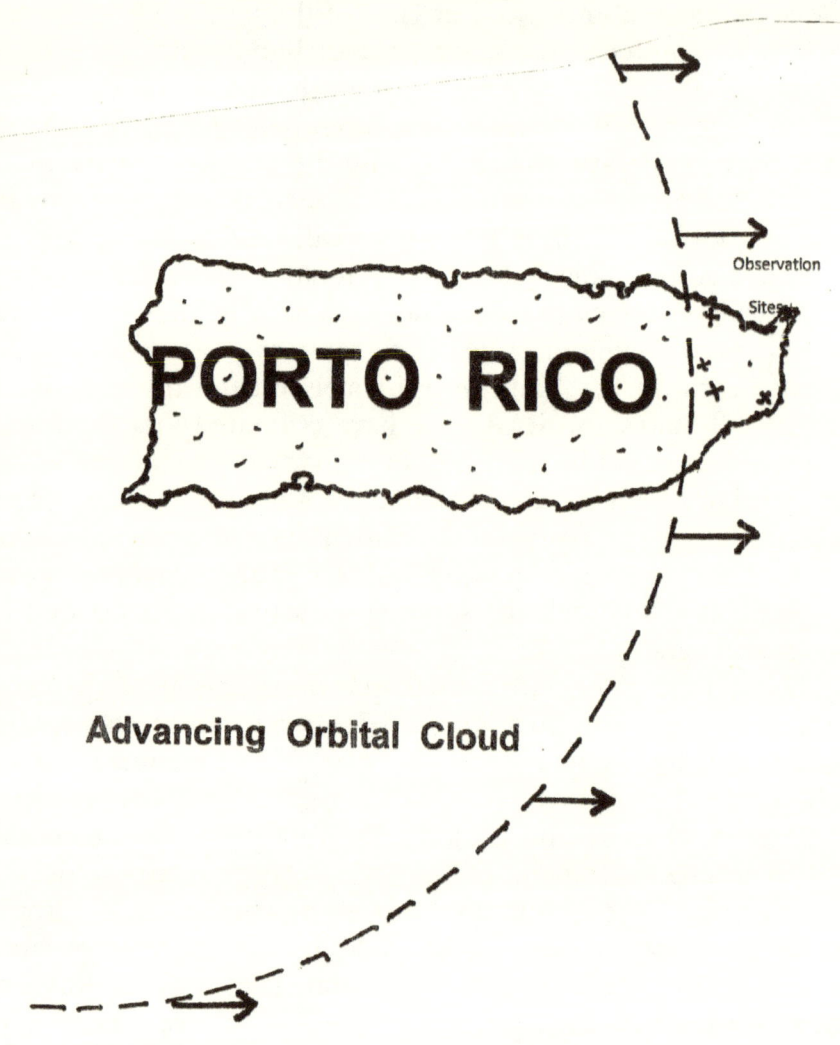

Ray turned to Meriwether and said, "Do you have any recommendations?"

"Yes, we definitely do," Meriwether answered. "We have given the two projects that have promise the names of 'Big Current' and 'High Cloud.' We recommend that the engineering phases of Big Current and High Cloud commence immediately and be carried through at least one prototype shot each. When ready, the production phases of both should also commence. We can, in the meantime, refine the simulations, particularly regarding the radioactive fallout of Big Current and make the deployment decisions downstream.

"We have two technology investigations we ought to pursue for future application. First is a possible sequestration of CO_2 for use in marine propulsion applications where it will be very difficult to develop alternatives to fossil fuels without going back to sails. Scrubbing CO_2 out of exhaust gases is a proven technology. The problem is what to do with the gas after it has been separated. The concept is to inject the gas directly into the seawater where it will end up eventually by absorption from the atmosphere at the sea/air interface. This is not a long-term solution as it ends up making the seawater more acidic which is damaging to corals and other similar sea life but would give us some leeway if we didn't reach our goal on CO_2 reductions to the atmosphere.

"The second investigation would be to study the seeding of clouds to get it to rain more in places where the water would not end up in diluting the North Atlantic seawater. The clouds reaching the North Atlantic would then have been milked of some of their rain, and the Gulf Stream pump would be weakened less."

Ray said, "All right, let's go with all that. Jim, I expect your directorate to lead the projects, with Boris's department doing most of the deployment." We will have energy look at CO_2 scrubbing technology and our security look at cloud-seeding technology. Boris nodded his agreement. Ray then turned to Roger and said, "Have we missed anything?"

Roger commented, "The plan looks good to me so far. We should have Son of NOAH up and running in a few months and be able to do a more accurate job of modeling the sea currents as well as the fallout patterns. That should give us better data before we have to decide on an all-out deployment." Seeing that the meeting was about to break up, Meriwether took the floor and began talking,

"We all know that there are high risks in certain areas, so we need to keep our eyes open for circumstances that might take us in wrong directions. Making natural gas our main bridge fuel to get us through the transition to sustainable energy has some risky aspects. Natural gas itself has forty times the greenhouse damage potential of carbon dioxide initially, although the damage will become less over time. From the leakage from wells, which amounts to 10 percent, it already has a significant presence in the atmosphere. In expanding its use significantly, we must tighten up our containment technology, particularly if we are going to use it directly in our automobiles, which will add tens of millions of potential leakage sources. We certainly can't allow simple venting as is the case in much of the present technology. We may need to require fail-safe devices and periodic monitoring of all potential leaks.

"Biofuels have been looked on with favor while they have not been a major source of our energy but should be viewed pragmatically as we come to depend on them more. Biofuels are not carbon-free, and we should not count them as so until their replacement has actually been harvested. If they are grown in place of something else that would not be burned, then they are adding as much carbon to the atmosphere as any fossil liquid fuel.

"We need to monitor all new processes and technologies to be sure that they don't have worse side effects that the ills they are presumably curing. Fracking to increase oil and gas supplies may introduce more long-term water supply contamination than has been supposed and must be brought under tight control. Sequestering carbon dioxide underground may only delay its entering the atmosphere. Sequestering it in the oceans may only be allowed on a short-term basis as it is known to make the water acidic with long-term damage to marine life.

"Good points," Ray said, and with that, the meeting ended.

From the meeting, Roger went with Lucille to help her move into her apartment. As they went into her apartment, which was a few corridors away from his, she said, "I'm so glad to get moved up here. I've been looking forward to you taking me around town. Have you got all the good places to eat spotted yet?"

The light banter created a good distraction from what was just under the surface of both their minds. Roger answered her, "Well, we have to be careful when we leave the SWG-controlled areas, because it isn't clear yet how the locals are going to react to the SWG invasion. So far, we haven't seen any major incidents, but there is a lot of ugly talk beginning to crop up again. People are beginning to realize that their lifestyles are really going to change, particularly the idle rich, who are going to have to go to work if they want to eat. There are a lot of people who are going to resent being told where to work when their present jobs in non-essential businesses come to an end. The owners of those businesses have already been stirring up a big fuss. They are particularly frustrated because there is no longer a way, simply by using their wealth, that they can get what they want." Roger remembered what Lucille had asked that got him started down this particular line of conversation. "There is a North-Indian restaurant called the Tandori Palace two blocks away that I haven't tried yet, but I am told it has a good selection of vegetarian dishes."

Lucille said lightly, "I haven't eaten Indian food, but I would be glad to try. I understand it is highly seasoned, which suits me fine."

He took her arm to escort her out.

In the Indian restaurant, which was decorated in Mogul style, she wondered at all the items on the menu but decided to go along with Roger and share family style with him. That way, he could do the ordering. Roger was glad to do so since he had eaten Indian food many times. They had muttar paneer, basmati rice, dal, and chapatis. The house contributed an additional curried vegetable dish that went unnamed, but Roger thought it was a combination of carrots, cauliflower, and eggplant. Roger had asked for medium seasoning, and the food came with just the right degree of flavor.

The conversation came around to what they both knew they were going to discuss. She smiled up at him. "When are we going to get married?"

"Well," he responded slowly, "the last time we talked about that, we agreed to get to know each other better. There are still so many things I don't know about you that you must tell me."

"Needing to know about me on the verbal level is just to satisfy your intellect," she pouted. "The real me and the real you already know each other completely, otherwise there wouldn't be this special thing between us. I know it may be hard for you to understand, but when I look at you in a certain way, you become all light, and your light and my light join together and are *one*. And this becomes a ball of fire that just flows and flows. I wish you could experience it too, and then you wouldn't have any questions."

She paused, but Roger was puzzling over what she had said, so she continued, "But if it would help, I'll tell you anything about me that you want to know." From his smile, she knew this was safer ground for Roger, so she embarked on the short story of her life.

"I was born thirty-two years ago in Illinois and went to the University of Chicago. I thought I wanted to be an engineer, but my dad convinced me that there was still a lot of prejudice out in industry against lady engineers, and he talked me into computer sciences. When I got ready to find a job, there was an opening right there at school. Later, I went to work for a research organization, also in Chicago, that was using computers to design better electric motors. They were mostly a bunch of old guys who didn't feel women have brains. When the government announcement of openings to work on Project NOAH came out, it looked so good that I only gave the Chicago firm two weeks notice. I packed up and went to Colorado before I knew I had the job."

She paused, but Roger didn't say anything, so she went on, "Let's see. You know I don't smoke, and I drink only occasionally. I've already told you I enjoy male company, no husbands or children. When I can, I like to go sailing and scuba diving. When

I can't do either of those, I will settle for reading or listening to music. I don't care for rock, it messes up your tranquility. The same for most TV."

"What kind of music is your favorite?" he asked.

"Classical," she said, and his face brightened. "You see, my mother used to play in the symphony orchestra, and I know it's not common these days, but somehow, maybe from hearing all that classical music so early, I just like it best."

Roger, who had lost both his parents when he was in college, asked, "Are your mother and father still living?"

"Yes," she answered, "they live near Chicago. Dad was planning to retire in a few years, before the climate change came up. Now, of course, things are uncertain. I expect the company he works for will be considered an essential industry. The policies announced so far have been vague about retirements. Mother hasn't played professionally for about five years."

"Any brothers or sisters?"

"Yes," she smiled. "I have an elder brother, who is an officer in the Navy, and a younger brother who ended up the engineer in the family."

They had finished eating, having had a very sweet rice pudding for dessert. Lucille didn't offer any more details about her life, and Roger didn't ask for any more.

When they got back to the old UN facility, they decided to go to Roger's apartment since Lucille hadn't really had a chance to move into hers. Once inside, they embraced long and hard until Roger drew her to the couch, where they settled into each other's arms.

"Well," she teased, "did I tell you enough?"

"Why that's just a start," he said, "you haven't begun to tell me what you think about. What goes on inside your pretty head is more important to me than all the things that have happened to you in the past. Like, what do you think about when I kiss you?"

"If I told you that," she laughed, "we would be moving into your bedroom, and I wouldn't be keeping my promise to you to keep my passions in check. What do you have in here to keep us distracted?"

"Well," he said, "we could watch a movie on cable TV, and when that good Indian food has settled, there are snacks in the refrigerator."

Later that night, they embraced for the last time in front of the door to her apartment. Roger, still puzzled, said, "About what you said how our two 'lights' combined into one and become a ball of flowing fire, when was the first time you felt that about us?"

Lucille looked at him through misting eyes. "The first time I saw you, when I was being interviewed at NOAA for the project. I never had that sense of oneness before with anyone else. That was when I knew we were destined to be together. Of course, I couldn't say anything at the time. In the beginning, you weren't ready, not until this year. I think something changed for you when the climate change came on for real. There may not really be so much time for us." Continuing to be surprised, Roger kissed her goodnight and reluctantly went back to his apartment.

*   *   *

Meanwhile in the Black Forest, many months had passed since Gertrude had put in her first conclusive report on saving the forests. She had heard nothing from her supervisor, Rudolph, except that they would discuss her report when he visited her post. This was now to be the following day. While she looked forward to any company, she had reservations about Rudolph. She normally enjoyed almost any male company anywhere near her age, but Rudolph was twice her age, and she always had to discourage his sexual advances. Suddenly he was there, a day early, driving up in his black VW. "So," he said, "I am here early. The meeting in Basil took a day less than expected. Shall we look at the trees you have written about?"

Gertrude was taken by surprise but arose to the occasion. "Surely," she answered, wondering about his lack of the usual amorous advances. "Let me get my coat."

Gertrude led him out to a ten-hectare patch of woods. In stark contrast to the surrounding forest, the trees in the treated patch were rich in foliage and very healthy appearing. There were no dying trees at all. The young trees showed remarkable yearly growth, three times more than Rudolph would have considered good.

"Remarkable, remarkable," Rudolph muttered. "There is no question as to the health and growth of these trees, but your explanation that it is all due to added fertilization goes against all reason. No! There must be some other answer. You must work more diligently to find it."

After Rudolph had left, Gertrude went over in her mind the futility of dealing with bureaucrats. Rudolph had implied he was up for promotion and transfer. Perhaps his replacement would be more rational, and she could get a fair hearing. Saving the forests should still be a first-class ticket for anyone who was associated with the effort, particularly now that a big effort was on to avoid another glacial period.

*   *   *

Slugger Williams was another who was not fairing as well as he would have liked. As the leader of his street gang in a backwater in Brooklyn, he was waiting in his apartment over a garage for his gang to gather. The Kings had come down a long way since the good old times when easy money was to be had in running drugs. With the Credo replacing the dollar, all their caches of money were useless. Most of the gang members had already spent all of the one thousand dollars they had been allowed to exchange for Credos. Not wanting to work in the few jobs available, they had no ration documents and had to spend much more time in the black market, buying food coupons when they couldn't steal them.

Slugger started his meeting by yelling, "OK, guys, knock it off. If I had asked you here for a social time, you woulda brought your old ladies. How's it going on the street?"

The response was grumbling and general reports of poor pickings. Also the fuzz were out in earnest, and none of the guys picked up had been sprung. A pimply faced kid said, "At this rate, the fuzz'll have us all in a month. I hear that the ones that got picked up last month were sent up to Alaska to plant trees. You try to escape up there, and you would freeze to death."

Slugger decided it was time to spring his new plan. "Yeah," he said, "we can't go on settling for the chickenfeed you get in a mugging. I'm thinking real big. We'll stage an accident on the parkway. Only rich dudes are riding around much anymore. There will be a lot of stalled cars. We'll hit them all at once before the fuzz even know about it. We'll be big time."

As the buzz of interest grew, Slugger said, "OK, OK, that's the general plan. Now let's get down to the details."

* * *

Times had changed even more drastically for Buddy Rustler now that no one was buying cars. With the coming of the glacial cold period, all but four of the city's car agencies had been declared non-essential. Buddy's employer had been closed down. The car business was down to driving for essential purposes only.

Buddy was at the Central Bar and Grill, nursing a beer. Even here, business was very slow. Buddy went over his options. There was really only one, to go to the employment office and see what work he could get. The thousand dollars he had converted to Credos was almost gone. Certainly he would have to have work by next week.

The next day, Buddy dragged himself down to the government employment office, where he had to wait four hours for an interview. The obviously overworked woman across the desk said, "What can you do that is useful?"

Buddy put on his best 'talk to the suckers Smile.' "I'm a very good salesman. I can sell anything: cars, furniture, hi-fi, insurance, even stocks."

"Can you do anything practical?" she interrupted.

Buddy knew what she meant but couldn't think of anything to say.

"Forest Service," she said in a loud voice and wrote it on his application. "Next," she said to conclude the interview.

CHAPTER 17

Turkmenistan

The Russian Prime Minister wondered if there was any solution to the problem he faced with the ambitious general in Kazakhstan. He would have liked just to turn the problem over to the SWG but knew that the SWG was just getting started, and that it was his problem for now. Certainly SWG would be in on it once action was initiated, but it was up to him to provide the lead. He missed the mature advice and experience of General Boris Metchnikoff and, as his meeting to review the situation in Kazakhstan got under way, wondered how his second string would cope.

He turned to the KGB representative and said, "What have we learned recently from our satellites on the situation in Kazakhstan, particularly what is General Mikhail Zellov doing?"

"Prime Minister Petrovich," was the reply, "the general now has moved most of his forces into Turkmenistan. We have been most fortunate that, while at this time of year there is usually considerable cloud cover over Turkmenistan, viewing conditions have been excellent for the past six days. From the satellite data, it is clear that General Zellov has his forces on a war alert. Twenty percent of the land-transportable IBM missiles are always on the move. Every missile is moved once in forty-eight hours. If we were to hit him with a pre-emptive strike, he could have at least ten missiles that would survive that could be used against us. From electronic monitoring, it appears that his command headquarters is moved once every twelve hours and is seldom at its nominal location, Ashkhabad. On the occasions we have been able to trigger the special beacon that we believe was planted in the general's car, it seems to be at the same location as his temporary headquarters.

"Because of limited airfields, he has not been able to disperse his aircraft, but he has built many protective revetments. There is no evidence that he is moving his tactical atomic weapons, but 50 percent must be hidden, because we can account for only half of them."

The Prime Minister mused, "He is, of course, familiar with our satellite capabilities so that he would know that we would eventually become aware of his actions. It must be that he intends for us to know, perhaps as a sort of warning to leave him alone."

The Defense Minister, an aging marshal, nodded. "I agree. Zellov would not take such a provocative action as moving into Turkmenistan unless he is prepared to use his weapons. The Americans, and from them the SWG, have also noticed this high level of war preparedness of the general's forces in Turkmenistan. I am surprised that they have not asked us for an explanation."

The Prime Minister commented on that, "I had anticipated problems in Turkmenistan, and I had alerted our recent colleague, General Metchnikoff before he left. No doubt he has passed on our concerns to the SWG and, in fact, must be coordinating the part that the SWG will play." Again addressing the marshal, he said, "What is your latest plan?" The marshal replied, "General Zellov seems to be staging his forces before moving on into Iran. When his forces seem to be more or less static, I suggest we hit them with a surprise attack. We would make the first attack with ballistic missiles and quickly follow it up with reconnaissance/attack aircraft to catch any missed targets."

The Russian leader shook his head. "In our war games, the reconnaissance/strike aircraft we have had a very poor record of being able to find moving targets. It is unlikely that they could find more than 50 percent of the moving missiles. That means that ten strategic IBM missiles with ten warheads apiece might escape our strikes, enough to completely destroy our country."

The marshal continued his advocacy, "I also, regrettably, know the numbers, but for the stealth strike aircraft, I had in mind that the American strike aircraft be used. They were designed for just such a mission, and our intelligence indicates an almost 100 percent success when used in this fashion in war gaming."

The Russian leader looked at his KGB representative, who nodded agreement.

The marshal warmed to his message, "The Americans would not need to use large warheads, creating excessive radioactivity. The missiles will be soft targets, being in the open. We must still expect some of the aircraft on the ground to escape damage and become airborne. The aircraft are not a very positive threat for Zellov to use, because once airborne, the air crews are likely to change their loyalties. To be safe, however, we must have a strong fighter screen to block any aircraft approaching Mother Russia. Any such aircraft would be told to land at once or be destroyed."

The Russian leader said, "Your plan has merit. Once hostilities are initiated, Zellov has lost. The only question remaining will be how badly Mother Russia is hurt. Very well, have the staff work up the plans and coordinate them with the SWG. The American aircraft are essential. For this whole operation, both in the military and in the KGB, I want a very small group in on what we are planning. In the event there is a leak somewhere, we must minimize the chances of alerting General Zellov."

The KGB representative wasn't finished. "Now that General Zellov has halted at Ashkhabad we have again been looking at the possibility of the success of surgical teams and feel there is now some chance of success. First, we would use independent planning teams to avoid a chance of a leak. Second, we could try using non-Russian ethnic attack personnel who would not be so quickly spotted."

The Russian leader, anxious for an easy way out said, "Yes, Yes, go on."

The KGB man continued, "I had in mind three teams. One to cross the Caspian Sea, and the other two would infiltrate across the Iranian and Afghanistan borders. It will be tight scheduling to make it before the planned strike."

The Russian leader closed out that topic. "We can't count on the surgical teams. Marshal's plan goes forward. Only if we learn of success by the surgical teams can the strikes be called off." He then turned to other matters. "What is the status of the arrival of assistance promised by the United States?"

The KGB representative took the initiative to respond. "The actual arrival of food from the United States has had a positive effect on the morale of our people. Only small stocks of meat have arrived so far, and these by air transport. They have been quickly moved into the stores in the most critical areas and are playing a major role in the improved attitudes that has been found from our sampling."

The representative for energy spoke next, "The oil stocks that have arrived in the Black Sea ports have already eased the energy crises in the southern areas. The pipelines don't run to all the right places when used for importing oil, so we should request that some of the long-haul transport that the United States is furnishing us be in the form of tanker trucks."

The Russian leader concurred, and then moved on to the next topic. "The SWG has decided to do most of the climatology change investigations, rather than depend on the United States or us. Director Ray has told me that this work will commence immediately in New York but will soon move to Puerto Rico. In order to staff this effort quickly, he has asked us to contribute one-half of the Project ARARAT staff, particularly the ones who have done climate change studies." He turned to his representative for climatology. "I would particularly like to accommodate Director Ray. I feel that the initiative in this area has passed out of our hands except for providing skilled personnel. Can we transfer half our personnel without it being a serious loss?"

His representative replied, "If, as we have previously discussed, our remaining responsibility is only to check on the adverse reactions that climate changes might have, then, for that purpose, one-half of our present staff would suffice. I presume they would want the English-speaking ones?"

"Naturally," the Russian leader said, "that has always been the case. Very good then, inform those of your choosing of their imminent departure, along with their immediate families.

If there are any that don't wish to go, which I can't imagine, make exceptions as hardship cases." Not all those present knew about the family rule, and he chose to explain. "We have agreed with the SWG, specifically Director Ray, that anyone making a permanent transfer to the SWG is to become a federal citizen rather than a citizen of his home country. Their ultimate loyalties must be to the SWG, and this can only be assured if there are no strings that can be used as leverage to sway loyalties. I know for many, this will be sad to give up the ties to Mother Russia, but it is the price that must be paid for the survival of the rest of us. That is all for today. Let us meet again when the plans to deal with General Zellov are complete."

That meeting took place two weeks later and, as usual, the KGB representative had the lead role. He started off quickly. "We have assembled the three surgical teams, and if approved in this meeting, they will leave tonight from their respective locations in the Ukraine, Afghanistan, and Iran. They have been briefed that their primary target is to eliminate first, General Zellov, and second, his security chief and, as far as possible, any members of their immediate staffs. The Iranian team has continuing contacts in Ashkhabad and reports disturbing news. Apparently, General Zellov has less fuel for his tanks than we had supposed. He has reportedly opened negotiations with the Iranians for diesel fuel. In exchange, he will provide tactical nuclear support to the Iranians, who would then be able to reopen the Iranian/Iraqi conflict on superior terms."

The Russian leader turned to the marshal of his defense establishment. "What is your assessment of this development?"

The marshal replied, "If it can be believed, it is certainly in keeping with his actions so far. He must know that he has burned his bridges as far as we are concerned and that he will get nothing from us in the future that help his armed potential. Cut off from supplies, he would eventually be brought into submission unless he can develop alternate sources. I see this as another step to take over Iran. Against his nuclear arms, Iran would have no choice but to agree to any demands he makes. Reopening the Iranian/Iraqi conflict can only confuse the issues in the area and give him a stronger hand in dictating to Iran."

The Russian leader then asked, "Will we be ready to make our strike?"

The marshal nodded, "Yes. The US stealth aircraft are already under SWG control and are being moved to bases that the Americans control in the western part of Germany. Our submarines are on station to make the surprise ballistic attack from the Black Sea. The blocking fighters that are to protect the homeland have been alerted and will operate from the bases to which they are normally assigned. We cannot pick an exact strike date until just before the time, because we must have clear weather in order to target the land-transportable IBM missiles."

The Russian leader turned to the KGB representative again. "What are the cloud-cover projections for January 31? What you have said so far is that normally this time of year, only one day in three is clear."

"This must not be a normal year, because we are getting excellent visibility two days out of three."

The Russian leader asked, "What is the most recent assessment of the potential danger to Mother Russia?"

The KGB representative looked at his leader. "We have used the most up-to-date success probabilities from the last war games and the inputs from the Americans for their aircraft. If we target two warheads for each land-transportable missile, we should destroy all but one of the non-moving missiles. The US aircraft have retargeting capabilities, so that they should kill all the missiles that they detect. We estimate that of the ten that will be on the move, they will not detect one. Therefore, there will likely be only one missile that survives our attack. We do not think that this remaining crew would psychologically be able to fire on Mother Russia."

The marshal added, "The AWACS that the Americans operate has not yet passed under SWG control, but the Americans will operate it to coordinate the aircraft battle. All our blocking fighters have been equipped with the proper communication systems and identification codes so that the AWACS command can distinguish all friendly from hostile aircraft. Those fighters have had English-speaking pilots assigned to us. AWACS will also have Russian-speaking personnel, who will try to divert any of General Zellov's surviving attack aircraft that might head for targets on our side. The engagement rule is that any aircraft taking off from Turkmenistan that does not land immediately, when so ordered, will be shot down."

"Well," the Russian Prime Minister said, "plans always sound good, but then the unexpected happens. I assume our staff has looked at all the possibilities and has contingency plans available for immediate execution?" He looked at the Marshal who nodded.

Prime Minister Petrovich had one last thought, "Can we take advantage of the beacon in General Zellov's staff car to attack him personally?"

"Probably not," the Marshal said. "The electromagnetic communication traffic will be so intense that it would be hard to pick out one low-power beacon and home a missile on it in the midst of a large battle."

As it turned out, the Ukrainian and Afghanistan surgical teams were identified and intercepted. Fortunately, neither of them was aware that there were other teams so that, even under torture, they could not compromise the other teams. General Zellov had expected some actions and instituted the highest level of readiness. The strikes scheduled for January 31 had to be called off due to cloud cover, but due to a missed communication, the Iranian team did not learn of the postponement and went ahead with their attack. They were unable to locate General Zellov's personal whereabouts, so they settled on blowing up his KGB headquarters, including 80 percent of the KGB staff. That was the only action on January 31, so General Zellov survived to carry on with his plans.

February 1 was partially clear, and February 2 was forecasted to be fully so by both the Russian and the US satellite systems. 9:00 a.m., GMT, was scheduled for issuance of the stealth aircraft force Go Code signal. Impact time of the warheads from the Black Sea-based submarines would be exactly two hours later. All forces involved were set into motion, including the alerting of the fighter blocking forces.

The first indication that something unusual was happening came to the attention of the Iranian air controller on duty, who noticed that the AWACS aircraft from Saudi Arabia was flying more to the north than usual. There was also more aircraft activity in Saudi Arabia airspace generally. This happened occasionally and was not sufficient cause to issue an alarm, at least in the beginning. The controller was not privy to the special arrangements that were being made between his government and General Zellov on his northern borders, so he had no reason to be suspicious. When the AWACS turned north and a large number of escorting low-flying fighters popped up on his screen, it was too late. A widely-broadcast warning to the Iranian Air Force that its aircraft would be safe if they did not take to the air was generally heeded, and the SWG forces had unquestioned air superiority in the battle with General Zellov.

At the same time, the warheads launched from the Black Sea submarines were falling on their targets in Turkmenistan. There was almost no warning because Zellov's radars had been oriented for an attack from the north, not the west. All of the land-transportable IBM missiles that General Zellov controlled that were not being moved were destroyed. This included fifteen that were being repaired and were hence not immediate threats. At the same time, hits were achieved on all the air bases, but with the dispersal of his aircraft, General Zellov managed to get twelve aircraft aloft, each carrying one nuclear bomb. Their pilots were given the vague orders to fly north and bomb Moscow. Within a few minutes, the general thought better of that and had radio commands sent to the twelve aircraft to fly to Iran and land as soon and wherever they could. In this, they were successful before they could be intercepted by fighters coming south from Mother Russia or those accompanying the AWACS.

Meanwhile, the stealth aircraft swept in looking for any surviving land-transportable IBM missiles, moving or not. The morning's location of each missile was known, and since each move was generally not greater than ten miles, the search areas were relatively small. Experience from the satellite photos had also shown that the usual locations for a new firing point would be near a road, and this narrowed the search still further. The urgency was to find the moving missiles before they stopped and could set up to launch. Of all the missiles on the move, all but two crews, on seeing atomic explosions around them, abandoned their missiles to take cover, thus making the job easier for the stealth aircraft. The two remaining missiles were destroyed before they could be set up and take any actions to launch.

The Russian Prime Minister, with aid from the SWG, had won the first round against the ambitious general.

The evening of the air strike, General Zellov decided with his staff that Turkmenistan could only get unhealthier, and orders were issued to move south toward Iran the following morning. The wounded, and those overly exposed to atomic radiation, including one headquarters staff orderly, Viktor Andropov, were to be left behind. General Zellov's forces were now reduced to a ground force of three armored divisions, with atomic warheads on ten tactical missiles. Twenty atomic warheads from those modified for aircraft were salvaged from the wreckage of the airfields, and General Zellov decided to take those as well. Even though he wasn't sure if he would regain control of any of the aircraft that had gone to Iran, he was sure that the atomic bombs would give him a lot of leverage. His attack helicopters had been widely dispersed, and most of them had survived. The general had his technical personnel looking at modifying them to carry the aircraft atomic bombs.

The general's Iranian contacts had been advised of his coming, and with an adventuresome spirit, he crossed into Iran to meet the waiting officials. General Zellov was confident of the future. He doubted that the SWG would wish to start a war with Iran even with him in a strong position of influence. He planned to keep his armored forces away from any large city so that there would be ample warning should they be attacked by Iranian ground forces. He had already conveyed to the Iranian officials that he had atomic weapons which they might find useful in a renewed war with Iraq. Also it was implied that he would use them on Iranian cities should he or his forces not be welcome. Besides the actual weapons, he had brought with him significant military technology, which he had already learned would be of extreme interest to the Chinese. With these as trading chips, he was looking for an alliance with China. Oil for the Chinese from the Iranian oilfields was a most logical outcome.

Meanwhile, an expeditionary force of land and airdrop troops from Russia was launched into Kazakhstan to insure that any atomic missiles left behind were quickly secured from possible use against Russia or any other state of the SWG. There was virtually no opposition. The civilian population and remaining armed forces looked upon the Russians as liberators from what had been a very oppressive regime.

CHAPTER 18

SWG in Review

It was Ray's management style to handle problems as they came up in one-on-one meetings with the appropriate director. He also encouraged the various directors to coordinate mutual problems between themselves as long as he got a memo summarizing the results. In addition, he made sure that all the directors got together formally, about once a week, to keep each other posted on things in which some other director might have an interest. Once a month, Ray had decided they would get together for a day-long meeting where the major programs in each directorship were reviewed. This was such an occasion in mid-March.

Ray was chairing the meeting, attended by the directors and several others with special interests, including Roger Foreman. The first report was from Boris Metchnikoff on security. "As you know, we are still in that phase of our development where the enforcement of our decisions is based on the strategic weapons we control. Until all such weapons are in our hands, we will continue in a very unstable situation, as was recently encountered in Turkmenistan. While not as dangerous as it was, that situation still is unresolved. Also, we have to recognize that China, with a large arsenal of atomic weapons, and her ally North Korea will probably remain outside our sphere of control for some time.

"In view of these and possible future threats, we have decided to locate SWG physically on four widely dispersed islands, Puerto Rico, Hawaii, New Zealand, and Sri Lanka. We were also invited to locate on Taiwan, but we consider that too close to China to be easily defended, at least for now. For the time being, we intend to retain only the submarine-launched ballistic missiles, and they will be based on three islands except Sri Lanka. The bomber and fighter forces that we retain will also be moved to these islands, along with the existing anti-ICBM defenses. The remaining naval units that are retained, as well as the land-armored forces, will eventually also be so based. We are well along in the planning of the expanded facilities needed and already have security forces in place. The completion of all major relocations is planned for June 1. The bottom line is that we want SWG to be sufficiently secure so that no one will seriously challenge its authority.

"Meanwhile, the forces of member states that are not planned for incorporation in the SWG are in the process of dismantlement. For the time being, certain rocket boosters and warheads are being held for possible utilization by the climate-change projects, which will be reported on later by Dr. Meriwether. Our reduction in conventional forces, as well as short-range tactical nuclear weapons, will be paced by the actions of those countries that are not yet member states and still maintain independent armed forces."

At this point, Ray interrupted with a question. "Could you give us a more detailed status of the situation in Iran at the present moment?"

"Yes, I was going to include that. The Russian land forces that cleaned up in Kazakhstan went on into Turkmenistan to neutralize any remnants of General Zellov's forces that he did not take into Iran. This was a slow process because of the general lack of usable roads and pockets of radioactivity. An analysis of the destruction in Turkmenistan, as well as the war materials left there, indicates that General Zellov has taken into Iran ten tactical nuclear missiles and an unknown number of ICBM warheads, not exceeding fifty, which he had been modifying for use from aircraft. From other intelligence, we know that ten aircraft capable of carrying these bombs landed safely in Iran. Whether he is using the carrot, the stick, or both, General Zellov is now the dominating controlling force in Iran. For now, he seems satisfied in maintaining the status quo, but we are at a high state of readiness in the area because of the sensitivity of several of Iran's neighbors who recently joined the SWG and look to us for protection. It also appears that General Zellov is in the process of trading military technology and possibly weapons with the Chinese in exchange for a mutual alliance treaty. It's imperative to pull General Zellov's fangs soon."

George Henson's report was second. "Boris has told you of the move of the security forces to the island sanctuaries, and our plan for moving the administrative functions of SWG falls in the same time period. Our facilities building and conversion program calls for the SWG headquarters to move from here in New York to Puerto Rico around April 1. I say 'around' because individual moves will be made over a three-week time span so that the business of the SWG continues smoothly during the transition. We have taken over two command and communication aircraft and have another on the way, so that SWG business can continue even when any of you are in transit. These aircraft have satellite links so that two-way video communications will be available. Satellite terminals for the SWG on all three islands will be in operation before April 1."

George saw interest was dropping and went on to a more personal subject. "We are building housing and other facilities for the SWG staff so that the SWG moves will not unduly inconvenience the populations already on these islands. With the drastic drop in tourist travel to Puerto Rico and Hawaii, both have a large surplus of tourist-type accommodations, and the locals are looking forward to the business that will come with the SWG's arrival. None of the leaders in Puerto Rico or Hawaii seem to have strong feelings either for or against becoming federal citizens, rather than citizens of the United States. In many ways, the case in New Zealand is quite different. We have chosen North Island for the SWG base since, after the climate changes, its weather will be less adversely affected than South Island. Being mostly agricultural, there are few facilities in existence that we can use, except for some port facilities. Initially it will be strictly a military base, with administrative functions added in time. The attitude of the locals is very positive since with the expected climate changes, New Zealand otherwise has very poor prospects, being much concerned about Chinese aggression. In the long term, we plan to have a presence in the western Indian Ocean on Sri Lanka but for the present that location has less priority."

George turned to his last topic. "Regarding personnel, we are still understaffed in all the SWG departments. As you know, our policy is to accomplish as much as we can through our member states, but there is a minimum of planning and coordination that must be done by SWG proper. The problem of understaffing is not for lack of applications, nearly everyone wants in, but is due to lengthy processing time to assess security risks and obtain equitable representation from all member states. The requirement to speak English has cost us a large number of excellent candidates."

As George sat down, Ray said, "Look at the feasibility of accepting top candidates who don't speak English and giving them a crash course in the subject. We must have the very best people joining the SWG."

Director of Energy, Akmed Hamid, was next. "Our first priority is in getting member countries to adhere to the energy quotas that we established for them. With partial compliance, there is a glut of oil, and people are prone to use it. The various member states are faced with a great inertia on the part of their citizens to change their life styles. If we are serious about these quotas, we will have to use stronger action than we have so far. In the current case of large importers of petroleum products, we can simply reduce their shipments and let them make allocations and do whatever rationing is necessary."

"As a passing note, our initial policy in setting energy usage quotas does not provide the right incentives and is more burdensome than it needs to be to meet our goals of CO_2 reduction. We are now going to establish quotas for each state on the amount of atmospheric CO_2 that they add. This will add a strong incentive for the short term to convert to fuels like natural gas and methyl alcohol that only produce one-half the CO_2 of traditional fossil fuels. It also provides an incentive which is very important in the long haul to convert motor vehicles to be battery powered. We are providing strong subsidies for research for not only lighter batteries but for ones that are cheap. We are currently processing an order that classifies manufacture of all but certain specialty vehicles that are powered by conventional motor fuels as nonessential.

Ray said, "Get Boris's help to intercept tankers if necessary."

Akmed looked uncomfortable with Ray's comment but went on, "There are many countries who are net energy exporters, and that strategy doesn't work with them. In this second category, if they are net food importers, it would be most direct to withhold food shipments if they don't comply with their energy quota."

"Right again," Ray smiled. "This time you will need the assistance of Director Kerensky. To avoid undue suffering, I suggest that the states from whom it is necessary to withhold food be given advance notice of the ratio of energy expended to food withheld." Ray sensed some of those present thought he was being overly harsh. "Remember," he said, "this is no game. The only reason for the SWG's existence is to make these hard decisions so that all of humanity has a chance of surviving. It goes the other way too. Those states consuming more of the food that they grow than they are entitled to should have energy withheld. For those states with a surplus of both food and energy, we will have to analyze their needs and find some leverage short of bombing them."

When he got the floor back, Akmed said, "Controlling the generation of electric power from the burning of fossil fuels will require the stationing of inspectors in all the major power-generation stations of the world that burn fossil fuels. Power allocation will be left to the local authorities within a state. However, we should set a date when burning liquid fossil fuels to generate electrical power will be discontinued.

"I would like to emphasize that our view of natural gas should be that it is only a bridge fuel to get us over the time period we are converting to a sustainable energy civilization, and its use should be curtailed as soon as possible. The major present sources are from the process known as fracking and can leave behind a legacy of an environmental disaster of permanently contaminated ground water. Also burning natural gas does not eliminate the production of CO_2, it just reduces it as compared to burning longer-chain hydrocarbons. Millions of conversion kits each month, worldwide, will be produced for converting existing automobiles. This rate will be expanded so that all the cars that are still on the roads at the end of two years will be converted away from gasoline. Methyl alcohol still produces some carbon dioxide and other products that are toxic, so it is not our long-term liquid fuel solution.

"We are making headway with hydrogen as a fuel for cars in the distant future which only makes water when it burns.

"As we build up a surplus of electricity generating capacity, particularly from solar voltaic farms, we will use some of it to produce hydrogen by electrolysis of water. Hydrogen can be moved around by pipeline and is a way to store energy for nighttime use and peak periods. It is most efficient when used in a fuel cell to generate electricity for driving an electric vehicle. Hydrogen will certainly be our fuel of the future, but we need to learn a lot more about it, such as its effect on the atmosphere from leakage.

"Carbon dioxide production from trucks will be greatly reduced as most long-haul freight shipments are forced onto the railroads. Those long-haul trucks still needed will be converted to natural gas.

"While my department is also involved, the report on solar and wind energy progress will come from Greta."

Ray then turned to Greta Schmidt for Science and Technology. With a smile, she started, "Actually, we are looking at a lot of new things, although, of course, solar energy and wind generation are the most important. Our main guiding light, so to speak, is that eventually we have to change all of the world's systems over to be sustainable and without polluting the planet. We also have to make these systems work under conditions which will be much closer to a glacial period climate than we have yet experienced. I'll give you a simple example of what I mean. A process that makes all the solar cells we need at next to nothing in cost is not a solution if it also generates toxic wastes which we cannot break down into harmless products. We recognize that almost all of the products and systems of the present day technology do not meet these goals, so we have a long way to go. In some cases, where the products or systems create high levels of environmental destruction, we may have to do without until a substitute technology is discovered. A case in point is the destruction of the ozone layer by chlorofluorocarbons. This also means we must test everything before it is put into production, rather than the old scenario of going into production first and waiting for the adverse effects to appear. We are also quickly moving into an approach of not producing materials that are planned to be discarded. The ideal is as much as possible to minimize products which have to be recycled. Where that doesn't happen, we plan to recycle everything, and we mean to make that happen everywhere, including human wastes that are valuable organic materials."

Shifting gears to what she knew they were waiting to hear, Greta said, "Fortunately for the future of our energy production, we have three processes for making low-cost, highly efficient solar cells that do not end up with permanent toxic by-products. These processes had already been invented before the SWG came into being but were not put to use for lack of financial support. Nobody had come up with large-enough needs to justify the building of large production facilities. Only with large-scale production facilities can the costs of the power generated from these solar systems become less than that from the burning of fossil fuels. I am happy to say that between our various member states, there will be fifteen large facilities producing solar cells by the middle of summer, and by fall, large quantities of completed solar panels will be leaving the fabrication plants. There are other elements that make up a complete power system, but these are conventional and are not the pacing items in our worldwide conversion away from fossil fuels. This will be no small feat. We are talking about producing literally hundreds of millions of square meters of solar panels per month.

"The companion to solar power is power produced by wind, a mature technology which has often previously not been utilized for aesthetic reasons. There are locations not so far utilized on the Great Plains and along the seashores where reasonably steady and strong winds are common. Winds complement solar power since they are not dependent on sunshine and when used together generally reduce the amount of energy that is needed to be stored.

"Hydrogen made during the day from surplus solar power electrolyzing water is a mature technology. Converting the hydrogen back to power will currently be done by using gas turbines similar to those now operated on natural gas. While a relatively efficient process, we envision in the long run using even more efficient fuel cells to generate power from the stored hydrogen. At some locations, when topography is favorable, stored energy, by elevating water to a considerable height during times of energy surplus, would be attractive and would use a technology that is decades old.

"With wind and solar production varying with the weather from location to location, to avoid the otherwise necessity of very large power storage, we anticipate building a smarter and more robust energy grid that would be capable of routing energy over long distances from areas of surplus power to areas of want. Some desert areas could be expected to be net energy exporters and large metropolitan areas to be net energy importers, sometimes thousands of miles apart. The power systems will be deployed as we make population moves so that the extra power-needs for the relocated populations can be provided for."

Greta used a number of charts to provide graphic detail regarding the solar and wind-power projects and distribution systems which in turn generated a number of lively questions. All-in-all, the directors were highly pleased with Greta's report.

Greta wasn't done but continued on to her other large project. "You all know that our master plan calls for relocation of millions of people, some to areas of the world that, even with the predicted climatic changes, will still have to be regarded as deserts. Fresh water in great quantity will be required, and the only practical source is to make it from sea water. Again, the economy of scale allows for low-cost methods that have not been used on a commercial basis before. The largest present existing plants use fossil fuels as their energy source, which is an unacceptable solution by our ground rules.

"We have identified two acceptable processes, distillation, and reverse osmosis. With regenerators of a recent design, the heat of condensation in the distillation process provides almost all the energy for evaporation, with the small loss due to friction and thermal losses being made up by a solar-energy plant.

"Low-energy needs in reverse-osmosis facilities can result from using very large area membranes. Since there are existing production facilities that can produce both systems, we will achieve the most capacity in the shortest time by pursuing both approaches." She dropped a small bombshell by closing her presentation with the remark, "We expect that the first installations will be in the Libyan and Australian deserts." Neither country was yet a member state.

Someone asked Ray if the Libyans or Australians had agreed to the relocation of millions of people to live in their deserts. "No," Ray responded, "we are working on that. The leverage to use on the Libyans is obvious. With the drastic reductions in oil use worldwide, they are getting desperate for trade, trying to figure out from where their food is coming. I'm sure when we show them how we can make them self-sufficient in food, then we can make a deal. It is harder with the Australians. They are self-sufficient in both food and energy. They are, however, very vulnerable strategically, being a logical place for the Chinese to put their excess populations. When that card gets played, they will need a big brother."

It was approaching lunch time, and Ray decided to finish the morning with an easy one, so he nodded to Lars Berg. Lars began, "In the end, whatever else we do, we must reduce the carbon dioxide content of the atmosphere. Some carbon dioxide is absorbed by the oceans, and maybe at a rate that we can increase in the future. The remainder CO_2 either stays in the atmosphere or is absorbed by all manner of plant life. In the past, we have been increasing the CO_2 content by burning fossil fuels and by reducing the plant life. The only solution is to greatly increase the plant life of the planet. We have been successful in stopping the wholesale cutting of the forests by buying off the cutters where they were agreeable and by threatening brute force where nothing else would work.

"The big thing for the long term is a large increase in the biomass. The only thing that makes enough difference is large-scale reforestation and increasing the health of the existing forests. We estimate that we must replant forty million square kilometers of forest eventually. This will take some five to 10 percent of the world's labor force, if it is to be done in a time period that will make a difference to the coming climate change. If we plant too slowly, it will get too cold for forests to grow where we need them. Forests do not do well growing on permafrost.

"To start this gigantic task, we are absorbing most of the manpower from the various armed forces as they are demobilized. I should say we are not taking critically skilled personnel when they are needed elsewhere. We are also absorbing the bulk of those individuals who are becoming unemployed, mainly from the luxury and service industries that are non-essential and are being phased out. Similar to the other areas that have reported, our department is not getting into the forest business directly but is working through the SWG member states.

"This is not a fast project and don't look for a major increase in tree planting this year. We have to start with the tree nurseries to get a lot of seedlings to plant in the future. We can, however, make a difference immediately with the existing forests. Many of them are dying or are unhealthy for reasons that are known but were previously not thought to be economical to correct. For example, we predict that acid rain will be down to only 20 percent of its past levels two months after we completely banned the burning of high sulfur-content coal. Stopping the acid rain will make a crucial difference for many forests. We have also started a program of re-mineralizing the soil of the major forests so that they will be healthier and increase the biomass faster. This has been pioneered in Europe, where it has been found that often a sick forest can be made healthy by the simple application of rock dust. They call it stone meal. This is the fastest way to remove carbon dioxide, but the logistics are mind boggling."

Lars closed his presentation with the statement, "If the glacial period can be held off a few years, the trees may yet save us." There were no questions for Lars, only enthusiasm for the massive effort that humanity was undertaking to heal the planet. At that they broke for lunch.

Julia and Roger happened to eat together, and Julia asked how Lucille was since she had not seen her for some time. Roger answered, "She is very busy getting the 'Son of NOAH' up and running for Meriwether. We do get together as often as we can, which is not that often. One thing," he added, hesitatingly, since no general announcement had been made, "we plan to get married as soon as the SWG headquarters moves to Puerto Rico."

Julia had been married when she and her previous husband had moved to the Washington, DC, area, but their respective careers had moved them apart, and they had now been divorced for five years. Roger's talking about getting married reminded her that recently she had been feeling that she was ready for a romantic attachment. Of all the people in the SWG that she regularly contacted, Olav Kerensky was the one that made her heart beat faster. So far, she had no opportunity to get to know him personally and wondered what kind of a man he was, coming from such a different background. As they walked back from lunch, each thinking personal thoughts, Julia made a conscious decision to find out more about Olav at the first opportunity. Maybe the planned socializing after the day's meeting would be the place.

The object of her thoughts was already waiting for the meeting to reconvene. Olav thought of all the turns of fate that had brought him to this point in his destiny. A jack-of-all-trades, and a master of many, he had started in the Manufacturing Institute at Kiev, apparently destined to spend his life in the unending battle of trying to squeeze ever-increasing production out of reluctant workers, who had no incentive to do much of any work. The system was doomed from the beginning because of the bureaucrats' greater interest in career advancement over the interests of the country or the workers. Olav felt sad that he would not see at firsthand a real market economy in Russia because he felt that with an interested and unfettered citizenry, a decent society should have been possible. In an open society, he felt it should be possible to devise mechanisms where the greed aspect of richer individuals could be sufficiently curbed so that all could share in the good life. In any event, all that was past for now as humanity was turning to a highly authoritarian survival society, which in some ways could not help but resemble what Olav had so recently left behind. He mused that one of the duties

Ray had asked him to perform was to provide a warning should they start down one of the unsuccessful paths that the Soviets had taken.

As Julia came in and sat down, Olav was somehow reminded of his now-dead wife and the early days in his climb in the Soviet power structure. He attributed his successes to an intuitive trait he had in understanding people, not just their surface desires, but the underlying motives, often hidden even to themselves. This was a very valuable asset in the dog-eat-dog environment he had been in, not only for himself but also for those for whom he worked. Some years ago, he had come to the attention of the present Russian Prime Minister and had followed his climb toward the top. On the whole, it had been a very interesting life so far, with the only sad point being when his wife had died. He knew why he had not remarried. In the years since Olga had died, most of the women he had met were party functionaries, looking for how they might best advance their careers. Perhaps in this new environment, there would be better opportunities. What he really wanted was companionship.

*   *   *

On the other side of the United States, Larry Owen was not paying much attention to world events. Trying to make a living under the new circumstances was quite a challenge. Art was not considered an essential business. It had taken quite a bit longer than he had expected for George Fox to set up the meeting with his potential customers for the diode art. As he neared George's store, he thought that it was very hard to continue his life as a pop-artist, and unless something materialized soon, he would have to register for some kind of work he would no doubt find most uninteresting. Often the optimist, he shifted to a positive attitude. Maybe there would be a nice market in his newest art form.

As he entered the store, Larry noticed that George had added a large inventory of practical items for sale in order to qualify as an essential business under the new rules. Better for George than planting trees he thought.

"Oh, there you are, Larry," George welcomed him. "Come into the back and meet two of my old friends."

The back room was a combination work and storage area, including a few chairs, two of which were occupied. "Larry," George said, "I want you to meet Dr. Ivan Wheeler and Dr. Gloria Wheeler, his wife. They teach and research para-psychology at the university. They are the ones that are interested in your unique form of art."

After a few minutes of small talk, Ivan Wheeler got down to business. "Where did you get the idea for these?" he asked, holding up one of Larry's creations, a round-shaped object with twelve triangular points around the periphery.

Larry answered, "The geometrical pattern was in a book on yoga depicting the chakras of the body. I saw it in the library. The idea to mechanize it using electronic parts just sort of came to me one day when I was visiting a friend who deals in surplus electronics. He has lots of stuff he couldn't get rid of and gave me a box full to play with. If I remember it right, the one you have is the heart chakra."

Ivan Wheeler continued his questioning. "Yes, but was there some special reason you soldered the parts together like you did?"

"Oh," said Larry. "I've dabbled in alternate art forms for years. You know, welded scrap iron, driftwood arrangements, mosaic tiles. This just seemed like something no one else had done, something new that might catch on. The parts cost nothing as they were surplus and soldering is the logical way to connect wires."

Gloria Wheeler couldn't restrain herself. "Then you don't know what they do?"

"You mean something besides just looking pretty?" Larry asked.

Ivan Wheeler took charge again. "We have found that when you are close to these patterns of yours, they activate the nervous system in interesting ways. You didn't know that?"

"No," Larry said. "They were just supposed to look pretty so that people would buy them."

Ivan Wheeler went on, "So far, we have found out that about one person in ten can feel the effects of one of these things within a few minutes. By electronic monitoring, we have found that they affect everyone, even if they don't feel them consciously. The results so far seem to be beneficial both physically and psychologically."

"That is amazing," Larry said. Thinking of his desperate financial situation, he added, "Would you like to buy my patterns? You've tried the four samples I left with George. I have eight more at home that are different that complete the set."

"Actually," Ivan Wheeler responded, "we would prefer to get you a job at the university. Several of our grants have been classified essential. That way, you could make more of these patterns for us as we expand our experimenting with them. I had half-time in mind, which would allow you to work some on your regular artistic endeavors."

That sounded like a real godsend to Larry, and they quickly reached an agreement on practical details. As they left the store, Larry joked with George, "No sale, no commission. Guess you will have to sell an extra dozen bars of soap to make up for it."

CHAPTER 19

The Reviews Continue

After their lunch, the directors continued their reviews with Olav's turn in the barrel. He began, feeling confident in his knowledge of the world food situation, "The world food stocks, production, and distribution are generally following our original plan. Because of the early slaughtering of grain-fed food animals throughout the SWG states, there has been a saving of untold millions of tons of grain. We are beginning to build up a surplus of food stocks. We will get twenty pounds of edible grain for each pound of beef not brought to market. By not raising pork, we get a smaller but still substantial saving. With chicken, it's four pounds per pound. These savings are being used to prevent starvation in all member states as well as nonmember states that wish to cooperate. China and North Korea are not one of these at the present.

"This buildup will continue for the next several years, even in the face of more crop failures because of the large amounts of grain that won't be consumed by food animals. You better start liking being a vegetarian because most of the meat will be gone in six months. When the world's temperate zones' food-growing capabilities are seriously reduced, we should have at that time a two years' surplus of grains. One challenge during this period will be having adequate storage facilities, and in fact, we are faced with adding significant facilities that will probably never be needed again. I might note that our demonstrated food surpluses have been a major factor in the decision process of many recent countries joining the SWG.

"Another factor, of course, has been our declaration that food is a basic human right, and that every person in the SWG states is entitled to a basic, healthy diet at no cost to the individual. Fortunately, we have been able to make good on our declaration in spite of the great economic upsets that the transition is causing.

"The great challenge for the future is to be able to replace the 50 percent or so of humanity's food that is currently grown in the temperate regions. It will be feasible to grow enough food for the world's population, providing that the people are willing to learn to eat foods with which they are not familiar. Eating habits and food preferences are established early in life and are one of the most difficult things for most people to change. Many people I know personally are dreading doing without meat when the meat from the recently slaughtered animals is consumed. This attitude persists in spite of the wealth of experience that demonstrates that a meatless diet is healthier. You have been bombarded with media information on excess fat and lack of fiber. On these two counts, meat, fish, and poultry are again generally losers. Another health problem with meat and poultry is that they tend to concentrate the toxic substances that have been used in modern farming. Fish concentrate the toxic substances that have been dumped in the oceans. It is also an old myth, not true by the way, that protein from meat and dairy sources is of more value to humans than protein from vegetable sources. To the cells of the body, protein is protein, no matter the source, as long as it is balanced. Also the amount of protein we need is much less than what has been thought for nearly a century. Most people have been eating so much protein that it has been a major source of toxicity, causing a great many degenerative diseases. If you are maintaining your weight you are probably getting more than enough protein in you diet."

Meriwether asked, "Weren't our ancestors largely meat eaters?"

Olav explained, "Well, bones are found around ancient campfires, proving that man ate meat on occasion. That is recent on the evolutionary time clock. The human body must have developed mostly on a vegetarian diet if you go by the evidence of our teeth, intestine length, and processes, as well as the weakness of our stomach acids, which cannot dissolve bones and feathers.

"Yes, getting people to change their diets is very difficult indeed. An example is that a number of the salt lakes in Africa naturally produce a very healthy plankton food rich in protein. This protein is largely eaten by fish and flamingos and spurned by the nearby humans, many of whom had been starving until we sent them food supplies.

A key to our future food supply is the growing of massive amounts of plankton as food. This plankton is to be grown in natural as well as artificial desert ponds and lakes, rapidly replacing our nearly exclusive great dependence on grains. Under the right conditions of sun and nutrients, vegetable plankton, spirulina, can nearly double in a day's time, providing a production rate many times greater than one of the most productive land crops, soy beans. Other than drying, essentially no processing is required of the Spirulina, and it can be stored indefinitely at room temperature. The world is full of deserts with the ideal sunlight conditions, so logically our second priority project after reforestation will be the construction of thousands of plankton ponds. These will, of course, need some of the power and water that were touched on earlier. Naturally some of the relocated populations will need to be settled near these ponds to provide a work force to tend the growing of the plankton. Already we have the appropriate industries fabricating the pumps and the machinery needed to dry the harvested plankton. Ordinary earth-moving machinery can be used for grading the ponds, and we are already moving quantities of equipment for this purpose. Assuming that political questions are settled, we hope to have our first large production facilities in operation this year on the natural lakes of Africa. The technology has been in place supporting the health food industry for several decades. It is just a matter of increasing the scale of operations."

One of the directors asked if there was a contamination problem with the growing of plankton for human consumption.

Olav answered, "No more than with growing other food stuffs. You need to pay attention to what else might be getting into the water, particularly into the natural lakes. They are so much larger than the average pond, which can be controlled precisely, that it may be necessary to move some nearby human populations that would otherwise contaminate the lakes. Another key to our future food supply is a variety of sweet potato developed for NASA for use on long space missions. While it has many characteristics of interest for space use, a key characteristic for us now on earth is that is has about three times the protein of normal sweet potatoes. As such, it provides a balanced diet essentially all by itself, important to us as we will now be doing without the protein previously provided for us by food animals. This potato is already doing service on our moon base at crater Perry where another of its characteristics, to accept the sun twenty-four hours a day, has greatly reduced the logistics problem of providing food from earth. Some of you may not know that our base at Perry is located on a mountain top at the crater rim which sees sunlight all year long.

"Within the next two years, we intend to introduce this variety of sweet potato to all the major sweet potato growers as well as other farmers willing to switch to them. While a subtropical plant, the sweet potato can be grown in green houses to extend its growing season."

Olav next took up his last main topic. "As Lars mentioned when he discussed the forests, we are moving quickly to harvest food from the tropical rain forests, particularly in Brazil. This is going to take an entirely new industry, because even though the forests produce a wide variety of human edible foods, gathering, processing, preserving, and then distributing them is only in its infancy. We are only beginning to get humans, other than the rain forest natives, to eat these new tasting foods. We will need to settle large populations in the rain forests in order to harvest and handle these new crops. Again, power will be needed where there is currently very little. Quantity of water is not a problem, although quality will be, in most places. In the long term, it is desirable to replant the sections of the rain forests that have been destroyed, but this is a very long-range effort that we will only plan for at the present so as to not dilute our efforts to survive in the short term. For the short term, we will locate our solar energy fields in the clear-cut areas adjacent to remaining areas of the rain forests."

Olav paused and smiled, then continued, "In closing, I would like to say something that is very much in harmony with what Greta said about the need to develop systems which don't harm the environment and are also sustainable indefinitely. This is a must in agriculture and goes under the name of permaculture. We must stop poisoning the planet and ourselves in the process of growing our food. It means going back to the proven systems of our ancestors, organic farming without pesticides, herbicides, and chemical fertilizers. What in the past has been termed organic wastes are in truth valuable materials that must be utilized. This kind of farming is less energy-intensive but more labor-intensive than modern agriculture. This is no problem for us since we will apparently have a labor surplus for the indefinite future, so we might as well use it in growing our food better. The bottom line on food growing must be quality to the consumer, not profit for the producer."

There were many questions after Olav finished talking, proving his contention that people are very much attached to food with which they are familiar. Questions included, "What does spirulina taste like? Can it be grown in the US southwest deserts? What is rain forest food like?"

To the question, "How are we able to produce spirulina drying machines so quickly?" Olav answered, "The machines are exactly the same as those made for drying milk, except that the air temperature is set slightly lower. We plan to add a solar pre-heat section, already proven on a pilot basis, to reduce the energy required."

Olav's report on the food situation was one of the bright points of the day's meeting. It was ironic that for the first time in history there was the prospect that none of the planet's humans would be starving, and that it took a threat of mass starvation to bring about that potential.

As Olav sat down, Julia gave him a particularly big smile, and Olav thought that perhaps now was the time to look for feminine company. His children, who had moved west with him, were a comfort, but still a man could be lonely without adult female companionship.

Jim Meriwether was next and took over from Olav promptly. "You have, of course, had a special briefing on our two main thrusts to modify the severity of the climate changes, so I won't repeat what was given in that briefing. We do have some developments since then, which I will cover. First, with regard to the increase of the warm water flow to the Arctic regions— Project Big Current. It appears that in both the Bering Strait and the Barrow Strait, a major blockage to the smooth flow of the currents is due to underwater seamounts. Leveling these seamounts would double the flow, meeting our goal set earlier but would require far fewer atomic explosions than our earlier projections. This is now the ongoing plan rather than the widening of the channels in general. We have established a base for the submarines at Hooper's Bay, Alaska, and should be in a position to make our first prototype trial shot by June 15. The companion plan to deepen the sills between the Norwegian Sea and the North Atlantic can also be done with many fewer shots by making notches in the sills rather than deepening them in general. We also now plan one prototype shot in the Atlantic from a base we are setting up at Reykjavik. We should be able to get that one off before the end of June. Review of underwater core sampling does not show any major faults to be located where we plan to do underwater sculpting. In response to Ray's request to reduce the radioactive fallout from these shots, we have a new plan which almost entirely eliminates the fallout. Rather than detonating the explosives on the sea bottom, we will use an underwater drilling barge in conjunction with the deploying submarine so that the explosives can be placed hundreds of feet below the sea bottom. We will still get the leveling of the seamounts, but the radioactivity will be trapped without venting into the air or the water." This was such good news that all the directors broke into applause.

Meriwether warmed to his subject when he moved to his second topic. "Second, with regard to the orbital screening cloud over the tropics, Project High Cloud, we will be making an experimental launch from Cape Kennedy using a Titan rocket and a prototype bubble dispenser. The operational cloud is designed to block 5 percent of the sun's rays over a limited range of latitudes 10° on each side of the equator. One shot will, of course, produce a very small fraction of this after the cloud disperses. However, by a very careful launch at a particular time of day, we can put up a small cloud between the sun and selected instrumentation points on the ground that can simulate the 5 percent screening for a short interval. This should give us a good calibration of our system before we commit to the large number of launches the full cloud will require."

Meriwether went on, "We have had some recent thoughts that simply the operational deployment by utilizing launch from ships. By launching from within 5° of the equator, we can use a single burn to orbit without the need, as from Kennedy, for two burns, one of which is initiated while coasting in space. Since precision is not required, a simple attitude pitch over until orbital velocity is reached would suffice for navigation. I also see a simpler cloud deployment likely by using a very thin but long cloud, perhaps thousands of miles long and taking many hours to put in place. Injection of the cloud matter would only be fore and aft along the orbital path.

"We are looking at modifying some of the large surplus container ships to act as the launch pads. Containers large enough to house the booster rocket with their dispersal container attached would be modified to include all the equipment for support of the launch. These containers would be loaded at the supplying port and stacked on the decks as regular cargo. Such a container would be moved to the front of the ship and erected vertically for launch.

"We envision launching from sheltered waters in two locations, the coast of Sri Lanka and the coast off French Guiana. These would be locations close enough to the ESA or Indian launch facilities that could provide range tracking abilities and also be within 5° of the equator.

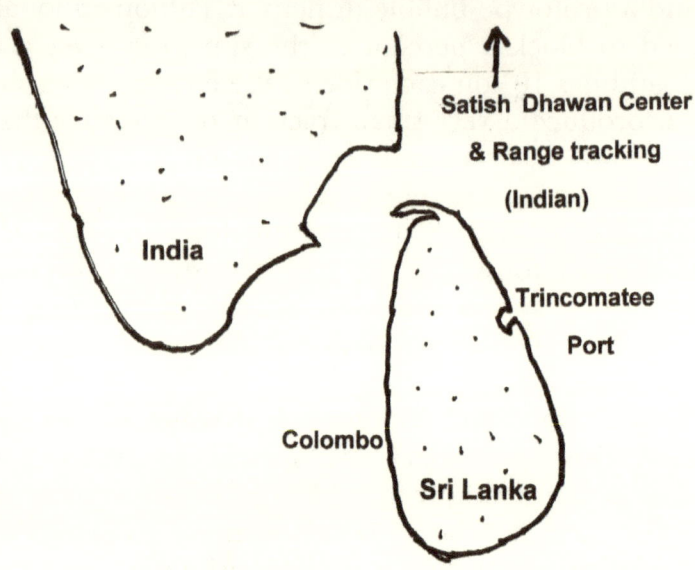

Sri Lanka and India

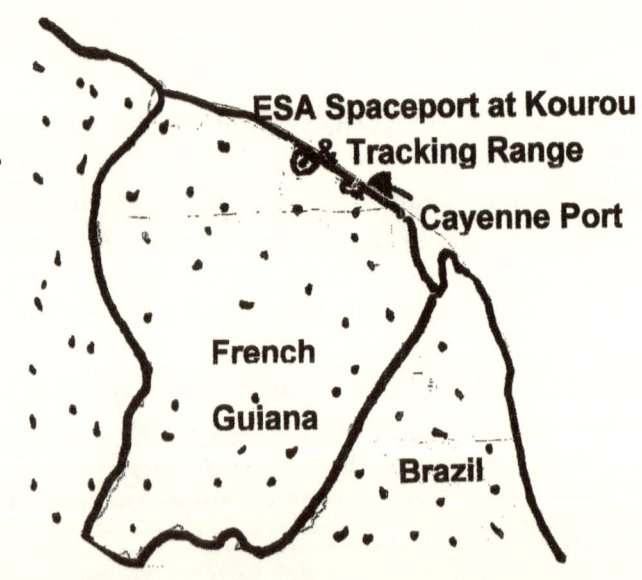

French Guiana, S. America

"Both the Sri Lanka and French Guiana locations have good harbors for ship shelter in the event of strong storms, Trincomalee and Cayenne respectively. For safety reasons launch would be from the open sea.

"As a footnote," he concluded, "we had scheduled to have Son of NOAH on line here by April 1. Since that is now the nominal move date of the SWG to Puerto Rico, we have decided to move Son of NOAH now and get it initially operational in Puerto Rico. Lucille and her staff will be leaving shortly for this purpose. I will stay here for now, where I am closer to Project NOAH, which we are still using extensively."

Roger decided that this expedited move of Son of NOAH, and hence Lucille, must have been a very recent decision, since she had said nothing about it to him when they had set the date to get married. Or maybe she knew they would be apart for a while and hadn't said anything because it might hurry them to get married before he thought they were ready. Well, he thought, if they were going to be apart until the SWG move, they might as well wait to get married until then. Dwelling on Lucille, and her sometimes puzzling ways, Roger almost missed the start of Benjamin Klein's report.

" . . . as you see, our population-move problems are compounded by the fact that there are many valuable industrial facilities in most of the areas from which populations will be evacuated." Benjamin illustrated his point by projecting charts depicting the locations of the facilities in question by categories. "To avoid the loss of production efficiency, we desire to locate the skilled personnel associated with a particular business in the vicinity of that business' new location. This requires extensive planning regarding the facilities to move, their new locations, and the particular personnel associated with them. This is a problem that transcends departments and must be worked well if we are to avoid the scattering and irrevocable loss of important skills.

"The initial population moves will be made to areas such as the Southwestern United States, where there are already infrastructures in place and adding to them will be faster and easier than where we are starting from scratch. Reduction of the large use of water for irrigation will be necessary in order to carry the additional people, but the tradeoff is a good one. However, using water for irrigation, particularly in desert areas, is very wasteful and generally is not economically sound. It is almost never done without large subsidies.

"The major population moves can be held off a few years so that we can prepare whole new cities in areas presently having no people at all. The reason we can wait is that urban populations can be temporarily maintained with, of course, an excessive expenditure of energy, in areas that have become too cold to grow crops by normal methods. It is obvious that agricultural, disabled, and unemployed groups would be moved first. Industrial personnel in essential occupations would move last. Locations that become so cold that there is a permanent and increasing ice or snow cover on the ground will at that point have to be abandoned. Without any change in the projected ice advancement, we see the need to eventually move up to five hundred million people. Even then, there would be hundreds of millions more living in areas that would not support traditional farming. The best long-term solution, which we are not addressing at this time, might be to move many of these additional millions closer to the location where the food is grown rather than pay the price of perpetual food transportation.

"Regarding population growth, we have made sure that all member states are being provided with the means and information to comply with the stated requirement for zero-population growth, beginning with the fall of this year. Some states have informed us that their citizens are refusing to comply because of social and religious customs that are strongly ingrained in their cultures. If we are to meet our goals on no population growth, the strong means discussed in the morning session for controlling food and energy use must be implemented also to motivate population control. At this time, there seems to be no alternative except for the member states to implement involuntary sterilization of those couples having two or more children. Voluntary sterilization should be encouraged of those with one or no children, possibly with financial incentives."

Ray commented at that point, "Population control is a major point in the agreement to become a member state, and if you think we should start enforcement now, based on your inputs from some of the states, I'm in agreement."

Benjamin nodded, and there seemed to be general agreement from the other directors. Greta suggested that the production of the French-developed abortion drug, RU-486 should be greatly increased and made freely available for those expecting couples not yet sterilized and already with two or more children. There being no more questions at that time, Benjamin sat down to be replaced by Bani Shinto.

"We have no immediate operational problems in transportation and logistics, because with the reduction in oil usage and the shipment of luxury goods, there is now a significant surplus in transportation capacity. We are using this surplus to move food stocks to areas of need and are finding the remaining problem to be local transportation. That again is largely being alleviated by moving the surplus motor transports in the western states to where there is a lack. With the elimination of recreational travel, three-quarters of the air transports are idle. We will maintain them for the time period when large populations will need to be moved. Since we have time to plan and prepare for the major population moves, we are converting many sea transport ships to passenger liner configurations. Sea transport is by far the most efficient by all counts except for the time taken."

Shinto continued, "For the long term, we are looking at transforming the world's transportation systems to more energy-efficient means. For land transportation, rail is generally the best for all but the most thinly populated areas. It may be a surprise to many of you that rail transportation is about ten times more fuel efficient than truck, automobile, or air. Therefore, the rail systems are to be expanded, with emphasis on conversion to electric and some to magnetic suspension systems where traffic levels justify it. Fortunately, most of the world still maintains a high level of rail usage, unlike the United States where large efforts will be necessary to revive the rail system to a high level of efficiency. These rail systems will largely be electrified. For less populous areas, particularly agricultural ones, trucks and cars will still be required, but in the long term, they will be converted to battery operation or natural gas and otherwise to the use of methyl alcohol, a liquid fuel refined from renewable sources. Future cities and additions to existing ones will be built as much as possible to eliminate the need for commuting that cannot be done by bicycle. In the new cities we will be building, and elsewhere for that matter, we must install attractive incentives which encourage people to live near their work, schools, and recreations.

"Air travel is probably the most energy-inefficient form of travel ever invented and will be phased down to a very small segment of the transportation system. Most business travel now-a-days is due to old habits and can be replaced by modern telecommunications. These will be expanded to fill the need. The fiber optics networks, in the process of being expanded, will allow economic, two-way video communications. Hopefully, in the future, most things can be manufactured close to where they will be consumed."

Shito had a last message to deliver. "Sea transport for large bulk commodities will be necessary for the indefinite future, particularly if we find it necessary to move large food stocks from the warmer to the colder climates. Sea transport is the most energy efficient of all but has historically been associated with a great deal of pollution of our planet's oceans. We are embarking on the design and building of a new kind of ship which will use airfoils to provide the majority of the driving power, thus eliminating a major burning of fossil fuels. Whether auxiliary power for these wind-driven ships should be atomic is a question that depends on finding a permanent answer to the disposal of atomic wastes. At this point, our preference is for solar power, backed up by methyl alcohol. The latter dissolves easily in saltwater, so in the case of a spill, it does not pollute the oceans as do fossil fuels. Also, for a given unit of energy delivered, methyl alcohol releases less carbon dioxide into the atmosphere than the current bunker grade oil. In the very long term, we anticipate that most populations will settle down in the vicinity of the food supplies and that manufacturing will be dispersed near the population centers. Therefore, over time, the need for sea transport will be reduced. The need for some sea transport will not disappear, however, because the world must maintain the capability to move reasonably large amounts of food in the event of catastrophes. As a technology initiative, we are investigating continuing the use of fossil fuels to power large ships if the CO_2 can be safely scrubbed from the exhaust and dispersed in the oceans."

Shito seemed to have covered his subject rather completely as there were no questions.

Ray next turned to Julia; Julia responded promptly, "With regard to communications of the normal business of the SWG, we are in excellent shape, taking over spare channels on the commercial comsats. As commercial advertising is being greatly eliminated, we expect many more channels to become surplus. With English the official SWG language, it appears easiest to take over the United States military communications system for use by our military forces. The Russian system will largely be scrapped except for some satellites that are in interesting orbits. Some ground equipment will need to be modified for Russian stations, but this will be minimized since we plan to use English-speaking personnel. As George mentioned earlier, we are adding ground stations at Puerto Rico, Hawaii, New Zealand, and Sri Lanka to handle the added volume we expect.

"The SWG What If, also assigned to my department, is operational to the extent that its inputs are the same as the one at the CIA. We are almost ready to go online with our own unique inputs. The usefulness of the CIA Unit is diverging downward because it is not getting all the planning and decision-making inputs that are going on at the SWG. We have taken on some of the CIA staff and are training others, so we can expect to make the first runs, including SWG inputs, by March 15. When our What If is proven operational, it is likely that the CIA facility will be converted to United States-use only, and we will transfer more of their staff to the SWG. We are, of course, taking over many of the CIA and KGB information sources, both overt and otherwise. As more of the countries of the world join the SWG, we will no doubt phase out most of the covert operations. These are large operations, and with the many dislocations that will be going on, some of the input networks will, no doubt, be lost to us.

"The compliance function, while small, is still quite important. This will largely be analytical and statistical, determining the compliance of the member states with the decisions of the SWG. We are already set up to monitor energy, food, and population."

Julia was finished and glanced at Ray, who said, "Thank you, Julia, for a good report." He then turned to Robert Schuman, "I have saved you for last, because some of your messages affect all of us personally, and I felt that after hearing your items, it would be distracting to go on to something else."

Robert Schuman, an international banker by profession, thought that his job was the hardest of all the directors. Most of the others were doing more or less what they had previously done professionally. In his world of economics, banking, and finance, everything had changed nearly overnight. Where there had been, in the free world, a wheeling and dealing market economy, there was now to be centralized, authoritarian control. Russia was certainly no model to copy, as it had failed to even provide the basic necessities for many of its people. As he stood up to talk, he thought that the only hope for success lay in the very large-scale application of computer modeling and data processing.

"In my department of Resource Allocation, I think everything has been included that is not specifically in some other department." This brought on a laugh from everyone, which was the first of the whole day. He continued, "It is hard for me to decide where to start. We can, of course, review our actions so far and some of the grosser results in the various states, but at the moment, to say where things are going and what other actions are needed are not clear."

Ray sympathized, "When Julia gets the new What If on line, it should be of help. The new What If will have more detailed economic factors programmed than the old CIA version."

Robert Schuman continued, "The SWG unit of exchange, the Credo, has now been issued for a month, and conversion rates have been established for all SWG member currencies which will eventually be phased out. All workers are now being paid in Credos. It is reported that there is a lively black market in certain currencies, as some people jockey for advantage. This is because the number of Credos any individual can obtain for his old currency is limited. Those businesses that have been defined as essential can convert as much currency as is necessary to maintain a reasonable cash flow. Those businesses that are not essential will not be able to convert their currency and will shortly have to go out of business. With the elimination of most private property as well as the profit motive, there have been wholesale disruptions in the economy. The financial markets are, of course, in complete ruin. Banking has been taken over by the SWG, and under it, by member states.

"The transition in business management is relatively slow, with those organizations still in business operating pretty much as they have been for the present. With the elimination of stockholders and extravagantly paid management teams, hopefully businesses will be operated to provide the services for which they are intended, as well as provide a better livelihood for their workers. In the United States, which seems to have moved the quickest, we are already seeing a shift to a form of management that is similar to what we used to call an employee-owned business. Some are very much like coops. The mom-and-pop businesses are changing very little but will be monitored to make sure that their prices are fair.

"A very rapid change has been a huge escalation in the unemployed, as luxury and other nonessential businesses have terminated operations. This includes a large segment of the service sector, such as stock brokers, insurance salesmen, real estate agents, in the United States represents at least half of the recent workforce. The time lag to transform this army of disgruntled beings into tree planters, solar-panel fabricators, and plankton-farm tenders is going to be long, and we will have a large segment of the population unproductive for some time. Food, housing, and clothing, where needed, will be provided at no cost to the unemployed, but without being productively employed, they represent an unstable element in the society. The bureaucracies needed to provide the services to the unemployed exist in most of our member states but not on the scale required. They are already swamped and are in great need of major staff increases in order to cope. Until these situations can be remedied, there will be hardship, confusion, and general dissatisfaction.

"One bright spot is that certain countries that were in critical condition before the advent of SWG, such as in Eastern Europe and certain of the developing countries, are actually better off now than they were, and in those areas, morale is good. Ironically, the countries that were relatively prosperous, particularly the Western democracies, are where the attitude crisis is the most severe. This is no doubt because the change has been the most drastic, going from a luxurious lifestyle to one of basic survival. Probably why there has not been a revolt is that, by and large, the Western democracies are the ones threatened the most and soonest by the coming climatic changes."

As he listened to Robert Schuman's descriptions of current society, Roger had to agree that even from his own viewpoint of relative isolation in the old UN facilities the summary being presented was reasonably accurate. Essentially all commercials had disappeared from the TV channels, which were rapidly beginning to resemble the old BBC format, an improvement from Roger's view. Cabs, to go on an infrequent restaurant outing, were becoming scarce, as gasoline rationing went into effect. The inconvenience of having to have his rationing card punched on such occasions was a reminder that change was here to stay. On his recent trip to Washington, he had encountered the need for filling out forms and obtaining signatures that were the hallmark of a controlled society. Making travel less attractive was no doubt one of the goals of the SWG.

Roger's thoughts came back to the present as Robert Schuman finished. " . . . so you see, authoritative, central economic control is not very viable in the long run as has been repeatedly proven whenever it has been tried. The economic decisions in a society are so many and varied, that they can only be made efficiently on the spot in a decentralized fashion, as is the case in a market economy. Assuming we get through the crises of the climate change, I strongly recommend that we plan to revert to some form of free economy."

"Well," said Ray, concluding the meeting, "I suggest your department model the various possible economic scenarios for our future world so that we can make reasonably informed decisions when the time comes."

As the directors began to rise to leave, Boris got everyone's attention. "One last precaution. As you have seen on the TV, the people living in the inner-core cities, who are the least capable of adapting under trying conditions, are getting quite ugly, particularly on the streets. We predict that they will turn their resentment toward the SWG personnel. For any travel you must make to any particularly dangerous location, please arrange an armed escort. Those of you trained in the use of weapons may wish to carry a gun with you, although having a gun may help you get shot. We are issuing special briefcases containing radio beacons to all directors and their important staff. In the event you are taken hostage, we will at least be able to locate where you are being held. Those of you who prefer may carry an alternate, which is a disguised beacon that fits in a pocket or purse. Be sure and use one or the other at all times when you leave this facility." On that note the meeting ended.

CHAPTER 20

Good Friends

After the meeting, Ray hosted his directors and other staff members who had been present to a social hour. Except for these meetings and when two directors got together for specific business, they didn't have much opportunity to get to know each other personally. In the course of the hour, Julia and Olav seemed to come together naturally, and Julia decided to start the conversation.

"I was really impressed with what you said we will be doing to feed the world, particularly with the cultured plankton. Tell me, what does it really taste like, I suppose a sort of salty seaweed?"

"Not really," he said, taking a small container from his pocket and handing it to her. "Have a couple of tablets. These happen to be spirulina, which has been sold in the health-food trade for decades. Try some. Most people just swallow them for an energy booster. Personally, I like the taste and chew them thoroughly first. They are really very bland. Spirulina is also available as a powder which you can put on or in almost any food. I particularly like it in soup and on salads."

Julia took two and gingerly chewed them. "Not bad," she said. "Sort of a nutty taste with a slight flavor of sardines. How did you get started on spirulina? I don't suppose it is common in Russia."

"Yes and no," he laughed. "Actually, Russia has done a lot of research on spirulina and even grown it in solar greenhouses. It has never been done on a scale large enough for it to be available to the general public. However, for people in the government, it was available."

After more small talk, the party began to break up, and Orlav asked Julia if she would like to come home to his apartment in a neighboring apartment hotel for supper.

"Why not?" she thought. "It's about time." Aloud she said, "Sure, I'm still hungry. Two spirulina tablets are not a complete substitute for dinner. Are you having something with plankton in it?"

"It's easy to arrange," he said, laughingly, and while she stopped by the rest room, he called ahead.

Julia had tried to prepare herself for anything, but she was still surprised when the door to Olav's apartment was opened by an elderly woman, who introduced herself as Ola, the family housekeeper. Behind her were a boy of twelve and a girl of ten whom Olav introduced as his children, Sergey and Sofia.

Olav commented, "Fortunately, Sergey and Sofia have always been in schools where English was taught, so adjusting to the American ways has been easier for them than for some of the other Russian children. Ola has been with us since my wife's death five years ago. I wanted my children to be fluent in English, so I was very happy to get Ola, who is a retired school teacher with a specialty in English. She has been very happy to come to America."

Feeling overly flattered, Ola blushed accommodatingly, thinking Olav was trying to impress this good-looking Western woman. She was right.

Supper was soon served, and the first course to come was a bright green soup. At Julia's raised eyebrows, Olav laughed. "This is really a lentil soup, a watered-down dal, with a heaping spoonful of spirulina added to each serving. I am sure you will like it." Julia had to agree that it was excellent.

The salad dressing was also green, being composed of spirulina mixed into an oil dressing, and again Julia found it agreeable.

The entrée was a nut casserole to which Julia herself deliberately added some spirulina powder and, again, found the taste very acceptable. "You certainly kept your word," she said to Olav afterward as they sat alone in the living room.

"Yes," he said, "not only can non-meat diets be tasty, but they can be very nutritious as well. In that one meal, you had more than a day's requirement of protein. If you had had significant protein in your breakfast and lunch, you would have taken an excess of protein for the day. Actually, did you know that researchers in both the United States and Russia and in many other countries as well have shown that excessive protein is a major cause of degenerative diseases that have become prevalent in the last generation?"

"No," said Julia, "most of what I have heard would suggest that the more protein you eat, like milk, eggs, meat, and cheese, the better."

"That," he retorted, "is just your Western free-market advertising." He laughed. "Those are old outdated ideas based on experiments made on rats nearly one hundred years ago. People have a different metabolism than that of rats and need about only one-fourth the protein that is eaten by the average Westerner. Eating too much protein builds up protein toxicity in the body. A good diet would consist of a large percentage of raw fruits and vegetables and only a little protein."

Olav warmed to one of his favorite subjects. "Most people on the planet who get enough calories in their diets, automatically get enough protein." Realizing he was losing the opportunity for which he had invited Julia home to dinner, Olav then said, "But what would you like to talk about?"

Julia smiled as the conversation turned in the direction she had in mind. Very straight forwardly she said, "I want to hear about you. What is your impression of the United States so far? I'm sure that it is very different from what you are used to in Russia."

"Well," he laughed, "here, in the United Nations' preserve, you don't really get much of an impression of the United States. However, one of my specialties back in Russia was to study the United States from afar but with the help of the extensive resources expended by Russia for that purpose. I probably knew the United States more objectively than any native possibly could. We were privy to many things that are not known to the general public. Of course, with the crisis of the coming climate change, the United States must have changed a lot from what it was like before I came here."

He paused and decided that she really did want to know what he was thinking on a serious level, so he continued, "As a way of serving its citizens, probably no country's government comes close to doing its job, although Sweden tries hardest. Most governments put their first priority on maintaining their officials in power and then in serving the special interests of whatever group put them there. In the United States, the country was run to benefit large corporations and those with money.

"In Russia," he continued, "in the past, it has been run, of course, for the benefit of the individuals in the Communist party, the higher the official's level the greater the benefits. In the restructuring that is happening currently, no doubt the benefits will be shifting to others who come into power. For the good of the people, of major importance to those in power should be not to be overly greedy for themselves, be efficient in the operations of the government, and not to forget that they are the servants of the people." Olav felt it was time to get feedback from Julia.

She sensed his questioning look. "Why is it that you feel that the Swedes have done the best job of government?"

"They have struck a reasonable balance, letting the marketplace efficiencies provide most of the goods and services, while the government or government-controlled entities produce in those areas not suited to private enterprise. They have strong laws which assure proper care for the people and at least one of the strongest set of controls in the world to protect the environment. Probably more than most, the Swedes have arranged things so that the workers in a given business control that business within reasonable constraints put on them by the rest of their people. Their major weakness is that the ethical and moral traditions that have served them well in the past are weakening, and they lack a replacement."

"I've often thought of that," she said, "with regard to the whole of the world in general. As the new generations reject their elders' religious beliefs and standards, what can be done to replace them with something appropriate for the changed circumstances?" Julia looked to Olav for an answer.

"The only societies that have been successful with this in the past have had a self-consistent set of standards, from whatever source, and have instilled them in their young people, starting in infancy. Do you not agree?"

"Yes," she answered, "of course, you are right in general terms, but, for example, what would be an appropriate set of standards for the new world we hope to create after we get beyond the glacial period crises, something specific?"

"You see," he said, "history and governments change, but human nature changes hardly at all. All of us need food, shelter, love, and a feeling of a place in the order of things, a purpose for being. These needs have been addressed in many past societies, some more successfully than others. Where successful, the societies have generally endured until internal or outside forces have no longer provided these needs. Of course, there is a big inertia to change that one must allow for under most circumstances.

"A prime example of such a system operating is how the standards and values of Confucius and Taoism in China maintained a stable society over thousands of years, even with the coming and going of different dynasties. By and large, the rulers realized that to stay in power, they had the responsibility of serving the people first. Such a system of standards and values would be suitable today with minimum change. These ancient Chinese systems established the relationships between the rulers and their people, between members of a family and their relations, between individuals and society at large, and most importantly, between the individual and what we in the West call God, what the Chinese called the Way, the Greeks called the Logos, and the Hindus called the Shabd."

Julia laughed. "You seem to have such a wide knowledge of the world and the history of its people, certainly more than one ever finds in a government official of the United States. How did you get such an education? It is my impression of Russia that many of the things you have been speaking of were not taught in any university or allowed to be discussed in the open, at least until recently."

"That has certainly been true in the past," Olav responded, "but, you see, as you rise in the government, the restrictions put on the general population don't apply, otherwise, vital decisions would be made in an atmosphere of such ignorance that the government of even the most brutal, totalitarian type would collapse. So I, and those other members of the government who chose to do so, had access to almost any information that existed in the world."

Julia's next question was one Olav knew would come up sometime in their conversation. "With the ethical views you have been expounding, how were you able to continue as an important member of the Russian government when its actions in the past have been in such strong opposition to them: the denial of human rights, the spoiling of the environment, the intimidation of neighboring countries?"

Olav paused before answering. He knew that a lot of their future relationship, which he hoped would develop substantially, depended on how she took his reply. He was slow and careful in his wording. "First was the accident of birth, over which, of course, no one has any control. Many years passed in my climb in the Communist Party before I was in a position to know what was really happening. By that time, I became convinced that by staying I could make things better for the people than if I left or defected. That is also the case of the present leader of Russia, Prime Minister Ivan Petrovich. He had to pay lip service to the true party line for many years until he was in a strong enough position to make the many changes he has recently made without being removed. Even now there are strong factions that will try to preserve their favored positions at any cost."

Julia seemed satisfied and returned to the main theme of their conversation. "But even if you can identify a workable set of standards and ethics, how can you go about implementing them in a society, such as the world society we will want to build after the crises are over, when those standards and ethics did not evolve naturally in the society?"

Olav's brow creased as he answered, "That is definitely a difficult problem but not, I feel, impossible. Once we start, it will probably take one generation to put into place. It would take longer were it not for the sacrifices and difficulties the world's people will have to make just to survive during the next few years. The best comes out in people when they are challenged out of their complacency. As for the details, we should leave them for now to Coordinator Carr who holds this as a very special personal project. He is greatly grieved at the present need to govern the world on a totalitarian basis, backed by the ultimate use of atomic weapons. I am glad that I do not carry his load."

The balance of the evening turned to lighter topics as it had first begun. Olav and Julia found that, in spite of coming from opposite sides of the world, they had many interests in common. Before the evening was over and Olav took Julia back to her apartment, they knew each other's life histories, likes, dislikes, and had had a thoroughly enjoyable time together. Julia resolved to see as much of Olav as she could arrange in the future. If it ended in marriage, she thought, a ready-made family would save her the chores of pregnancy and interrupting her career.

For his part, Olav considered that life had been kind to him. While his wife had been a model Russian wife and mother, Olav could see that they had never really been friends, with their common interest being mainly their children. Russian society was still male-dominated, and women and men usually did not relate as equals. With Julia, he had felt a true friendship growing, as between equals, something new that he attributed to women's liberation in the West. It was exhilarating and full of promise. Perhaps it would develop into love as well. What more could he ask for than that?

*　　*　　*

Back in the Black Forest, Gertrude was not faring as well as Olav or Julia. The forestry service had been greatly expanded with the objective to plant billions of trees. Gertrude had been offered the supervision of one planting team, a change she considered a step backward, and she had declined the offer. She was then summarily assigned to a construction crew on its way to North Africa. The crew's work was to build new cities in North Africa for the northern Europeans who would be forced to leave their homes in the coming years in the face of the advancing ice.

CHAPTER 21

Kidnapped

Of all the people in the world, Meriwether was one whose life so far had changed very little. He had been to Washington, and was now on his way back to SWG headquarters from LaGuardia Airport. He was winding up his affairs in New York and would soon be moving his operations to Puerto Rico. At the moment, he was relaxing as much as one could in a New York cab and not paying much attention until he saw that traffic was blocked ahead. It appeared that a semitrailer had overturned, spilling some of its cargo and blocking all the lanes on his side of the parkway. Meriwether thought it must have just happened because as yet there was no sign of a police car.

As he looked closer, what seemed unusual was a large crowd of bystanders who were opening the doors of the stopped cars and pulling the people out of them. His cab driver was taking it all in too and attempted to turn around, but it was too late; the lanes behind them were already packed solid. It was apparently a deliberate gang operation, as Meriwether could see them approaching, smashing windows where people had locked their doors in an attempt at protection. Meriwether decided it was best to vacate the cab and depart as quickly as possible on foot. Even that proved to be too late as an alert gang member spied him, pulled out a gun, and ordered, "Over here, mister." Apparently, the operation was a desperate effort by a large street gang, not wanting to comply with the policy that everyone must work, to obtain a quantity of the new currency. The rough-looking character with the gun took Meriwether's wallet and gave him a quick body search, coming up with Meriwether's SWG credentials.

To the apparent leader of the gang, he called out, "Slugger, look here, we got us a big shot. They will probably pay big to get him back. We need to get his stuff from that cab. It might be worth a lot, too."

The sound of approaching sirens in the distance could be heard, a sound not lost on the gang. The gang members gathered up the wallets and other loot in plastic bags and moved quickly to a side street where they seemed to melt into the alleys. Four of the gang members, who had all the bags, dragged Meriwether into an old van and drove off slowly.

The man with the gun had assumed the role of Meriwether's keeper and growled, "Stay quiet and do what I tell you, and you won't get hurt." After about ten minutes, they drove up to a building with a garage door that opened onto the alley. The building seemed to have a small garage-repair business on the ground floor and apartments on the upper floors. Someone inside the garage must have been waiting because the door was opened quickly so that the van did not even have to stop. The door was closed immediately behind them.

Meriwether was now seriously concerned for his own safety. He knew that the gang would quickly be traced to the location of the garage by means of the beacon in his briefcase that they had taken from the cab, but that didn't mean he would necessarily get out unhurt. He calculated that the forces of law and order would arrive in less than an hour. He knew and agreed with the policy of the SWG that there would be no negotiations with terrorists, which his kidnappers would certainly be classified as. To negotiate would only promote future incidents.

This was the first time that a member of the SWG had been seriously molested in the city, so Meriwether decided his case would set a precedent. With most of the world now a part of SWG, there were very few havens left for terrorists, and the incidents of terrorism had dropped dramatically. Maybe the SWG would pretend to negotiate to improve the chances of his rescue. Certainly his capture had been a fluke and incidental to the gang's main operation, which had been simply to take viable cash off the passing motorists.

While one gang member kept Meriwether covered with a gun in the corner of an apartment living room, the others were systematically going through the wallets and purses that they had taken out of the bags. The Credos being removed from the wallets and purses were piled on the carpet. As the counting neared its end, Meriwether, who was watching, estimated that their haul amounted to the pay for about fifty man-months of work at today's average salary. Under the new economic policies, nobody would be carrying large amounts of Credos around even though in previous times it was not unusual to carry large amounts of dollars. The gang apparently considered it a small haul, knowing it would be split about twenty-five different ways. Their attitude turned sullen and mean.

The leader whom everyone called Slugger turned and addressed Meriwether's guard. "Have you gone through his stuff?"

The guard answered, "Yeah, not much of value there, the usual things a guy takes on a trip. The briefcase was locked, but I forced it. Full of papers about weather and useless stuff like that. A small personal computer you could probably pawn."

Slugger turned to Meriwether. "So, what do you do for the crapping SWG, those guys who are lording it over everybody?"

"I'm a weatherman," Meriwether responded, "you know, the guys on the local news that tell you when it's going to rain or snow. Well, the SWG wants to know a little farther into the future, so they hire guys like me."

"Well," Slugger grunted, "they probably would like to have you back in one piece." Turning to a small man on his right, he ordered, "Jerry, go to the pay phone down at Jim's bar and call the fuzz. Tell them to get word to the SWG bigwigs we got one of their fellows, name of Meriwether. If they want him back, they are to put one hundred thousand Credos in a briefcase. We will call them back in two hours and tell them how they can trade for Meriwether."

When an hour had passed and Jerry hadn't returned, Slugger began to show obvious nervousness. What he didn't know was that Jerry had walked into a police blockade around the block and wasn't coming back. Finally Slugger turned to one of his two remaining assistants and told him to go find out what had happened to Jerry. The second man didn't return either. Two hours after Meriwether had been taken captive, the sound of a bullhorn broke the silence of the night. "This is the police. We have you surrounded. Your errand boys have told us you are holding Meriwether. If you want to live, leave your weapons inside and come out with your hands raised." Suddenly, banks of floodlights were turned on, and the building was lit on all sides.

Ray and Boris were a block away at the command post of the antiterrorist unit that was conducting the rescue operation. They were talking to Captain Rodregus who was in charge. "We don't want anything to happen to Meriwether," Ray said. He repeated what he had said earlier. "But even more important, we can't have them leave here with him as a hostage. What is your latest plan?"

Captain Rodregus looked very capable in his assault fatigues. "We've got the swat team in position around the building. The kidnappers haven't responded to our instructions, so apparently they are planning something. A neighbor says he saw a van drive into the garage in back. We have to disable the van so that if they try to leave using Meriwether as a shield, they will be out in the open, where our guys can take them out. There are lights on only on the second floor in the left front apartment, and we have the telephone number for it. In five minutes, I will call and see what kind of a deal they want. If it involves Meriwether, I want you to verify his voice so we know that he is alive. When you are talking to him and we know that he is not in the garage, we will take out the van."

Five minutes later, the phone rang in the gang's apartment, and a nervous Slugger answered it. "Yeah, what do you want?"

Rodregus said into the phone, "This is Captain Rodregus of the New York Police, Antiterrorist Section. Like we said on the bullhorn, come out without your weapons with your hands up, and Meriwether better be with you."

Slugger bellowed back. "I'm telling you what you are going to do. If you want Meriwether back alive, when we come out of the garage in a grey van, you let us go pretty as we please. No following us, or Meriwether gets it. Understand?"

The captain, expecting this development, responded, "I can't talk a deal unless I know Meriwether is OK. Put him on the phone." He handed the phone to Ray.

Meriwether came on soon with, "Hello, hello, who is this?"

Ray nodded at the captain and then said, "This is Ray. Don't worry, we will get you out of this all right."

At the same time, Rodregus said, "Go" into his handheld communicator, and the assault team broke down the garage door and disabled the van with a burst of gunfire from their assault rifles. The team then withdrew to avoid a possible counterattack from the second floor. They had not so far gained access to the front of the building, which apparently contained the stairway.

Ray passed the phone back to the captain, who found he was talking to a highly enraged man on the other end. When Slugger calmed down a little, the captain said, "So much for your grey van. Now do what I said to start with and come out with your hands up. If anything happens to Meriwether, there will be an unforeseen accident, and you'll never get to see the inside of a jailhouse."

Slugger responded, "You'll never get us alive. If you want Meriwether alive, move a police car to the front door and leave the engine running. In five minutes, we are coming out with Meriwether, and if there is any shooting, he gets it first."

Slugger wasn't familiar with the competency of the swat team who had all been shown photos of Meriwether. Before the four of them were more than halfway to the police car, Meriwether was the only one of them left alive.

Ray had alerted the various TV and news services who gave the incident full coverage. He wanted other, would-be terrorists to know that the SWG was not an organization to fool with. When interviewed, he repeated the SWG policy of not negotiating with terrorists.

CHAPTER 22

Puerto Rico

Lucille had arrived in Puerto Rico in March, and she found it a very pleasant change from the New York winter she had left, a winter which was still in full swing. The SWG had selected an area for its headquarters that was east of San Juan near Carolina, reasonably close to the San Juan Airport. For Lucille, it was also a happy choice, being near the sandy beaches and close enough to the shore to get a steady breeze from the trade winds, an important consideration in the tropics. While many existing buildings were to be used by the SWG through modification, there was also a lot of new construction in progress. There seemed to be a mix of Navy Seabees, Army engineers, and civilian contractors. Ray was apparently using whatever it took to get the SWG headquarters ready as fast as possible. The living quarters Lucille had been assigned to, as well as the building to house Julia's new What If, were finished. So was the facility for the Son of NOAH. Most of the components for the Son of NOAH had arrived and were in the process of being checked out. A lot of the debug for the new software programs had already been done back at NOAA so that getting it online shouldn't take long. Fred and some of his staff were scheduled to come down toward the end of the month to help. Some of them were joining the SWG and would stay on permanently. There would still not be enough staff, and Lucille was reviewing local applications as well as interviewing likely prospects.

Lucille reflected that changes were coming very fast. With the conversion to a survival economy, there were many out of work in Puerto Rico, but with the arrival of the SWG headquarters, most of these would find employment. There was first the large increase in construction activity as well as providing services for the SWG staff that had begun to arrive.

Planting in the tropical rain forests would take up much of the unskilled labor. Fortunately, environmental activists had prevented much clear-cutting of the forests, but much cutting had still been done in anticipation of building condos and other wasteful uses of the land, such as golf courses. On several of the level areas, plankton ponds were being built in order to do experimental cultivation of spirulina right at the headquarters. Normally grown on desert areas, the SWG wanted to find out the practicality of growing the plankton in high rainfall, tropical areas. If successful, this would be the prototype of the ponds that it had been proposed to build in Brazil on a large-scale basis.

Lucille was part of the climatology department's advance party, and she had taken on an extra assignment. This was to scout out ground locations for special sensors to be used to observe the High Cloud test shot that was to be made soon. The test cloud would be deployed in an inclined orbit such that it would pass directly overhead. The date chosen for the test would also place the sun directly overhead so that conditions would come close to simulating conditions near the equator where the operational orbit would be. As dispersed, the test cloud when passing over Puerto Rico would be approximately 150 miles long, traveling west to east.

Being in low earth orbit, the test cloud would be traveling at approximately 4.3 miles/sec and pass a point on the ground in the center of its track in just under forty seconds. Lucille had made arrangements to take a car and drive around the east end of the island, looking for suitable spots. Meriwether had suggested that they plan on five locations, approximately twenty miles apart. Clear visibility was an important factor, so Lucille had already ruled out anything downwind from all the SWG construction where there was quite a bit of dust. She had selected her first location and marked it on the map, a point northeast of the SWG headquarters right on the beach. As she drove on the coastal road, she added a lighthouse and the Roosevelt Roads Naval Air Station as the second and third points.

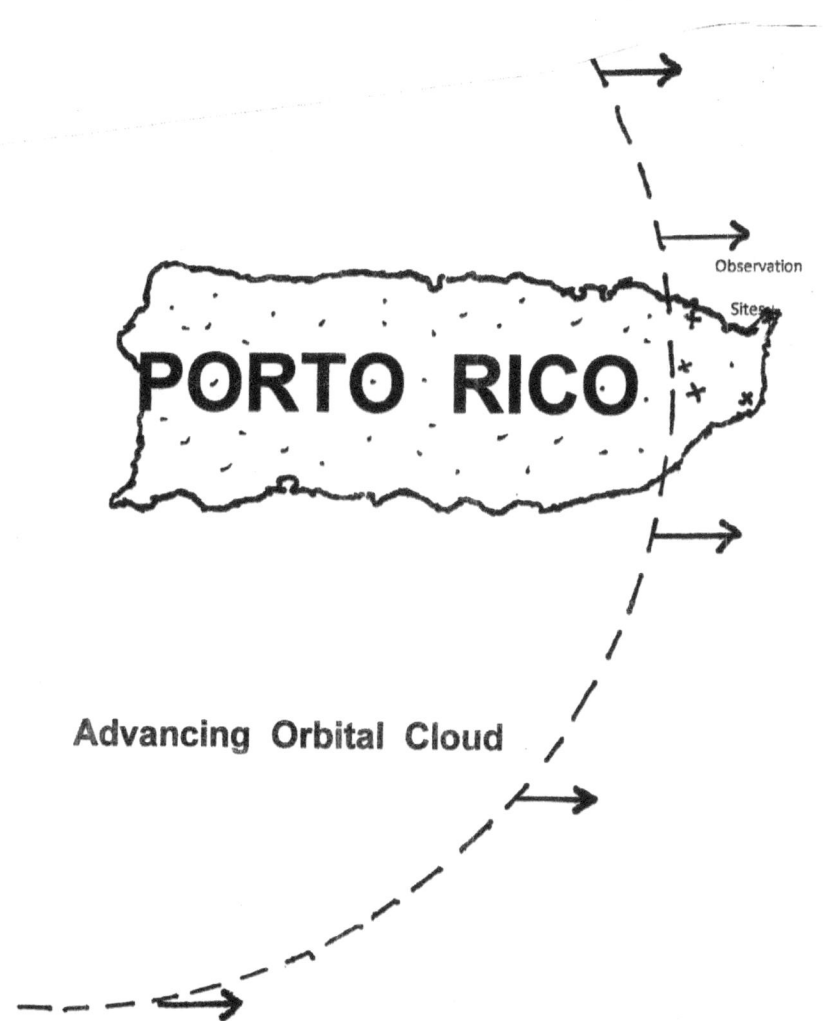

Observation Sites

PORTO RICO

Advancing Orbital Cloud

Orbital Test Launch

To keep the observation points no more than a few miles apart, she next turned inland, traveling in a circle. This took her into the tropical rain forest. She picked two more sites with clear viewing near the tops of two of the rain-forest mountains, El Toro and El Yunque.

As she drove back toward the SWG facilities, Lucille felt quite pleased with her trip, getting a feel for the island outside the immediate area of San Juan. What she had seen was a nice mix of beach living, small tropical farms, banana plantations, and best of all, the parts of the rain forest that as yet had not been destroyed. She decided it would be a lot of fun to show it to Roger when he came, maybe on their honeymoon.

A few days after her little trip, things really began to pick up on Son of NOAH. All the equipment had now arrived and was powered up. NOAH team members from Washington began straggling in, one of the first of whom was Fred. He was very glad to see a familiar face and have someone to show him around. Much had changed in the last two weeks. The open trenches around the buildings were covered over. Power lines were now neatly strung. The rough construction had been completed, and most of what was left on the new buildings was just finishing work. A large cafeteria had just been opened, replacing the temporary canteen. Over refreshments, Fred was telling Lucille about the latest runs on NOAH.

"Well, we are not home free yet," he said. "When the two climatic change operations are completed, the yearly move of the perennial snow line is cut in half, and the final location of the permanent snow cover ends up about two hundred miles north of the Canadian border. In Europe, the permanent snow cover goes through Oslo, Stockholm, and then passes about two hundred miles north of Moscow. Significant quantities of food will still be able to be grown in the United States and Europe, but not the present types of grains. Many vegetables will only be able to be grown under cover, like in greenhouses."

"That's wonderful!" Lucille responded. "Is there anything else being considered?"

Fred shook his head. "Not that I know of, only the possible sequestering of CO_2 exhaust in the oceans. Of course, even these new projections are based on a big effort in fertilizing the present forests as well as on a massive reforestation program so that the excessive carbon dioxide in the atmosphere can be reduced, not to mention the big cutback in burning fossil fuels. Without building a lot more rockets, Project High Cloud is a one-time operation, and when those bubbles begin to drop into the atmosphere and the cloud goes away, we better have the greenhouse effect closer to normal."

Lucille asked, "Has anyone looked at building more rockets?"

He replied, "Well, of course we could, but it would take a lot of energy, resources, and skilled manpower. I seem to remember hearing someone tell Ray that to build enough rockets for a second cloud would probably keep us from completely converting over to solar power and prevent us from building enough plankton facilities to feed everybody."

Lucille wasn't ready to give up. "Why can't the Arctic currents be increased further? We aren't using all the atomic warheads we were going to use in the beginning."

Fred shook his head again. "You see, what we are planning to do now to the two Arctic channels is like removing rust in a pipe that is slowing down the flow. Once that is done, you have reached a limit and to do any more would be like increasing the size of the pipe. That would take thousands of warheads and probably do us in with radioactivity. Lowering the sill notches in the Atlantic further would only be a temporary help. The cold water in the Norwegian Sea would flow out faster but still would eventually reach the old equilibrium. No, the real solution is in cutting way back on the carbon dioxide we are putting into the air and greatly increasing the plant life that can remove carbon dioxide. That way, the greenhouse effect is reduced, and then it eventually will be back where it was two hundred years ago. The bottom line is that in the long term, only the trees can save us."

By the end of March, half of the SWG personnel had arrived from New York, and they were getting the business of governing the planet from Puerto Rico underway. The most recent arrivals included Meriwether and Roger. Lucille and Roger had a long public embrace, which they continued in private as soon as they could.

Roger finally managed to say, "It's been a very long month. We talked about getting married when we moved here. Why don't we do it while Fred and the rest of the gang are here, before they leave? You won't be needed by Son of NOAH as much until Fred goes back. Ray isn't here yet, so I can probably play hooky for the next week."

Lucille smiled and rubbed her nose on Roger's. "I've been ready for a long time, so tomorrow would be great! I've located a VW camper we can borrow, and with our two gas rations, we should be able to drive around the island. It would be partly on business, since I will show you the places I've picked out for the instrumentation for the test shot of Project High Cloud."

Roger laughed. "I'll bet you've had the whole thing all planned. You're so smart, I suppose you've already made our wedding arrangements?"

"No," she said, joining his laughter, "I thought I'd leave something for you to decide. I did find out, though, that there won't be any long waiting period."

"It's so close to tomorrow," Roger said, pulling Lucille hard against him. "Why don't we spend the night together?"

"No," she said, "I promised you we would wait, and we can certainly wait one more day."

The next morning, they found Olav and Julia and asked them to be their witnesses, collected the VW camper, had a quick civil ceremony, and by noon were headed east along the coast. They passed the nearby beach and the lighthouse that Lucille had spotted before, and Roger agreed that both were good locations. Turning south, they were soon at Playa de Fajardo. The beach and weather looked so attractive that they decided to set up camp nearby and spend their first night together right on the beach. Swimming in the clean water of the Caribbean would always be a treat, but the first time for Roger was especially so. Later, they luxuriated in the late-afternoon sun, watching a few of the Puerto Ricans with whom they shared the beach.

Roger couldn't help saying, "They don't act like they know that the glacial period is coming."

Lucille responded, "Well, I've talked to a few long-time residents and, although they know about it, to them it is just a great imposition by the northern Yankees. It's changing their whole economy more than most places. Already there are almost no tourists as you can see, and no foreigners in the casinos to sweeten the economy. The changes in the money and mandatory work have just happened, so they are going through that upheaval right now. Food and gas rationing has just started but haven't been implemented very well by their bureaucrats. Down here, they are just beginning to designate the essential and nonessential businesses. Also they are trying to understand what no private property means, such as who controls the property today that was privately owned yesterday. The reason that there are no riots is that, underneath, they are very perceptive. They see that with the SWG coming, they will be very important in the world. Psychologically, this is very important to them, because, throughout their history, they have been in a colonial or backwater status."

Roger said, "You seemed to have learned a lot in the short time you have been here. What say we go back to the camper and have something to eat while you tell me more?"

They snacked on the fruit and other goodies that they had picked up along the road. No one had asked for a ration card. Since they weren't plugged into power, as it got dark, they decided it would be a good idea to settle in while they could still see. Roger finally figured out how to pop the top tent so they could use the sleeping quarters of the camper. Neither had camped in a VW camper before, so it took a couple of tries climbing into the upper bed to get the right technique down to avoid risking a chance of falling.

There was no hesitation in moving into each other's arms. Roger kissed her passionately, and she kissed him back, feeling the oneness of their union. During a pause in their lovemaking, Lucille asked Roger to become very relaxed and see if he could sense the combined energy flows that she was now feeling more strongly than ever before, the combining of their energy fields in one large, white ball of flame.

Roger responded that when he closed his eyes, he seemed to see a white pulsating star in a purple background.

Lucille said softly, "That's the beginning."

Later, they both remembered Roger's prophecy that they would be very good together in bed, a prophecy they surely exceeded.

On the second day of their honeymoon, they found a sheltered cove on the northeast coast that in better times looked like it had been a busy marina. As they drove up, it looked nearly deserted. After walking all around the place, they finally found a middle-aged man, browned by the sun and wearing tattered white trousers. At first, when Roger said they wanted to rent a sailboat, the man said no, but when Roger told him that he would be paying in Credos, the man became all smiles.

They selected a day-sailor with a wide beam, popular in the rental trade because it was nearly impossible to turn over. Their new friend supplied them with cushions, face masks, snorkel tubes, fins, and drinking water, giving them directions on sailing to the most colorful reef.

The trade winds were blowing nearly from the direction that they were headed, which made the outbound trip longer and more exciting as they sailed as close to the wind as they could in their wide boat. To maintain a reasonable line of advance, Roger, who was at the helm, tacked about every ten minutes, keeping his eye on the small island where the reef was. Both Roger and Lucille were careful to keep covered in the tropical sun, but even so, their faces began to show a little sunburn.

At about noon, they beached their boat on the island that was their destination and had lunch under some palms. "Out here," Lucille said, "it just doesn't seem like anything has changed at all."

"Yes, I know," he answered. "There is something about water and sailing that focuses your consciousness on being in the present as if there had never been a yesterday, and no tomorrow will ever come."

A little later, they sailed the boat out to the reef and, after dropping their anchor, Roger swam down the anchor line to make sure it was secure and wouldn't drift off. Then they snorkeled over the reef. What a kaleidoscope of color and shapes with the multicolored, tropical fish darting here and there on the coral and the bright green seaweed swaying back and forth to the slow rhythm of the gentle swells!

Later, an afternoon squall seemed to be forming, so they up-anchored and ran before the wind back to the marina.

The next day was a repeat of the previous outing, except to a different island where the reef was not quite so dramatic but had the varied interest of an old wreck. With only snorkels, they had to be satisfied with exploring the wreck from a distance and were glad they had when they saw both barracudas and eels that seemed to have made the wreck their home.

The following day, they decided to move on. They only had a week and, besides looking over the other sites for High Cloud, they wanted to see as much as they could of the rest of the island. After a leisurely dip and some bananas for breakfast, they stowed the pop-top of the camper and broke camp.

Their first stop was the Roosevelt Roads Naval Air Station where their SWG credentials got them promptly escorted to the commanding officer. He had received advance notice of their visit from SWG security and gave them a warm welcome. Roger explained that the purpose of Project High Cloud was to insert a vast number of bubbles into orbit to act as a screen in the tropics to reduce the energy received from the sun by a small percent. Roger described the sensing experiment they planned to make in several months when the test rocket for Project High Cloud would be launched and that they had selected the base as one site. The commanding officer promised all cooperation needed, and then he turned them over to his executive officer for a tour of potential locations. They settled on an unused shed as the best tentative site, with its most attractive feature being that it was upwind from the runways which could be a source of dust. Although the executive officer apologized for the primitive condition of the shed, Roger said that since it had power, it would be quite adequate. Actually they were prepared to use sites without power if it came to that.

Leaving the Naval Air Station, they drove first west and then angled northwest toward the Caribbean National Forest, which contained the two rain forest peaks, El Toro and El Yunque. Again, Roger agreed with the selections that Lucille had made. There was a parking lot for each site, and with gas rationing, there would be little traffic to stir up any dust.

Having finished the business part of their adventure, they found a good campsite just below the peak of El Toro and resumed their honeymoon. During the rest of their week's trip, they drifted around the island, staying where their fancy dictated, always only a short distance from good swimming beaches. Roger, as a dedicated respecter of all forms of life, particularly enjoyed the Cabo Rojo bird sanctuary at the southwestern corner of Puerto Rico. The Caribbean seabirds were so interesting to watch by the hour, so graceful in the water and also in the air. Particularly fascinating were the fishers who spotted their fish from the air and dove into the water nearly vertically, folding their wings just before entering. Roger never saw one come back up without a fish.

So as not to miss anything they might be asked about, on the last day, they took in the old fort the Spaniards had built at the entrance to the San Juan harbor. From there, reluctantly, they returned to the SWG headquarters and made arrangements to trade in their two small single apartments for a larger one in the married quarters' area.

*   *   *

In contrast, Buddy Rustler felt that destiny had dealt him a poor deal. He groaned as he struggled up a steep hill in central Colorado with a pack of seedlings on his back. He had been planting seedlings in clear cut areas of a national forest for a month and still was not adjusted to the life. His muscles ached all the time.

Besides being a tough life, Buddy didn't even consider it fair. When he had pointed out to the crew chief that he was being given more seedlings to plant than his quota, the crew chief had said nothing and only shrugged. Buddy had retaliated by burying the extra seedlings. For minimum wage, he wasn't going to give them any extra work. He couldn't anyway, he was too tired.

The trouble was that Buddy saw no end in sight, nothing to live for and just more trees to plant for the indefinite future. He had decided to end it all and suddenly hit on a plan. Just ahead was a sheer drop in the rocks of over one hundred feet with boulders at the bottom. He could just walk over, and they would think it was an accident. His last thought as he sailed through the air was he would leave them with a mystery.

Back at the tree-planting camp, when Buddy didn't show up for the second day, the crew chief made a notation against his name in a small notebook, "AWOL—couldn't cope." No one went looking for him.

CHAPTER 23

Iran

Toward the end of April, Ray called the first full directors' meeting since all of the directors had moved to Puerto Rico. "I thought," he began, "that it was time we had a full meeting, particularly since we need to deal with the problem of Iran. First, though, I would like to hear from any director who has anything specific that should be brought to the group's attention, either in the form of information or a question. If things in your department are pretty much on schedule, as they have been discussed before, it won't be necessary to make a report. Then we will do the Iranian thing last." Ray liked an informal meeting as they were having on this occasion; they were sitting around in a circle. He nodded to Akmed Hamid, Director of Energy, who was sitting on his left and had indicated he had something.

Akmed said, "We still have a number of SWG states that are exceeding their energy quotas. After the mid-February meeting, we threatened to intercept tankers or withhold food supplies. All the states that are net importers of either energy or food have generally complied. The problems we are having now are with states that have a surplus of both. There are seven states in default of their quotas; even the United States is in default by generating too much electric power. Without installing new metering systems, they have not figured out how to ration electric power without having either brownouts or, worse, blackouts. So far we have not insisted on these because it would disrupt too many essential programs we have in the works to deal with the climate change."

Ray responded, "I'll talk to President Morgan and give them one more month to get their power usage down. I'll have him tell his people that if they don't individually reduce their power usage, that selective brownouts will be applied in residential areas. I believe that the United States will comply. I've seen your list of the other countries and their flagrant violations. In the modern world, no people are completely self-sufficient. In each case, find out what essential commodity they are most dependent on that they import and give them one month to comply. If they don't, let's cut off that commodity or commodities as the case may be. If that doesn't work, the following month, we will cut off all trade between them and the rest of the planet."

Ray turned to Olav. "I suppose you have a similar story on food?"

"Yes," Olav said, "and the countries are the same ones. Why don't we handle the energy and food quota violations in concert?" Ray nodded.

Ray next recognized Benjamin Klein who said, "I think I have the third big problem, lack of compliance on population control. Of course, the after-the-fact statistics will not be in until a year after our initial directive was issued. Projections based on feedback on family planning usage already indicate, however, 30 percent of the SWG states will be out of compliance. We have to assume that the sexual appetite of the planet will remain constant." There was an outbreak of laughter at his last comment.

Ray was pensive. "Well, we can't wait nine months to put pressure on the likely offenders. Why don't we require pregnancy statistics from each member state so that they will have the data ahead of time and see that they are likely to be out of compliance. Also we should have each member state review its tax and social welfare laws and replace existing incentives for childbearing with disincentives. Another thing, and something I was hoping we could avoid, but I don't see a way around it. We are going to have to come down hard on those religious organizations that are against family planning."

Benjamin asked, "What do you suggest there?"

Ray said cynically, "Most of the religious organizations are also businesses. So far, to reduce potential unrest, we have allowed all, but the most flagrant money-making religious organizations to be classed as essential businesses. On a selective basis, we could reverse their classifications, after due notice of course, to allow for a change in their stand on family planning. Benjamin, this is one you should work jointly with Schuman. Keep up the pressure for sterilization and the use of abortion-inducing drugs as we have discussed before."

Greta, for Science and Technology, was next. "The only thing I have to bring up has to do with the fresh water-extraction plants we are locating on the shores of oceans and seas. The planned new population centers, where the water is to be used are, on average, twice as far away from the water plants as was in the old plan. The large-diameter pipe production as well as the pumping stations must be doubled unless we move the settlements back to where they were supposed to be. I have been coordinating this with George."

Ray responded, "You have done the right thing. I know about the changes of the locations of the settlements. We are building for the long term, and some of the original locations just weren't suitable. We don't want people to live in malaria swamps just because we didn't know they were there. I presume you can handle the increases, George?"

George nodded, and then said, "I don't have something specific in my department, but something that does affect us. With the conversion to a survival economy, we are getting more unemployed than was planned for. Some of the businesses that had been classified as essential have gone out of business on their own initiatives, putting their employees out of work. Without a big profit motive, the previous owners don't want to bother running a business. We can get the governments involved to restart those businesses, but it takes time. Our concept of businesses managed by the workers is a good one for the long term, but in the short term many of these businesses don't have any workers with the right training in management. Meanwhile, the skilled workers are scattered and picked up somewhere else, making it hard to revive the business if it is really in an important area."

Ray looked puzzled for a moment, reflecting on the problem. "Well," he finally said, "if it is a key business, we should have the government branch involved pay the workers to stay on the job, even if they aren't currently productive. Then when a new management can be brought in or, where possible, the employees involved are appropriately trained, the business can quickly become viable. I know we are bound to have inefficiencies and losses, but we must do what we can to minimize them."

Lars Berg had no comment on the reforestation progress.

Julia was next. "For those of you who don't know it, the SWG What If is up and running. We have been checking it out and have declared it to be operational. It is, of course, open to the use of all departments on a first-come first-served basis. If we have a priority conflict, Ray has given me some ground rules on how to resolve that. Boris has been the main user, working the Iranian situation, but there is a lot of free time right now."

Olav, who had come in with Julia, was sitting next to her and was next with a regular report, even though he had spoken in conjunction with Hamid earlier. "To balance the bad news about the food quotas you already heard about, I have some good news. We have had some breakthroughs in our plankton research. Mainly, we have isolated a strain of spirulina that will grow rapidly in colder climates as long as there is good sunlight. This will simplify our long-term food-distribution problem, since it will allow the growing of more food closer to the major population centers. You may have noticed that we are building scaled-down growing facilities right here at the SWG headquarters, for both the regular and cold-water spirulina."

"Good work," Ray exclaimed, and then turned to Bani Shinto, who was next. Bani had nothing to report, so it was Meriwether's turn.

"Preparations for our experimental shots are coming along well. In May, with the sun directly overhead Costa Rica, we should be ready at Cape Kennedy to launch the test vehicle for Project High Cloud. The first of the two prototype underwater shots for

Project Big Current should be ready later in the month or at least early June.

Ray next turned to Robert Schuman, who spoke in a clear voice. "The economic part of SWG's overall plan continues to fall behind the schedule we initiated. Most of the old Western democracies just don't have the central planning and control bureaucracies in place to implement what we have asked for. They have to create them ad hoc, and some are less successful at it than others. The eastern European countries are even in worse shape, having dismantled their bureaucracies but without yet replacing them with anything effective. Those member states that joined the SWG as totalitarian states with strong central control have been able to continue doing what they have been doing all along, although not very efficiently. I predict that they will be even less as time passes, as the benefits of personally being in the bureaucracy are diminished or eliminated altogether. The once developing countries, particularly those with large, illiterate populations and primitive institutions, will be very difficult problems. We will have to deal with them on a simplified basis. Their own communications are primitive by any standards. The bottom line, there, is that it will take a lot of education before the desired standards of individual treatment are realized by all their people, in spite of the SWG goals."

"I know," said Ray. "We may not get there for some time, but we need to hold up the ideal, the standard, so that people can strive for it in a world that will no doubt always have imperfections. Boris, would you now please share with us the imperfection you have been dealing with recently?" That drew a laugh that eased the tensions that were building with the picture that Robert Schuman had been painting.

Boris, the director for security, took the cue. "Our show of force in Turkmenistan against General Zellov, mainly implemented by Russia, had a remarkable effect on the then holdouts. The only important countries still not joining the SWG are China, North Korea, and Iran. Australia, still dragging its feet, has just joined, being persuaded personally by our coordinator, Ray. Iran is a high-priority problem because of the atomic weapons Zellov took with him when his forces moved into Iran. Since we did not immediately pursue him and force a further atomic confrontation, it appears that Iran has wrongly concluded that we have lost our will to act. Also, no doubt, much of Iran's policy these days is dictated by the general.

"The situation in Iran is building to a crisis due to the world oil glut, which has greatly diminished Iran's trade. Also our embargo on trading with Iran has almost stopped all trade with them. They depend on a lot of things from the outside, which they have no way of getting at present, including food. In the last four days, with the force of atomic weapons behind them, Iran has demanded certain trade items from Turkey and Pakistan in exchange for oil which no one wants. Iran has let it be known that she will take these items by force, if necessary, using atomic weapons. These neighbors of Iran are well within the range of General Zellov's weapons, particularly if the bombs he moved to Iran have been fitted to Iranian planes.

"Turkey and Pakistan are SWG member states, and there is no question that they will be defended. We have been maintaining a high level of readiness in the area since the Turkmenistan episode and have the forces available for a number of options. You may recall our decision not to strike Iran immediately on humanitarian grounds, giving Iran time to see the true great imbalance of forces and make an accommodation. Religious zeal and national egotism, blind to realities, combined with what must be insanity on the part of General Zellov, have led them to conclude that we will remain indecisive."

Boris, who had everyone's rapt attention, continued, "I have spent considerable time with Julia and her new What If, looking for a solution that avoids a serious confrontation and large loss of life. A preemptive strike is not a desirable solution, because too many of the weapons are concealed from our observation satellites. In a fanatical backlash, they would launch the surviving weapons at the cities of their neighbors, including those in Saudi Arabia and even India, causing a loss of life of over one hundred million. The key to the problem is shown by the What If to be a show of force that splits the Iranian leaders from General Zellov. Our intelligence informs us that Zellov controls his armored divisions with their limited range tactical weapons, but not the

Iranian planes armed with his bombs. Without the planes, he can only inflict limited damage on his neighbors and could quickly be contained by our forces. The What If predicts a successful outcome to an atomic show of force, coupled with an immediate demand for the delivery of General Zellov and all atomic weapons to the SWG. In exchange, Iran could immediately join the SWG and receive food and other trade items that they desperately need. The perceptive Iranian leaders are ready to join the SWG now but need a face saving mechanism to swing the unthinking mobs."

Boris paused to let what he had said sink in before he went on to particulars. "The show of force must be personally experienced by the majority of the Teheran population, so we propose to set off, during nighttime hours, a large, hydrogen bomb over the salt flats to the south of Teheran. The Iranians will be given several minutes warning to make the largest possible impression, as well as to protect their eyesight. Fallout from the prevailing winds this time of year is over a very sparsely inhabited area. I feel we must implement this plan promptly before Iran carries out the threats she has made against her neighbors."

Ray asked, "Are you still sure there are no other less forceful alternatives?"

Boris responded, "Julia and I, and also members of our staffs, have looked very diligently. All other successful scenarios are even more forceful. This conclusion is, of course, based on what we know and have programmed into the What If." Julia nodded her agreement.

"Well," Ray said, "I would like a record of the opinions of all the other directors. Please raise your hand if you are in favor of this action." All the directors raised their hands. "Very well," Ray concluded, "let's get it over with."

"And one last thing," he added. "Russian Prime Minister Petrovich has requested we also commit to the flight, one of the stealth fighters armed with two small homing air-to-ground missiles that he will supply. This has to do with a radar beacon planted in General Zellov's car. Boris, will you coordinate this with the Russians?" Boris nodded.

The next day, a missile rose from a location along the trans-Siberian railway and arched southward. Shortly thereafter, on twenty radio bands receivable in Teheran, a message was broadcast in English, then repeated in Persian.

"This message is from the Supreme World Government to the people and government of Iran. At this moment, a large, nuclear warhead has been launched at your country as a warning to desist from attacking your neighbors. It will detonate over the salt flats south of Teheran at 2015 hours Teheran time. Do not look at the explosion directly, or your eyes may be permanently damaged. You will immediately take the required action to turn General Zellov and all nuclear warheads located in your country over to the SWG. Air transports will begin arriving at Teheran Airport at zero eight hundred tomorrow to take delivery of General Zellov and the weapons. If this request is not complied with, or our transports are interfered with, other missiles will be launched toward the cities of Iran. Be assured that we are taking precautions against any ill-advised use of the subject weapons. If all terms of this message are complied with, immediate membership in the SWG is still open to Iran, which will include the immediate shipment of all needed relief supplies. To minimize further possible complications, broadcast your intentions to comply on Teheran Radio at your earliest opportunity."

The message was repeated until twenty-fifteen, when a brilliant display of awesome power shook the salt flats south of Teheran. At 2200 hours, Teheran Radio was broadcasting in English and Persian, Iran's acceptance of the SWG terms and the decision by Iran to join the rest of the World community. The expected SWG transports were requested to contact Iranian Airspace Control for identification and routing upon their arrival in Iranian airspace.

By 1600 hours the next day, all of the requested weapons had been loaded on the SWG transports. The body of General Zellov was offered, with the explanation that he had been killed by a bolt from heaven that demolished his car just before Iranian security forces arrived to arrest him. The SWG headquarters was notified that an Iranian delegation would be arriving in Puerto Rico in several days.

CHAPTER 24

High Cloud

While it was only May 29 in a NASA briefing room at Cape Kennedy, to Roger, it seemed like the middle of August. Actually, that year summer came to Florida in April to stay. The chief of public relations for the Cape was just starting a pre-launch press conference. Roger and Meriwether had come for the launch and were attending the press conference in case there were questions for which NASA didn't have the answers.

The public relations chief began, "Ladies and gentlemen." He paused to look out at the sea of faces, many of whom were part-time press representatives, including housewives, who covered NASA launches for press organizations which couldn't afford to send seasoned veterans. "We will be launching for the first time a very critical prototype payload for the Supreme World Government. This will be the start of humanity's attempt to control the weather." At Meriwether's frown, he quickly corrected himself. "I mean, the climate. Called Project High Cloud, this launch, as many past ones, has a very critical launch window because of the need to deploy the payload over a very specific geographical location at noon and in an orbit with very tight parameters. We will be using a standard Titan launch vehicle, originally built to launch military payloads. The Titan will travel down-range for a few minutes after main engine cut-off, coasting in a circular orbit at three hundred miles altitude. Over the equator, there will be a second burn to reduce the inclination of the orbit so that the payload will pass directly over the island of

Puerto Rico at the end of its first orbit, traveling in an easterly direction."

The chief didn't understand everything he was reading, but he liked to pretend that he did and went on with the confidence that the press knew even less.

"Once in the proper orbit, on the far side of the earth, the payload will be released and on command from our control center in Goddard, relayed by satellite, will dispense a special cloud, which will grow to about 150 miles in length. The cloud will be composed of thin-walled bubbles which will reduce the amount of sunlight that reaches the earth's surface. Of course, one launch will not make enough difference to change the climate, but precise instrumentation can show its effectiveness. If all works out like the scientists have calculated, this launch will be followed by two thousand more, which will make a difference. Are there any questions so far?"

"What do you mean by inclination?" asked one of the lady members of the press corps, who was wearing a very strange hat that looked very much like a pineapple.

The press chief smiled. He had been briefed for that question and a few more that were expected to be asked. "Inclination is the angle the plane of the orbit makes with the equator. In a zero-degree inclination orbit, the spacecraft would circle the earth over the equator. In a ninety-degree inclination orbit, the spacecraft would pass over the earth from pole to pole. You see, the greater the inclination, the farther north and south the track of the spacecraft will be and also the bubble cloud to be released from the spacecraft. For this experiment, we want the shadow of the cloud to pass over the SWG headquarters on its first orbit, traveling from west to east."

The chief liked to use up the time on safe questions, so he continued, "Tomorrow, the sun will be nearly overhead at SWG headquarters in Puerto Rico, so in effect, we would have arranged for the bubble cloud to eclipse the sun, locally." That was a setup for the next question.

"Why is it important for the cloud to travel from west to east?"

Again the chief smiled. "It isn't essential. It just makes it easier for the people on the ground to acquire the cloud with their instrumentation." That wasn't exactly the right answer, but Meriwether decided it didn't make any difference, and he said nothing.

Another question came from a full-time professional who had traveled from New York City for the launch. "What are they going to measure on the ground?"

Again the chief was pleased with the question. If the questions continued to go well, he would not have to call on the SWG specialists that were standing by, and he would look good. He paused deliberately, before answering, to make it look like he was going through a complicated thought process. "The instrumentation measures the amount of sunlight before, during, and after the cloud passes overhead. At the first passage, the cloud should have expanded to a size such that the amount of light measured is 95 percent of normal. On each subsequent pass, the cloud will, of course, have expanded some, and the reduction in light will be less."

The chief frowned as the next question was asked, because he would obviously have to have Meriwether answer it. "How will the cloud be useful if the reduction in light is less with time?"

Meriwether picked up his cue and took the microphone. "In the operational system, we will have approximately two thousand clouds which are overlapping, so since they intermingle, the attenuation is constant."

The representative from *Aviation Week* asked a critical question which again the chief knew he couldn't answer. "I know that there are a few Titans in the inventory and that Martin can make about ten a year. How can you possibly launch so many of these bubble clouds in a reasonable period of time?"

Meriwether chuckled, knowing the game the chief was playing. Again he was called on to answer. "We are using the Titan for this prototype shot because of its immediate availability and flexible targeting as a multipurpose launch vehicle. For the operational shots to put up the two thousand bubble clouds, we will be using the larger Russian military rockets that no longer have any other purpose."

One of the Cocoa Beach housewives asked the next question. The chief decided that it definitely wasn't one of his days. "I don't understand the point of Project High Cloud in the first place. If we are supposed to be going into a glacial period, it would seem to make things worse to keep some of the sun's heat from reaching the earth."

Meriwether had taken over responding to the questions and didn't wait for his cue from the chief. He said, "We have with us today Roger Foreman, the scientist who first discovered we are moving into a glacial period. I think you might enjoy having him answer that question." He nodded to Roger and handed him the microphone.

"You see," Roger began, "It takes a lot of energy to move water vapor in the form of clouds from the tropics to the higher latitudes where it is deposited as snow. We now know that a warming of the tropics is necessary to provide the extra energy to initiate a glacial period. It's very simple." He turned to the chief and smiled as if to a small child. "Only after much moisture is moved toward the poles does it get hotter in the tropics and colder in the higher latitudes. The bubble clouds will compensate for the excess heat that would otherwise be retained by the greenhouse gases."

The *Aviation Week* representative was still hung up on rockets. "Do the Russians really have enough ICBM boosters for two thousand clouds?"

"Not quite," responded Meriwether. "They still have their assembly line open, and we will probably make some more, depending on the results of tomorrow's test. The United States has some large surplus rockets too."

One of the more astute members of the press corps said, "It seems to me that what you are planning to do is sort of like putting up a ring around the earth, like the rings of Saturn."

"Yes," said Meriwether, "similar, but different in detail. Our ring will be much broader, extending ten degrees north and south of the equator. Also our ring will be in a low orbit where the bubbles will soon collide with the upper atmosphere and eventually fall back to earth. To put the cloud higher would take more rockets, and it would then permanently contaminate the space around earth. Since the cloud will have a half-life of ten years, this part of space will be dirty anyway for quite a while.

Fortunately, the bubble walls will be so thin that one of them hitting a spacecraft having even modest protection should do no damage." Meriwether thought that an answer should be given to a question that hadn't been asked. "It should be recognized that Project High Cloud will only help delay the onset of the next glacial period. It will not permanently change the climate. It will, however, give us a little extra time to do other things, like reduce the carbon dioxide in the atmosphere. It will also give us a little more time to adjust to whatever changes are ahead of us."

A gentleman from World News Service asked, "What else is being planned to make permanent changes in the climate?"

Meriwether answered that question as well. "There will be timely announcements when the SWG is ready with other plans to modify the climate. I am not authorized to divulge what these may be at this time." Meriwether knew that careful public relations preparations would be needed before announcing a program that involved firing off over one hundred large nuclear warheads. The gentlemen persisted, "Then there are other projects being considered?"

Meriwether smiled. "I didn't say that."

The next question was asked by the lady with a pineapple for a hat. "I don't see how the bubbles will do any good. Light goes right through bubbles, doesn't it?" This drew a laugh from everyone. It was nearly the time scheduled for the end of the news conference, and most were getting restless.

Meriwether had a good answer for that. "It depends on the material and how thick the bubble wall is compared to the average wavelength of the sun's light. The bubbles for this prototype shot are designed to be nearly perfect mirrors."

There were no more questions, and those assembled adjourned to join a planned social event scheduled at one of the nearby beach motels. Meriwether never did find out who was hosting the event. Roger didn't go, preferring to take advantage of the ideal ocean conditions obtaining that day to go surfing at the beach.

The countdown for the next day's launch of the Titan started that afternoon. Roger and Meriwether were not involved until the last several hours the next day when the payload was scheduled to be checked out. Both were a bit restless after supper at their motel and began to talk of the morning's launch to come.

Meriwether had noticed at the press conference, earlier, a map which showed that a large part of the Cape would be evacuated. He said to Roger. "You have been to launches before. What is so dangerous that so much of the Cape will be evacuated?"

Roger answered, "Well, this is a launch with a Titan vehicle. If it blew up on the pad, that would be the same class of explosion as if the same weight of TNT were to be detonated. The major concern for a Titan, though, as compared to an Atlas, is that propellants, nitric acid and hydrazine, are lethal at a few parts per million. They won't even launch unless the prevailing wind is blowing out to sea. You can't go to the Titan pad without a special chemical briefing, and they have gas masks all around the pad to be handy to use just in case of a leak."

Meriwether was puzzled. "Why would anyone choose such deadly propellants when there are safe ones, like kerosene and liquid oxygen, or liquid hydrogen and liquid oxygen?"

"It is a matter of heritage," Roger said. "The Titan was developed for the military where the overriding requirement was storable propellants that would allow a fast reaction launch. Any system using liquid oxygen has to load oxygen during the launch sequence, a bad scene for military rockets. Titan came before the development of large solid propellants, a more recent technology at least in large sizes. The military had a big investment in the system, so it was continued. With the end of the Apollo program, the ability to build alternate, large launch vehicles, was no longer necessary except to support the shuttle."

The next morning, they were both at mission control, Roger in the visitor-viewing area and Meriwether at a communication console, representing the payload launch team. Meriwether was tuned in to the payload checkout team's network, and it was his responsibility to advise the mission director of the payload's status at appropriate points in the countdown.

Suddenly there was a forceful announcement on the countdown network. "At T-55 minutes we have a hold. Safety monitors indicate we have an armed destruct package on the Titan. It should have been in the safe mode until T-5 seconds. A conference is scheduled immediately in the launch conference room, with the launch director, the missile engineer, and all of the safety team members. We have a dangerous condition on the pad. Evacuate all areas back to the road blocks or block house and secure the block house."

Meriwether had asked for Roger to join him, and when he arrived asked, "What does all that mean?"

Roger replied, "Apparently the destruct package on the Titan is in the armed position, presumably as indicated by telemetry and ground lines. Should a destruct signal be transmitted, the Titan would be blown up on the pad. Being fully fueled, that would be one big explosion."

The sound system activated again. "This is Launch Control. We will not be able to pick up the count in time to make today's window. The launch is scrubbed for today. Recycle all systems except the destruct package and secure power on the bird. We have rescheduled the launch for tomorrow, assuming that the problem with the destruct package will be resolved."

Later that day back at the motel, Roger and Meriwether were told that the launch for the next day was confirmed. After hours of studying the circuits and documentation, it was postulated that the wiring in the destruct package had been modified without the corresponding changes being made in the Titan. The missile engineer had ventured out to the pad and visually confirmed that the destruct package was actually in the safe mode.

The next day on the second launch attempt, even from the viewpoint of a casual bystander, it was a very trouble-free countdown. The built-in holds were more than sufficient to recover from the several minor instrumentation anomalies that were experienced. Roger held his breath as the countdown proceeded to the point of lift-off, paced by the voice of mission control, "five, four, three, two, one, zero. We have lift-off . . . the Titan has cleared the tower . . . We have a very smooth launch . . . The roll program has been initiated . . . Everything is Go at this time."

Roger looked at the TV monitor and could see the angle of the Titan changing as the launch proceeded. The nose slowly dipped as the rocket climbed and moved down range. The roar of the rocket had reached mission control for some time and then began to diminish. Roger again became aware of the voice of mission control. "We now have booster burnout and separation; telemetry reports a clean separation." There was a small cheer from the launch team at this point, which was one of the most critical of the whole mission. Roger looked at the TV monitor, and he could clearly see the two trails from the spent boosters falling behind the central body of the Titan. Then the TV monitor shifted to another camera which was down-range, and about all that Roger could make out was the flame of the rocket burning and the exhaust trail.

Soon the voice of mission control was saying, "Telemetry indicates the shroud has successfully separated." Roger wasn't sure he saw that event on his monitor, because the picture was getting very small and blurry. Mostly all they were getting now was the rocket plume.

Pretty soon, the voice of mission control said, "We are coming up on MECO, main engine cut-off, in about ten seconds . . . Yes, we have MECO." There was a larger shout this time from the launch team, followed by a hushed silence and plain waiting. They all knew they still had the burn over the equator before the rocket's job would be over.

During the coast, the voice of mission control was more subdued, if not actually bored. "Telemetry indicates all mission parameters are nominal. Ground tracking as well as computer simulation indicate we have a one sigma orbit, a good orbit. We have just lost telemetry as the Titan has gone over the horizon. The next events will be reported from telemetry on Ascension Island, down-range." With nothing else to report, the voice of mission control fell silent.

It seemed to Roger that the burn over the equator should have taken place, but looking at the mission clock, he could see that it was just his anxiety changing his subjective time.

The voice of mission control came on again. "Ascension telemetry and tracking radar have acquired the Titan. All telemetry is nominal. We are coming up on the second burn . . . We have main engine start, we have a smooth burn, and all parameters are nominal." Roger knew that this second burn was going to be short compared with the first one, but it still seemed a long time before the voice of mission control came on with, "We have second MECO!"

This time the cheering was loudest of all and didn't end for some time. Many members of the launch team shook hands or even slapped each other across the back. They had done their job. Whether the payload did its job did not seriously concern them. The voice of mission control continued, "Telemetry indicates that the payload has separated from the Titan and that the cloud dispenser has initiated operations."

Roger was familiar with the dispenser design, so he knew it would take several minutes for the whole cloud to be put into place. At this point, he was not worried about the mission being unsuccessful because this part was redundant and would be completed in spite of any single failure. The procedure had been checked out on a small scale in the world's largest vacuum chamber, and there had been no problems. The only difference was that the dispenser was now in free fall instead of at one gravity. The voice of mission control returned briefly. "This is the voice of mission control. Just before we lost telemetry, telemetry showed the cloud had reached the 50 percent point . . . . We now have airborne telemetry from farther downrange. The signal was breaking up, but now we have a good signal. We just had the dispenser complete mark. There are no more scheduled events. As a matter of information, the cloud should pass over Puerto Rico in approximately forty-five minutes. This completes the operations of the voice of mission control."

There was again a shout of success and handshaking all around. Dr. Meriwether left his console and came out to collect Roger. "Well," he said, "there is nothing more to do here. The rest depends on our teams back on Puerto Rico at the observation sites. If we leave right now, we can be back this evening and see how things came out."

Roger responded, "I thought the mission director said everyone was supposed to stay over for the debriefing."

Meriwether chuckled as they got into their rental car, "That's for everyone who works for him. In this operation, he works for us, and we make the rules."

On Puerto Rico, the five monitoring teams had been in place for the second day for over four hours. Their only part in the launch was to be sure that four of the five sensors were Go and that weather conditions were clear for good viewing of the sun. They had been in touch with Meriwether and given their Go's during the countdown and the critical Go two minutes before the Titan lifted off. The monitoring teams were being coordinated by Lucille, who was at the Roosevelt Roads Naval Air Station site because that was where their link to mission control was. She was in touch with the other four teams by portable radios they had borrowed from the Air Station.

The operation had been scheduled so that the pass of the cloud over Puerto Rico would occur close to noon, local sun time. Weather reports indicated that there would be an 80 percent chance of no cloud cover up to that time of day. With five observation points, Lucille felt confident of success once the word was passed to them that their cloud had been created. There were some big, billowy clouds beginning to build up to the south but nothing close. For sentimental reasons, Lucille would have liked to have been at the El Toro site but knew that her place was here where there were good communications.

They were only ten minutes away from cloud encounter, and Lucille called all her teams to have them make a last check of their instrumentation. The monitoring equipment was relatively simple, consisting of a solar light-level detector feeding a recorder that was also getting time ticks from a time station. Each setup was battery-operated and mounted in a walk-in van which had been modified for the operation. Lucille thought it strange that the vans still had their UPS markings, indicating their previous owner. In a survival economy, UPS soon found that there weren't many essential packages being sent and had reduced its fleet accordingly.

The checks were made by placing a calibrated filter in the path of the sun's rays striking the detector. All teams reported ready. The El Toro site, being the most westerly, was expected to detect the cloud first.

At five minutes before the nominal time of first encounter, Lucille called to all her teams. "The event encounter will be in five minutes, mark." She continued to call off the minutes as the time approached. At thirty seconds, she said, "Set recorders to 'fast,'" and proceeded to count down by the second.

At one second after nominal encounter, El Toro came up on the net, "This is El Toro. Our sunlight output is dropping. It has now steadied out at 94.9 percent." In turn, each of the other sites came up on the net reporting light outputs all very close to the 95 percent. Just over a half minute later, El Toro came up on the net again. "This is El Toro. Our light output is steadily increasing. It is now back to its pre-encounter value." The same thing happened at all the other sites.

Lucille got on the radio net and said, "All stations, recalibrate your sensors and then stand down until a possible next pass." The Roosevelt Roads team, after making their calibration, relaxed and had some of the refreshments they had brought. There was general exhilaration that even if they got no more observations, the project would be declared a success.

About ten minutes before the time of the next expected encounter, both El Toro and El Yunque sites reported large cloud buildups and no current viewing of the sun. Lucille acknowledged their situations and had the other sites stand by for the next encounter. At the command, "Recorders fast," the Air Station recorder malfunctioned, so on the second pass, measurements were made only at the beach and lighthouse sites. These gave sun readings as expected lower than before and for a shorter period. All sites were clouding up, and Lucille instructed all teams to return to the SWG headquarters. With the amount of dispersion seen, they cancelled the plan to return on each of the next several days to take more measurements. Lucille hadn't known how many days they would get anything, because the amount the test cloud that would be thinning out was uncertain.

That evening, everyone was back, and Ray called the directors together to hear about their success and do a little celebrating. He first called on Roger and Meriwether to report on their

jaunt to Cape Kennedy Space Flight Center and the mysteries
of rocketry. Everyone was amused to hear about the lady from
Cocoa Beach with a pineapple for a hat. Ray made mental notes
to send off messages of thanks and congratulations to all the
many organizations that had made the launch a success.

Next, Lucille reported on their measurements on the east
end of the island and how the results had been very close to what
was expected. Meriwether commented that it all looked very
good, and it was unfortunate they didn't have at least another
day's observations to find out how fast the cloud was spreading.
Just one day's observations, however, had provided the basic data,
how good a mirror the cloud was, and from its time of passage,
how big it had been at that moment.

Meriwether summed up the operation at a celebration party
"From what we have already seen, the number of launches we will
need is within 10 percent of the two thousand we had calculated.
The Russian boosters will, of course, be able to put up more
payload than we did in our test launch. A toast to our success and
may we look forward to a successful operational High Cloud."
They were all flushed with the aura of success and raised their
glasses in the toast.

Julia and Olav had been sitting together, and to any observer,
it was obvious that they were as much interested in each other as
they were in the party. As the party was starting to break up, they
slipped out and found a quiet place to talk. They had spent the
night together on a number of occasions during the past month,
and Olav was ready to make it permanent.

"You know," he started, "my children are very fond of you.
They have been asking me when you are going to become their
'mommy.'"

Jokingly, she answered, "Well, I hope you would have other
reasons besides satisfying your children for marrying me."

"Of course," he rejoined, "I just wanted you to know that
there is no reason on the part of the children not to get
married."

"What about Ola?" Julia asked.

He responded warmly, "With you and me so busy with the
SWG, nothing should change there. We would still need a

housekeeper. With both of us as directors, we certainly rate the space and can afford her."

Julia had been over all this ground in her own mind weeks before, but it was comforting to hear it from Olav. So it just came down to a matter of when, and the answer to that came quickly as Olav continued, "I have just agreed with Ray that in a week I will leave on a tour of the facilities for growing plankton that are under construction in Libya and Australia. It would be too long for you to go on the whole trip with me, but if you take the first week and go as far as Libya, we could also make it a honeymoon."

She responded, "That would work out just fine. We are installing a major communication center on Malta for our naval forces in that area, and I would like to look in on it on the way back from Libya." Her voice softened. "We could get married the day before we leave."

"Yes, I agree," he nodded. "What kind of a marriage ceremony would you like?"

"There is that small, old chapel just inside the main entrance to the SWG facilities," she answered. "I think that would be perfect. We would want to invite the other directors, and since it is on the grounds, there would be no special fuss about security."

"It sounds beautiful," Olav said, and they sealed their decision with a lengthy kiss.

CHAPTER 25

Big Current

It was June 25, and the SWG public relations officer at Oahu was giving the press and media an unusual briefing. Because no big buildup had been given for the briefing, it was very lightly attended, the way the SWG wanted it. A subject for the briefing had not been given since the SWG was going to use the briefing for the first public disclosure of Project Big Current. Besides being a SWG bastion, Hawaii had been chosen for the briefing as being the nearest convenient point of civilization to the Bering Strait where the operation was to take place.

The officer started his briefing by displaying a map of the Arctic. "This is a briefing concerning an operation the SWG is initiating as part of the efforts to change the climate. On this map of the Arctic, we have drawn in red the major Arctic warm water ocean current. It starts in the northwestern Pacific as a branch of the warm-current that comes up the coast of Japan. It eventually works its way up through this first narrow point, the Bering Strait. Even when the sea is frozen over, warm water flows under the ice. When we say warm in the Arctic, we are talking relatively. It flows past a number of these islands and then through the Barrow Strait. From there, it goes out into Baffin Bay and down the west side of Greenland. At this point, it has given up all its heat and can't be called a warm-water current any longer. Before it gets to this point, it has moderated the otherwise frigid temperatures of the Arctic, which is one reason the Arctic weather is not as severe as the Antarctic. Now, if more warm water could be made to flow around the Arctic, the glacial period climate that is coming would be less severe."

One of the reporters raised a question at that point. "You mean the SWG intends to change this ocean current?"

"Exactly," the officer responded. "Our simulations of the currents show that the Bering Strait and the Barrow Strait are the choke points that limit the current flow. They are both narrow and shallow. This next chart is an underwater topological map showing both of the straits. Notice there are a number of places where the bottom comes toward the surface, what in nautical terms are called seamounts and ridges. They cause the current to swirl and branch, which slows it down. If we were to flatten the seamounts and ridges to provide a smoother channel, the currents would significantly increase, and we would get a warmer Arctic. A warmer Arctic would reduce the moisture that is transferred from the tropics, hence a less severe glacial period. Any questions?"

"Yes," another reporter said. "How much flow increase are you talking about?"

The officer answered, "For what we are planning to do, the increase might be 100 percent, based on computer simulations. The amount of underwater sediment and rock that need to be moved is on a magnitude that is only feasible by the use of atomic explosions. In order to validate our simulations, we are first planning a prototype explosion on this seamount just south of the entrance to the Bering Strait. Depending on the outcome, we will later explode between one hundred and two hundred atomic devices altogether."

The officer saw his audience was getting nervous, as he had expected, so he hurried on to the safety aspects of the operation. "We are calling this operation 'Big Current.' The explosions will be set off a distance down below the seafloor so that the radioactivity resulting will be trapped in the earth, so you see, we are planning the utmost in safety precautions. The timing of the explosions will be carefully controlled so that should some radioactivity leak out, it will not come into generally inhabited areas. The few individuals who live in the affected areas will, of course, be evacuated. They will be later anyway as the cold glacial period proceeds. There is also a possibility that earthquakes might be triggered by an atomic explosion, so populations living near fault lines will be alerted before the explosions are initiated."

There were at this point a number of questions on how the SWG could be sure that there would be no danger from either the fallout or earthquakes. They eventually were only partly satisfied and had to settle for the officer's statement. "Of course, there is some danger that things won't happen exactly as predicted, but I'm sure any problems will be minimized. Besides, the benefit of reducing the severity of the glacial period will far outweigh the slight danger."

The officer ended the briefing by saying, "The test operation I spoke of will proceed in five days' time. Those individuals who are being evacuated for this shot have already been notified." The press wondered how notification had been given without them getting word of it.

Both Meriwether and Roger were going to monitor the test explosion from the SWG facilities on Hawaii and were observing the countdown from a control room that had been set up at Pearl Harbor. The United States Navy, now under command of the SWG, was in charge of the actual operation. The test site was an oval-shaped seamount, and two warheads were actually going to be set off at the same time. The warheads had been placed one-half mile apart in holes bored in the seamount some days earlier. Both a specially equipped submarine and an underwater drilling barge were used in the deployment. The warhead detonators were actually overpressure sensitive devices, set to activate on receipt of a sharp pressure wave. A small conventional explosive device suspended from a moored buoy would be detonated by radio command, thus setting off the two atomic devices simultaneously.

Meriwether commented to Roger that he thought the system was overly complicated. A Navy expert, overhearing the comment, assured them that this system gave good synchronization between the two atomic devices and had been thoroughly checked out.

Everything was in readiness. The several explosive devices were all armed. The deploying submarine was safely out of the way, using Hooper's Bay, Alaska, as a temporary port. The population along the Alaskan coast and the Aleutian Islands had been alerted to a possible earthquake. A few isolated Eskimos had been evacuated. Meriwether had insisted that the operation take place at the time of the half moon when earth stresses would be at a minimum, reducing the chances of an earthquake. He had surprised a number of scientists with statistics which showed that earthquakes are only one-half as likely to happen at the half-moon times as compared to the full or new moons. With the tidal stresses minimized, Meriwether was of the opinion that the stresses from this particular explosion would not in themselves be sufficient to trigger an earthquake.

The time set for the detonation was to coincide with the passing overhead of an observation satellite so that the event could be monitored visually in real time without endangering an aircraft. Several drones were planned to be flown in the vicinity in order to monitor any stray radioactivity. The weather predictions called for any stray cloud from the explosions to go north through the Bering Strait into the Chukchi Sea. As the satellite crossed over the pole and started south toward the Bering Strait, the countdown continued. ". . . We are now at T minus ten minutes and counting," came the announcement in the control center where Meriwether and Roger were observing. At the same time the countdown wall clock showed T minus ten minutes and continued down. Roger thought it would not be long now before the detonation command was radioed from a transmitter on St. Lawrence Island.

The count continued. "It is now T minus five minutes and counting. All systems are Go at this time." The large screen on the front wall of the control room had just been activated and showed a view of what Roger assumed was polar ice. He had been told that the satellite was in such a low orbit that its transmissions had to be relayed to a higher satellite before they were beamed down to Hawaii. He hadn't been told that it was the TDRSS, so assumed it was some undisclosed military system instead.

The voice of the announcer continued, "T minus three minutes and counting. All systems remain GO at this time." The northern approaches to the Bering Strait came into view with an obvious contrast of land and what was now apparently broken sea ice. The scene zoomed in and started to track a particular spot just south of the Bering Strait. Roger assumed that somewhere an operator was being

given information on the geographical location of what the camera was viewing and was maintaining it centered on where the explosion was to take place. His thoughts were broken into by an increase in the urgency of the announcer's voice. " . . . T minus ten seconds, nine, eight, seven, six, five, four, three, two, one, zero."

There was no great flash as would have been expected from a surface explosion or even from one in shallow water. It was more like the bottom dropped out and water rushed in to fill the void. A lot of spray shot up into the air and a ring pattern of water formed which moved outward in all directions from the center. As the satellite moved away to the south, the viewing point was switched to a ground camera on the point Spencer lighthouse which was perhaps twenty-five miles from the target location.

Because of haze, the view was not nearly as clear as it had been from the satellite, but nevertheless, it could be seen that the spray had spent itself. Only a small cloud was slowly moving off toward the north.

The announcer came back on the sound system. "Our drones have successfully completed their sampling and will be retrieved as planned. Except for the monitoring of the cloud as it moves north, this completes Operation Big Current for today. Tomorrow, surface ships will monitor for residual radioactivity and make depth soundings across the target seamount. The admiral has invited visitors to a reception this evening in the Officer's Mess at 2000 hours Hawaii time."

The only apparent problem with the test was that the spray thrown up above the ground zero points indicated that a small part of the explosion might have escaped. In the future, Meriwether thought that perhaps the type of rock in the sea bottom would have to be considered in more detail.

Later, in the Officer's Mess, Meriwether had champagne while Roger had a fruit drink which was a mixture of exotic tropical fruit juices. They had already decided to catch the morning plane back to Puerto Rico. With stops and plane changes, it would be a grueling twenty hours, and seven time zones earlier. There was no reason to hang around Hawaii because the important data they were waiting for would get to Puerto Rico as fast as it would get to Hawaii.

It was early afternoon of the next day by the time Meriwether and Roger were back at the SWG headquarters and had checked in at the Son of NOAH office. Lucille was glad to see them, particularly Roger, even though they had talked nearly every day while he was gone. She handed each of them a package of papers. "These just came in on the wire, and I made a copy for each of you. It looks good to me, but you guys are the experts."

The papers gave the actual soundings by track across the seamount as well as a plot of the new topology. The old topology was also included for reference. "Not bad," Roger said. "Except for these two saucers which must have been right above the ground zeros, the bottom smoothness is about the same as the surrounding area."

"Hum" was all Meriwether said at first. Then, "Look at how one saucer seems to register over the other. I'll bet the right warhead went off about one microsecond before the other."

Roger laughed, "That's pretty good for government work."

*   *   *

Meanwhile, on the opposite side of the earth, Wong Lee was completely unaware that attempts were in process to tailor the climate. His only concern was with the success of his meditation, or rather the lack of success. He had occasion to talk privately with his companion monk as they walked to a particular sampan on the Huangpu River in Shanghai Harbor. They were apparently delivering a message from the head monk to the family who lived on the sampan. What the message was and where it would eventually go was of no concern of theirs.

As they walked back to the monastery, Wong, looking to his older companion for advice, said, "I find it even more difficult to meditate properly now that there is a shortage of food in the land. When I try to still the mind, my attention goes to my feeling of hunger, which is greatly intensified. What is to be done?"

His companion answered, "These are just the trials of the body. There is no answer to what to do when you can't meditate properly except to try to meditate even more. Someday Heaven will smile on you, and all this will be forgotten. The only true reality is the Way of Heaven."

CHAPTER 26

Algeria

A year had passed since the creation of the SWG, and Olav and George Henson were on tour of inland Algeria. While Libya had been their earlier choice for the implementation of large-scale plankton farming in Africa, the emphasis had shifted to Algeria. For one thing, the Algerians had been more receptive, including the idea of hosting millions of new inhabitants from northern Europe. As it turned out, even more than Libya, Algeria was particularly suited to the rapid establishment of the plankton farms due to the existence of a great many old, dried-up lake beds. Little would be needed to be added besides water and, of course, harvesting facilities.

They had just arrived at a point about one hundred miles south of the city of Algiers where a new city was under construction, a short way off the highway from the north. The construction was the most intense on a rise of ground midway between two old lake beds. Temporary housing had been erected for the construction crews from Germany, who were the first of the new immigrants. The local site manager was pointing out progress and referring to a map.

"The desalination plant for the city will be just west of Algiers, and the pipeline will come south on the left side of the highway. You probably noticed the ditching operations as you drove in?" Olav nodded.

The site manager continued, "We have all the pumping stations under construction, which you probably also noticed on the drive down from Algiers. We have completed the large

storage facility for fresh water, which you can see on that hill to
your left beyond the city, which we have named New Bergen.
The water storage volume is exceedingly large for two reasons.
The primary power for pumping will be solar, so pumping will
be only during the day. We also want to allow for breakdowns
and occasional times of cloudy weather. In that flat area you
passed on the way in where there was that forest of aluminum
framework, we will be installing the solar-panel farm. The
batteries, inverters, and controllers will also be housed in that
area. This will be largely for power needed by the city. Each of
the lakes will have its own solar-power facility for driving the
pumps, driers, and other plankton-support needs. Most of the
plankton-farm requirements are daylight only, so the power
systems there are quite simple. All the systems will, of course, be
cross connected to handle any breakdowns."

The site manager paused to see if he was properly impressing
his important visitors. George said, "I see you have diesel
generators for support of the construction work. Will those be
kept for emergency use after the construction is completed?"

The site manager answered, "Yes, initially. But when natural
gas engines which produce less carbon dioxide become available,
and a pipeline is run in, the diesels will be replaced."

The site manager continued, "We are trying to benefit to
the maximum from the excellent solar exposure we have here.
For example, the plankton drying will be almost exclusively
dependent on solar heating as will our residential needs. Would
you like to go over to the edge of the city where we can look at
some of the finished living units?"

Olav and George nodded showing their interest. The
site manager picked up another map showing the city plan.
"Actually," he said as they got into an open jeep and started
toward the city, 'small town' would be more correct by most
people's standards. The city has been sized so that most
inhabitants will be able to get everywhere by just walking or by
bicycle. Powered vehicles, other than electric vans for moving
heavy loads or supporting maintenance, are banned from the
city and will be parked on the periphery. Public buildings for
hospitals, schools, shops, cafeterias, and entertainment will be at

the center, surrounded by residential areas. New Bergen is sized at ten thousand people. There will be a number of public parks because a water shortage will not allow the luxury of individual gardens and lawns. Community gardens and greenhouses will be available for the raising of vegetables."

Olav said, "I'm sure that, in spite of the low humidity, summer afternoons can get quite warm." Looking at the buildings, he continued, "I have noticed those funny looking towers built into all the buildings. Is their function that which is referred to in the Middle East as 'wind towers'?"

The site manager smiled. "Yes, you are very perceptive. The openings in the towers are aligned with the summer prevailing wind. The design is such that the wind going through the tower will pull air out of the building, providing natural ventilation." As they drove up, he added, "Would you like to look at a typical living unit?"

Olav and George nodded again, and all three of them moved toward the group of buildings that were obviously finished. Olav asked as they approached, "Why is the construction so massive?" noting the thickness of the masonry walls.

This time, George answered, "While we will have reasonable amounts of power for the foreseeable future, we will not have enough for air-conditioning. We are therefore adopting the desert designs that have proven effective over thousands of years. Nights are cold here, even in summer when the days get very hot. Massive masonry is the cheapest thermal mass and evens out the temperatures. With proper solar design, where the sun shines almost every day, there is really no need to heat in the winter. With masonry heat sinks and natural convection, the summers will be tolerable."

The living units they were approaching were grouped closely together like town houses and sported bright red-tile roofs. The site manager said, "These are family units, with varying numbers of bedrooms to accommodate families of different sizes. Some units don't need to connect to a wind tower because of the way they are sited. With high ceilings and high-opening windows, they will have good natural convective cooling. The wide overhangs are worked out to give solar heating in the winter, but not in the summer. Now, those larger buildings across the way have efficiencies for single persons."

Olav noticed a small railway still under construction, terminating near the center of the city. "What is that for?" he asked.

The site manager answered, "The primary industry here will be the growing of the plankton on the old lake beds. These are beyond a reasonable walking distance, particularly during the heat of a summer day. So we will have an electric trolley to both lakes. The plankton industry will only occupy about one-half of the working adults that will live here. Another quarter will be needed in service industries, minding the children, keeping stores, the cafeterias, maintenance, and so forth. Other light industries are planned to occupy the last quarter of the working adults. A bicycle assembly plant is already under construction. One plant that is in operation already, and will continue after the city is completed, is the assembly of photo-voltaic solar panels. Fresh produce for local consumption will be grown on the south periphery of the town, some in the open, and some in greenhouses. Other light industries are yet to be decided on, mostly dependent on the skills available from among the settlers."

As they drove in the jeep back to the site construction office, the site manager asked if they had any other questions.

George wanted to know and asked, "How soon will you have the first lake in production turning out plankton? I notice that one appears to be a bit ahead of the other."

"Everything here is on schedule, and the last item should be finished by July 15. We will be ready for plankton production in two months if the water is available and if we can get the plankton driers. They are being built in Germany and, I have been told, are in great demand all over the world. They are a three-story piece of machinery, and it has been difficult to convert factories to build more of them in a hurry."

George said he would look into what could be done to expedite the building of plankton driers. Perhaps they should be moved up on the SWG's list of priorities.

Olav and George thanked their host and walked toward their car to be driven to the next location. As they walked, they were accosted by a young woman in overalls who asked, "Are you from the SWG headquarters?" At Olav's nod, she went on hurriedly, "I was a forester from the Black Forest in Germany. There I learned how to make the forests grow back and become healthy again. Is this not important to be used to make the earth whole again?"

Olav was somewhat taken back by the woman's forceful approach but was not one to miss any bets. Before getting into the car he gave her Lars Berg's address and urged her to write Lars about how to make the forests grow back.

SWG headquarters, of course, had reports of progress from all the construction sites but had selected a few to be visited to get a hands-on feel for how things were developing. They had decided to select places to visit at random and without advance notice.

The last site was about forty miles north-east of New Bergen and was actually several sites since the old lake bed there was very large and would allow for several settlements. Being closer to the coast, the desalination plant and its pipeline were scheduled for earlier completion as were all the other aspects of the project. They were disappointed to learn that everything was significantly behind schedule. The site manager not only blamed everything on his workers, bad material, or late deliveries but also had no plan to make up his lost schedules. As far as Olav and George could tell, conditions were the same as those they had seen at New Bergen, and they concluded that the critical difference was an incompetent site manager. They made an on-the-spot decision to replace him with the site manager from New Bergen. New Bergen's manager had a competent deputy who could probably take over there. A strategic decision was also made that the old spy satellites, which were not very busy these days, should be used to verify the field progress reports, which apparently were not always accurate. That could save a lot of traveling.

On the way to the airport, Olav thought that this trip to Africa had not been nearly as enjoyable as the earlier trip to Libya he had made with Julia, which had also been their honeymoon.

CHAPTER 27

Darwin

At the same time that Olav and George were headed back to the SWG headquarters in Puerto Rico, Ray was on his way to transact some unpleasant business in Australia. As his plane started its approach to Darwin Airport, Ray came out of a short nap and began to think again about his mission to Australia and his important meeting with Douglas Barrington, the Prime Minister. Australia had joined the SWG reluctantly and only after Ray had made it clear to them that only as a state of the SWG would they be protected from the threat of Chinese expansion. China was beginning to hurt badly from the loss of food-growing capability in the Northern provinces and was looking elsewhere for food and land.

As a growing superpower, China had sufficient atomic weapons to make it a no-contest with any country, such as Australia, that did not. China had refused to join the SWG, and SWG had decided that as long as she remained passive, it was not worth a nuclear confrontation to force her to do so. Time was against her. In a year or two, with more crop failures, she would have nowhere else to go for food besides the SWG.

Meanwhile, Australia was the immediate problem. While committed to carrying out development plans formulated by the SWG to absorb essentially the entire population of Canada, everything seemed to be dragging. The meeting with Barrington was an exercise in personal diplomacy to see if in a one-on-one meeting, the Australian attitude could be changed to one of enthusiastic cooperation. Ray intended first to convince him that the Canadian transplant was really going to happen on schedule and make him see that it would be easier for them if they cooperated rather than if they were forced. His strategy, as worked out for him by the What If, was to show them what an Australia would look like when married to a transplanted Canada as compared to a significant portion of China.

As the plane pulled up at the terminal, it looked like Barrington had some strategy of his own in mind. Instead of pulling up to a normal jet way, the plane was stopped in an open space on the tarmac, and a set of stairs were rolled up to the plane. A large crowd had been assembled as a greeting party, with good coverage by the press and the media. Ray decided this was definitely being staged to play well back in Sidney. He smiled to himself. It didn't matter what external ego satisfaction Barrington needed, when it came to the showdown, the SWG had the cards.

Since it was already midafternoon, nothing was scheduled until the next day except for a ceremonial dinner, just the right time Ray decided, to play his winning card. As Ray descended to the tarmac, he thought there was more than the usual amount of security. Maybe the extra security was because Australian emotions were running high about the expected influx of Canadians that was bound to reduce the lifestyle the Australians had previously enjoyed.

None of this showed in Barrington's welcome, which appeared genuine as he greeted Ray. "We are very pleased to greet you and have you visit the great state of Australia," he said, shaking hands and holding Ray's shoulder briefly with his other arm. "It has not been often that a director of the SWG has visited us."

After they were settled in the limousine, Barrington continued. "If you aren't tired, I have planned to have the motorcade go past the harbor so you can see the progress there."

"Fine," Ray replied. He knew that the harbor project was the only major effort in Darwin that was close to being on schedule, so he was not surprised at the suggestion. Not close to schedule was the building of a second harbor, roads to the interior, the desalination plants, the laying of pipeline, and the construction of the solar-power farms. Until these were completed, no major progress could be made on the new cities and agricultural projects.

Ray had to admit that the progress at the Port of Darwin was impressive. The harbor had been more than doubled in its capacity to handle ships and further construction was still under way. Barrington said in a strong voice, "We have been utilizing overtime for the past two months, and we project that we will finish the port expansion on schedule. As you saw at the Darwin Airport, we have added the new runways, and the planned increase in gate capacity will be finished by the end of the month."

The motorcade came to its destination, a large hotel adjacent to the Northern Territory government house where the SWG party was being hosted. In the suite reserved for Ray, they were met by Tom Hamilton, the SWG chief representative in Australia. Barrington bowed out with a reminder of the time dinner would be served, and that in the subtropics, formal attire was not practiced. Ray and Tom were left alone.

While Tom had been sending the SWG regular factual reports, Ray felt that perhaps there was more he could say in person. "Tom, what is the real problem here? We have done much better almost everywhere else, including Algeria, where we were even faced with religious prejudice."

Tom hesitated a few seconds, gauging the other man, one with a very direct style whom he had met previously in a large group but he had not engaged him in a personal conversation before. "The basic problem, it seems to me, goes back to the Australian work force which has lived 95 percent in the luxury of the very urban, large cities of the southern coast, Sidney, Melbourne, Adelaide, and to a lesser extent, Perth and Brisbane as you come around the coast. They hate the climate around Darwin and the austere living conditions in the interior, where most of the construction needs to be done. While the Australians have met their manpower quotas, the productivity of this displaced workforce has been very low. Barrington's party has only a very small, working majority in the government, and he has avoided actions that are controversial in order not to risk loss of control of the government."

Ray responded, "I thought it was something like that. Barrington seems to be very politically sensitive. I guess I know how to make him sensitive to the needs of the SWG. Let's have our first meeting tomorrow with just you, me, and Barrington. I'll put it to him in a way he will have no choice, and neither will the Australians. I think I'll give him a hint tonight at dinner." With that they parted, agreeing to get together an hour later to go down together for dinner with Barrington and the other participants.

At dinner, Ray and Barrington were seated at the end of the table where they could talk in reasonable privacy if they so chose. It was apparent to Ray that, unless he took the initiative, Barrington, who had initiated all manner of small talk, was going to avoid talking business. After the main course was over, Ray broke the ice on that. "I know that you have prepared a long review of the Australian effort on behalf of SWG for me tomorrow, and I am looking forward to it. That, however, is not my main reason for this visit. The SWG is quite disappointed in the lack of progress, and it is rethinking whether, perhaps, it would be better to resettle the Canadians in the southwestern United States and northern Mexico. This would leave Australia open for the northern Chinese, who will, no doubt, someday join the SWG and need a place to relocate some two hundred million or more people. It is my primary purpose to discuss this alternative to the present plan with you tomorrow and, on my return to the SWG, render a recommendation. I know that the alternative to the present plan would be very unpopular and cause unpleasant reactions, so I suggest we keep it quiet for now and limit the meeting to discuss it to you, me, and Tom Hamilton."

The Prime Minister nodded his agreement and said almost nothing for the rest of the evening, It was apparent to anyone sitting nearby that he was definitely not enjoying himself.

At the special meeting the next morning, Ray took charge immediately. "Tom will not need to take an active part in the meeting, but I want him present, because he needs to know the situation firsthand and will be speaking for me in the future after I leave."

Turning to address Barrington directly, Ray continued, "The situation is quite simple. The change to a glacial period in Canada is following our climatic predictions very closely. The grain harvest in Canada this past summer was 10 percent of normal and won't be worth planting next year. The SWG intends to move the Canadian population as scheduled, and if it appears that Australia will not be ready, then, as I told you last night, we will absorb them in the United States and Mexico. The logical population then to resettle in Australia would be the northern Chinese."

Ray had expected Barrington to say something at that point, so he paused, but Barrington remained silent. Ray continued, "It is not well known, but at the SWG headquarters, we have a fantastic computer that we call the What If which can accurately predict a future situation based on the decisions made at an earlier time. Perhaps we should have divulged its predictions for Australia to you before now. If the Canadians are relocated here, the What If shows that within fifteen years Australia will become the leading element of the SWG. The climate changes will bring more moisture to what are now desert areas. The Canadians, who are generally a very hard-working lot, will transform the Australian laid-back attitude. Their agricultural skills will make Australia a major surplus area for food production. Also with the Canadians come much of their technology and a considerable amount of light industry, all that is practical to relocate. This is a very attractive scenario considering what most parts of the world are facing."

Ray could see this was going to be a short meeting with Barrington doing nothing but listening. Ray went on, "On the other hand, the picture of Australia, if made the home to several hundred million Chinese, is not the same at all. Because of the greater cultural differences, the What If shows that there will be great unrest in the transition years. The Chinese are much less demanding than most, so it will be possible to settle a great many more of them than the Canadians. They are, however, very tenacious in maintaining their culture and language. While a very difficult time for all concerned, the What If in the long-term sees Australia becoming more Chinese than Australian. From the

SWG's point of view, it might be the better solution, because the Chinese will have to go somewhere eventually."

Still Barrington said nothing, so Ray went on to his conclusion, "So you see, to a large extent, the future of Australia is up to the Australians, at least between these two scenarios. Most of them don't know it yet, so it is up to you to tell them and motivate them. Recognizing that it takes time to get the word out to so many people, I will withhold my recommendation for a month and see what you are able to do. I feel that your primary problem is to get your city people out of the cities to where the work is. You need to figure out how to get your best people out there. Also I think it is time to get some Canadians over here as examples. At this point, they are certainly motivated."

With Barrington's assurances that he would get all the projects on schedule within a year, they went on to the planned review meetings. In an aside to Tom, Ray said, "I don't think he's tough enough to make it happen. Too bad."

CHAPTER 28

Auckland

The next day, Ray continued his tour which was to take him to his second destination, Auckland on New Zealand's North Island. General Boris Metchnikoff was waiting for him, and together they were going to review the readiness of this, the third military base for SWG. It was the most important of the three, being closest to the main remaining military opponent, China.

The base had been declared fully operational two weeks before, and Boris had been there for that time to make sure it really was. He was waiting for Ray at the airport and was going over in his mind the decisions that had led to what in SWG parlance was now called Auckland Base. The New Zealanders were quick to see disaster ahead for them with the expected climatic changes and so were one of the charter members of the SWG. Becoming one of the SWG's safe island enclaves had looked like a good way to go for a small country, besides obtaining a sure thing to replace much of the declining sheep industry.

From the SWG point of view, the sheltered waters around Auckland had looked like an ideal place to base the one third of the atomic missile submarines that SWG was retaining to enforce its decisions on a restive world. Pulling the fangs of national armed forces was not yet complete with China still maintaining its sovereignty, so the base needed a strong defense against any possible attack.

Antiballistic missiles had been brought in from the Russians and were the first line of defense against the Chinese ICBMs.

Traditional naval forces obtained from the navies of a number
of previously sovereign countries were also based in and around
North Island. The emphasis was on antisubmarine units since the
Chinese did not have overpowering naval surface forces.

Lastly, a number of new airfields had been established and
manned by interceptors to provide defense against an air strike.
As the last island stronghold to be commissioned, Auckland
Base was probably not as large as Hawaii Base but probably more
strategically located. Of the three bases, Boris reflected that the
weather on North Island suited him best. After spending most
of his life as close to the pole as the equator, the tropics did not
agree with him.

North Island, New Zealand

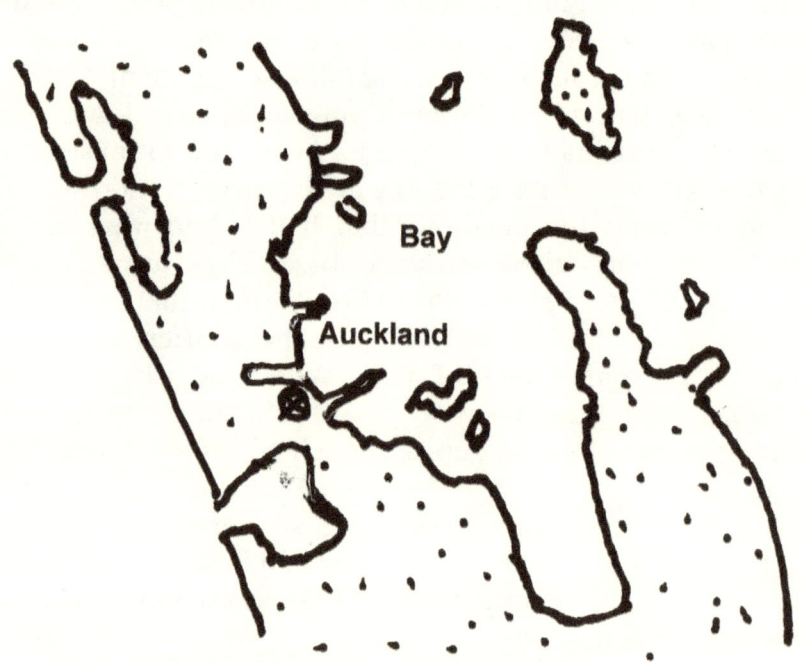

A plane was landing, coming in low from the south, and Boris
was sure it would be Ray's plane. At Boris's insistence that he
should always be able to get in touch with Ray at any moment,

Ray flew in one of the airplanes the United States had previously used for top VIPs. Boris himself always flew in military aircraft. Sure enough, as it taxied up, he could make out the markings of a SWG command aircraft.

Construction had been going on at a furious pace ever since the decision had been made to make New Zealand one of the SWG's secure bases. Boris wanted Ray to see the physical plant of the base first, and for that, they headed for Auckland proper. They first toured past a city district that had been a depressed industrial area, which the SWG had taken over for its command center. Beyond was a hotel and apartment district where the SWG personnel had been temporarily settled.

They next drove out to the other side of town, and Boris commented, "We are coming up on one of the antiballistic missile installations on our right. Because we anticipate no attack weapons will ever leak through, we have settled for a relatively soft installation from the point of an atomic attack, although quite hard if attacked by conventional means. Each missile is well dispersed from its nearest neighbor so that a conventional bomb could at most take out only a single missile. There were many surplus control radars when the Russian ABMs were dismantled, so we have put in three times the usual number to provide much redundancy. The command center is duplicated at each ABM site and hardened against anything but a direct atomic hit."

Ray laughed, "You're like a kid in a candy store. If anything, you have erred on the safe side."

Next they visited an interceptor base where, just like the ABM site, the crews were on a continuous alert status. Covered revetments had been constructed so that each airplane was secure from anything but a direct hit. Boris showed Ray a special part of the field where some of the stealth fighters that had been developed by the United States were kept. Boris commented, "When we took over the stealth fighters, we decided they would be most useful in action with China, and so we are basing most of them here. For certain operations, we would need a forward base in readiness and have arranged for one in Japan. No stealth fighters are kept there, however, on a regular basis." Ray nodded his understanding.

The next part of the tour took them to dock areas of the port where a torpedo motorboat (TMB) was waiting for them, its engines turning over at idle. Boris apologized, "We don't anticipate using the TMBs as they were originally intended but have converted them to an antisubmarine warfare role. They also happen to be the fastest way to get around the water, short of flying. In the future, we expect to have some hovercraft." As the TMB got underway, they moved up to the wheelhouse, where Boris could better point out the various features of interest to Ray.

Pointing, Boris said, "Over on the left, we have new facilities for the submarine ICBMs. Currently we have four based here, two always on station at sea and the other two in port for repairs and crew R and R. We also have six attack submarines for protection of the anchorage and the harbor. Of course, we have set up sonar picket fences across all the approaches to the anchorage, so it is not necessary to have the attack submarines at sea stations at all times. Nevertheless, to keep them on their toes, we divide them into teams and run practice exercises." The boat's course took them past some new housing, and Boris commented, "As is the policy for all military personnel, regardless of the country of origin, their families are located with them. This housing for military personnel and their families is in a secured area that has just been completed."

The TMB picked up speed with a corresponding increase in the roar of its engines, causing Boris to speak louder to be heard. "To the right we keep the bulk of the ASW fleet and the larger surface ships we still have in commission. Most of these are already out in the anchorage or open sea in preparation for the exercise we are going to run tomorrow. The center part of the port has been retained for cargo and other civilian activities."

Over the next hour, they had a fast, water tour of the protected anchorage at Auckland, and they then returned to the dock they had left from and went ashore. On the way back to the SWG base headquarters, where they were going to spend the night, they passed an area where elements of an armored division were being billeted.

"What unit is that?" Ray asked.

"Actually that is one of the new federated divisions made up of nationals from many member states," Boris answered. "We will be doing a lot more of that in the future so that we don't run into the problem of a unit being used against a state where a large number of the personnel originated. A number of the males have already married New Zealand girls. We also encourage females, even in combat roles, which helps keep up the average intelligence."

"The morale too, I bet," Ray laughed.

The next morning, Ray and Boris were present at the base command center to observe the practice operation. It was planned as realistic a situation as could be arranged without overly endangering the personnel.

The beginning of the mock attack was the launch toward Auckland of five surplus minuteman ICBMs from Hawaii. These were picked up on the surveillance satellite system and later by long-range radar, which showed predicted impact points centered on a bay a few miles north of Auckland. Boris commented as the countdown for the ABM missile launches preceded. "For practice, we are targeting one ABM per incoming target so as to save on missiles. In a real attack, we would target two each to improve the probability of the intercept."

The ABMs were launched, and in only a few seconds, four of the five incoming missiles were destroyed. The surviving attacker splashed in the middle of the target bay. Telemetry showed that one ABM warhead had not exploded due to a defective fuse. Boris said, "In the future, if we don't improve, we will have to increase our response to three ABMs per incoming target."

Next, to give them practice, each of the ICBM submarines that were on station north of the Philippines, launched one missile each, targeted on the center of the anchorage. As with the missiles launched from Hawaii, these had no active warheads. They were both destroyed with a single ABM each, bringing the score up to six out of seven for the ABMs.

All went well in the other exercises. Three attack submarines, simulating enemy boats, were all detected by the sonar fence. The ASW forces, dropping dummy depth charges, would have destroyed all three had they been using live ammunition. A low-level flight of bombers, from a base on South Island made a simulated attack on the base and was easily detected. Fighters were vectored into positions where the bombers would have either been destroyed in a real-life situation or would have been forced to break off their attacks. The air intercept was successful, even without an AWAC's plane, which they were scheduled to receive soon.

At the end of the exercise, Boris commented, "Most of the time, we will exercise the various teams with computer simulators, which will save a lot of wear and tear on the hardware, as well as fuel. There is also some danger to personnel on any live exercise. However, we need occasional real exercises, and, overall, today's went quite well."

"Yes," responded Ray, "I am sure we are good enough for the threat that we face, and once the Chinese join the SWG, we should be able to cut back further in our forces by perhaps a factor of ten."

"What are your travel plans now?" asked Boris, changing the subject.

"I'm going to Brazil right away," Ray answered. "The Amazon team is there, putting together their recommendations. Want to fly with me and get updated on the spot?"

"Sure," said Boris, always glad for a chance to spend time with his boss.

CHAPTER 29

Amazon

The Amazon project was probably the most difficult and complex operation that the SWG had undertaken so far. Not only had it not been clear what to do about the areas of the rain forest that had already been clear-cut, but also there was a basic question as to whether it was feasible to settle urban populations in the rain forest areas. Also, the political climate in Brazil was difficult. The majority of the SWG directors were gathered in the Amazon at the project headquarters to review progress so far and decide the direction the project should take in the future.

Director Lars Berg was first on reforestation. "When we were able to stop the clear-cutting of the rain forests, approximately half the forests had been destroyed. In the long term, we need to replant them, if for no other reason than we need the forests' capability for removing carbon dioxide from the atmosphere. In this regard, the tropical rain forests are more efficient than the temperate ones because they absorb carbon dioxide year-round and have more sunlight for photosynthesis.

"Since we set up the inducements for Brazil to harvest human edible foods from the rain forest, they have put in place a major effort to set up harvesting facilities. This has been a difficult process, because only recently has information on the rain forest species, such as what is edible, how they propagate, etc. been systematically collected. This job has just begun, and we are supporting Brazil in a major push to complete it.

"Certain desirable species have already been selected for their known food value and means of propagation, and extensive nurseries are being established in many of the clear-cut areas. There will be problems in reestablishing growth in many of the clear-cut areas since many of the nutrients were in the tree growth and the land is quite deficient. Also the loss of the natural growth has resulted in considerable erosion. Soil rebuilding and land erosion control will be essential. All this is very labor-intensive, so it is necessary to build extensive facilities for housing people, and all the other needs that come with them, including hospitals, schools, power, sanitation, the works." Lars concluded with, "The bottom line is that the rain forests can be made useful with a lot of effort in labor, capital, and time." He sat down.

Akmed Hamid on energy was second. "We are looking at a three-point program to expand the energy available in the Amazon basin. First, there are a number of ideal sites for the generation of hydro-electric power that have not yet been tapped. The potential is about ten times the power generated from the Aswan high dam. We estimate this power, which gives us a night-and-day base capability, can all be on line in five years. This will still not be enough power for the projected needs, so second, we are recommending the same kind of solar-voltaic farms that are currently being installed in North Africa and Australia. These would be located in clear-cut areas that are close to where settlements are projected. The Amazon power needs will be significantly less than in the desert areas since water desalination will not be required, nor the pumping of water great distances. Third, for transport, we will need energy in the form of liquid fuel, and here we will be converting to biomass, a technology which was first pioneered here on a large scale decades ago."

Akmed concluded, "So far, nothing has surfaced that would prevent us from reaching the energy goals set for the Amazon. One important consideration to remember is that our projected needs for energy do not include extensive application of air-conditioning. It is well established, as you can personally testify, that humans brought up in a temperate climate will find the Amazon quite uncomfortable." That drew a laugh from a sweating audience. He had one parting comment, "There is promise of solar-powered air-conditioning, but it is too low on the priority list to be implemented now."

Bani Shinto took his turn. "I don't have much to say about new technology. In the Amazon, there is a lot of water, and the rivers that make up all this water are the most efficient way to transport things if you aren't in a hurry. The Brazilians have greatly expanded their capability to build shallow draft tugs and barges. Our planned needs will not be met even so, and we are also having them built in the United States where there is an overcapacity. For the time being, we are stuck with using diesel fuel, but in the longer term will convert over to the same fuel that is already a major one for ground transport, methyl alcohol.

"Some of our transportation needs to cross from one river to the next, so we are adding to the existing canals at strategic locations where the terrain permits such construction." Bani projected a map of the Amazon basin showing the locations of the existing and projected canals. "Amazing, isn't it? When we are done, you will be able to go almost everywhere by water. Actually, if you looked carefully, you may have seen that there are several rivers that are not connected by canals to the others, and that is because of high ridges of land between the rivers. In those cases, there are existing roads, mostly quite primitive, which we will be expanding, also some rail lines." Again he projected a map, this one showing the roads and railways, present and planned. "In most cases, the roads and railways will be used by people and perishables only. As you know from the inconvenience of getting here, almost all the air transport systems have been greatly reduced. I should make a point here that applies worldwide. We have started a technology program of great promise in the area of lighter-than-air vehicles, dirigibles. Particularly in places where there are not many existing roads or railways, they are a very promising, energy-efficient form of transportation for the future. The age of artificially cheap energy robbed the dirigible in the past of its rightful place in the scheme of things."

Olav opened jokingly, "It seems that I always get to talk when it is just before or just after lunch when you are thinking about food." It got the laugh he intended. "Here in the basin, there are two major food initiatives with which the SWG is involved. First, we have been investigating the human edible food that grows naturally in the rain forests. There is actually a wide variety of fruits, nuts, and meaty plants that can be harvested essentially year-round. Unfortunately, except for the native population, no one to speak of has been utilizing these foods with the exception of the Brazil nut with which you are all familiar." Olav projected a series of pictures showing this wide variety of tropical foods which no one else in the meeting was familiar with or could even name. "A completely balanced diet can be had from these foods," he added. "The only trouble is getting people's tastes to accept them. We estimate that eventually we can harvest enough food from the rain forests to feed five hundred million people. New machines are needed to harvest and process the rain forest foods. We already have some proven designs but need to put them into quantity production.

"Yes," Olav smiled as several directors groaned on seeing his next slide. "I am going to talk about plankton again. We have been experimenting with growing plankton in ponds built on some of the eroded land in the clear-cut areas. We will continue to conduct research in this area but at the present time are not ready to commit to the growing of plankton in the wet tropics. The primary problem is that in the humid tropics there are so many airborne microorganisms, molds, yeasts, and so forth, that the open ponds we use in the deserts allow far too much contamination. Also the insect population is so prolific that we get a lot of insect parts in with the plankton, some of which are mildly toxic to humans. There is still another problem, in that the extensive rainfall tends to dilute from the pond's salts that are needed for the optimum plankton growth. We can grow the plankton in covered ponds, but if you are building hundreds of square miles of ponds, it might be better to build more ponds in the deserts."

To close his presentation, Olav passed around samples of the foods from the rain forests which were candidates for large-scale utilization. The reactions varied from ohs and ahs, to quizzical looks, and in the extreme, a puckered face.

George Henson got immediate attention with, "I have the shortest report about the largest effort. To harvest the potential food in the Amazon rain forest, we need to build about two hundred thousand villages, each holding about three hundred people. Most of the villages would be within walking distance of their neighbors, but big enough to be self-sufficient for basic services. For every forty villages, we need a central town for processing the food and providing supplies to the villagers, perhaps ten thousand towns. For each fifty towns, we need a small city to act as a major shipping and distribution center, some two hundred or so, mostly located on the larger rivers. Many of these small cities already exist but must be expanded to provide the new services required of them. The creation of the new, small towns and villages will take a fantastic amount of construction that can only be handled by prefabrication in existing factories in the developed countries. It is fortunate that a great surplus of sea transportation is available to move all these new towns and villages to the Amazon." George decided he had handed around enough numbers and sat down.

Ray had been scribbling away and then said, "You didn't say how many people would live in the towns and cities, but I estimate you are talking about housing for something like seventy-five million people. Is that right?" George nodded.

Ray said, "That's as many as living in Germany, for instance."

"Yes," George commented, "And Germany is much smaller geographically and took about a thousand years to build. We have five years."

Boris asked, "Who is going to get resettled here?"

Ray answered that one. "We haven't decided entirely. Certainly a lot of northern Europeans will be left over after we fill up the places we are preparing in North Africa. It will have to be a mix. We are studying which ethnic groups can be combined most harmoniously. Let's go on to Benjamin's report since he has been looking at this."

"Yes, thank you, Ray." Benjamin Klein had the last report. "At first blush, we are thinking of settling the northern Europeans with urban skills in the expanded cities and new towns of the Amazon basin. Assuming China joins the SWG soon, we would also settle some of the Chinese with urban skills in the cities and towns. For the farm labor for doing the actual harvesting in the rain forests, we are planning on displaced agricultural workers from elsewhere in Brazil, northern Europe, and China." Each time Benjamin used the word China or Chinese, he had a question in his voice and looked at Ray.

Recognizing Benjamin's problem, Ray commented, "In our model for future world events, we show the Chinese requesting SWG membership two calendar years from now. The confidence level of that prediction hinges on several unpredictable events and is only 50 percent. That is the best we can do for now. We have a study in the works to see what can be done to make that a certainty."

The review meeting was over, and most everyone hurried off to get ready to go on the tours of the various things they had heard about.

Benjamin and Ray were the last to leave. As they walked out, Benjamin asked Ray, "Which of the two, the Chinese or the Canadians, are moving to Australia?"

Ray said, "Ask me again in a month and then I will know for sure. As you know, I have just been to Australia, and it is clear that they are too much behind schedule to likely take the Canadians, so the Canadians likely will go to the southwest United States and Mexico. Don't worry about not having enough people. There will be enough Chinese for both Australia and Brazil, and probably some left over besides."

Ray was right about the Australians. Barrington was unsuccessful in his attempts to motivate his people and, at the end of the month Ray had given him, resigned from the government, causing the fall of his party from power. The leadership of the government passed to the opposition. The SWG announced the change in plans that the Canadians would now move to the United States and Mexico. The plan included having all car owners moving their own families. The exodus started two years after the SWG came into being and took place over a five-year period. The five years was just long enough to build the new homes and facilities needed and to move those industries that would be useful in the future.

CHAPTER 30

Climate Change

Two years had passed since the creation of the SWG, and Meriwether was conducting a progress review on his major climate-change projects. Boris, Roger, and Lucille were also present as well as a panel of climatic scientists. Now that they were in the operational stage, Boris had the lead since his department had operational responsibility.

Boris said, "First, with regard to Project High Cloud.

"We changed our plans a year ago to go to sea launch using container ships. Launching off the Sri Lanka east coast, we are using the Indian tracking range. The same thing is being done off the coast of French Guiana using the ESA Spaceport range.

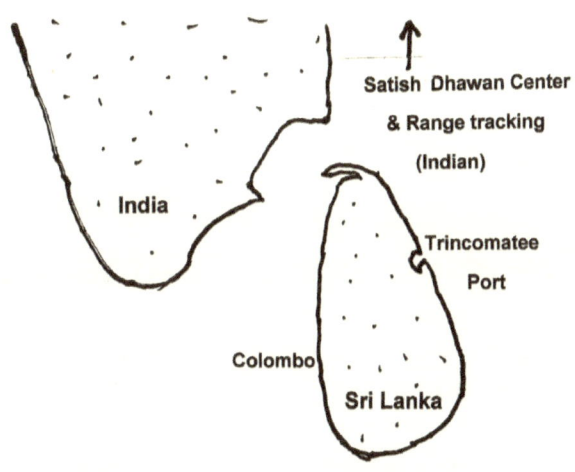

Sri Lanka and India

From last summer until now, we have launched 796 modified, large ICBMs, deploying the bubble dispensers into low, near-equatorial orbits. If our schedules hold, the remainder of the two thousand planned launches will be completed by the end of this coming January. Our schedule is paced by the delivery of the dispensers. So far, only three of the systems have either failed to make orbit or dispense the bubble clouds, which speaks well of the original booster design as well as the new payload."

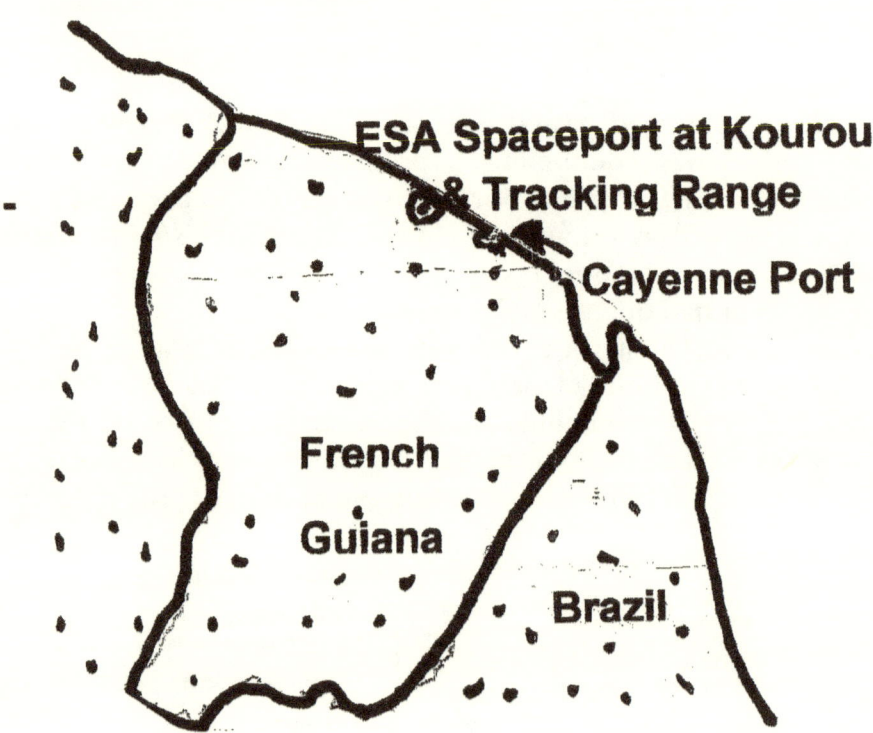

French Guiana, S. America

At this point, Ray, who had planned to attend, joined the group. Boris summarized what he had already said and continued, "You may remember from the last review that, due to the sun going into a quiescent time for the next few years, we have been able to lower the nominal orbit and hence get some increase in payload to orbit. Lucille, I believe at this time, has experimental results from our monitoring stations."

"Yes," Lucille said as she walked to the head of the table and put her first chart on the projector. "We are definitely seeing the predicted results. In fact, the attenuation factor is just a bit greater than our design value, no doubt due to the slightly greater payload Boris discussed. The orbits are such that the attenuation should apply in a band from latitude 10° south to latitude 10° north, and our instrumentation shows this to be the case. So far, the edge of the band is about half a degree wide, where it goes from maximum attenuation to no attenuation. With time, we expect this to spread slowly. The graphs you see show some variation, part of which is due to the cloud not being quite homogenous, but mostly due to variations in dust and haze that are equal to our calibration error. We have a baseline which represents measurements made before the cloud deployment was initiated, shown in these other charts. We are continually monitoring the sun's output from a number of locations, including satellites in orbit, and the sun's output has been normalized in the results. This includes the variations due to the changes in the orbit of the earth around the sun. Extrapolating to the completion of the two thousand launches, we predict an initial reduction in the sun's energy reaching the atmosphere in the affected band, equal to 5.1 percent." Lucille sat down and one of the scientists knew it was his turn.

The scientist displayed a chart showing the percentage of carbon dioxide in the atmosphere plotted against year. "You see here," he said, "The history of the culprit. In the early industrial period, the baseline carbon dioxide content was around 250 parts per million, that is a quarter-of-a-tenth of 1 percent. At the beginning of the 1900s, it had reached three hundred parts, and last year peaked at about four hundred parts per million. Seasonal variations put noise on the curve over a short time period, but we still think we see a major change in the increase. In fact, it appears that we have stopped the increase at this level. Until the level is brought back down, we are still at risk that some random event can trigger us into a fast transition into an irreversible glacial period. Even if we continue the planned further reductions in the burning of fossil fuels, it might take one hundred years to return to a safe level. The oceans only take up carbon dioxide at a fixed, small rate, and our reforestation program has a very long time constant. Only mature, healthy trees remove significant amounts of carbon dioxide."

Ray interjected a comment. "What you are saying is that although High Cloud buys us some time, we will still be at high risk for a long time."

"Yes," the scientist responded, "and that applies to at least part of the other good things we are doing. I just wanted to emphasize this so that you will recognize the importance of fertilizing the existing forests. The High Cloud project has a temporary effect due to a half-life of ten years. During that time, its effect is similar to reducing the carbon dioxide by only fifty parts per million."

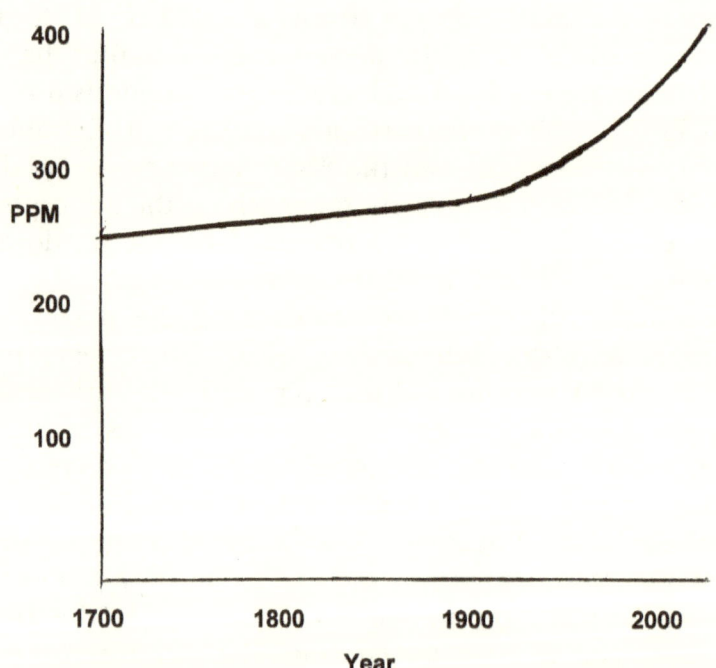

Atmospheric CO$_2$ (ppm) Verses Year

Meriwether was a little irked to have the smooth flow of his presentation interrupted and said, "We are saving the good news about the fertilization of the existing forests until the end of the review. Let's first go on to Project Big Current."

Boris again took the floor. "The easiest, and again a temporary change, is to increase certain of the ocean's currents by deepening the sills between the Norwegian Sea and the North Atlantic. We are doing this by detonating atomic warheads under the channels between the two bodies of water. Using submarines and an underwater drilling barge, we have so far successfully detonated thirty seven warheads between Greenland and Iceland. Our monitoring indicates a 95 percent increase in the cold bottom-water flow into the Atlantic. To balance it, there must be a 95 percent increase in the surface warm water flow in the opposite direction. By early spring, we will have finished detonating thirteen more in the Greenland-to-Iceland channel and fifty in the channel between Iceland and the Faeroe Islands. The original plan called for deepening the channel between the Faeroe Islands and Scotland, but that has been ruled as too dangerous if a shot breached the surface and we had radioactive fallout. This last gave less additional flow as well, so it is best left out. Lucille, do you want to comment on the effect on the climate?"

"Sure," she said and went up to the front with another chart. "This shows the effect on the climate in terms of the equivalent reduction in the carbon dioxide content of the atmosphere. As you can see, when the channel deepening is done, it will initially be the same as a reduction of thirty parts per million in the carbon dioxide. It doesn't last as long as High Cloud, having a half-life of only three years. By half-life, I mean its carbon dioxide equivalent effect will be down to fifteen parts per million in three years."

There being no questions at that point, Boris moved on to the main part of Project Big Current. "The main effort of Big Current is to make a permanent change in the climate by permanently increasing the flow of warm water into the Arctic through the Bering Strait into the Beaufort Sea and from there through the Barrow Strait. Here we plan to level sea mounts and ridges in the two straits and double the flow of warm water. The exact mapping and targets of the underwater objects has just been completed, and the actual detonations will start in two months. We hope to complete this work by the end of next summer, allowing some delays for adverse weather. To avoid submarines having to pass through radioactive debris from earlier shots, we will start at the east end of the Barrow Strait and work upstream through the Bering Strait. The spring and summer seasons are the best time in the event of a radioactive breach because spring and summer polar air currents are more likely to keep the radioactive fallout from reaching lower latitudes. The Bering Strait will give us the most problems because there are more humans in the areas of possible fallout, who will have to be evacuated. Do you have any comments on this, Lucille?"

"Yes," she said. "We are assuming a doubling of the permanent warm water current. As a bottom line, with the two delaying tactics already described, Son of NOAH shows that the permanent snow line will stabilize twelve years from now. The line would run across Canada, three hundred miles north of the United States' border. In Europe, it will cut off the top half of Scotland, the top half of Scandinavia, and the northern part of Russia from Leningrad north. This is, of course, much better than the projections we were running two years ago without any climate modifications. I should add that, if no random events cause us to go into a deep glacial period, we will see the permanent snow line move back slowly as the reforestation programs take hold and remove carbon dioxide from the atmosphere. After one hundred years, the climate should be back as it was eighty years ago. Because of land erosion and loss of nutrients, the forests will never be as strong as they used to be, but this will be balanced by the permanent increase in warm water to the Arctic."

Ray shook his head. "That is a very long time to be at risk on the edge of a glacial period. Tell me about the fertilization of the forests."

Meriwether said, "I was saving that for the end. Replacing lost nutrients in the forests has been a part of our program, but not a major one. The problem had been that the application of rock dust as a general fertilizer to replace lost nutrients is a massive logistics undertaking. Many parts of the forests are inaccessible for the desired application of what amounts to tons of rock dust per acre. We now have a solution. You remember Gertrude Vogel whom Olav met in Algeria, the German forester?"

Ray smiled recognition. "Oh yes, the one with the construction crew at New Bergen. She was told to get in touch with Lars. I seem to remember. She's now managing our re-fertilization program."

"Well," Meriwether went on. "She had done some remarkable demonstrations on forest renewal in the Black Forest, which she wrote us about. After we moved her to Puerto Rico, we incorporated her techniques of identifying and adding trace minerals to forest soils instead of the traditional application of the complete rock dust. For the average forest, this may now only amount to a hundred pounds to an acre, a logistics problem that is within reason. Her work was really first rate and is making an amazing difference in forest growth where it is applied.

"It now appears that almost all the forests are lacking in trace elements and with the application of the right elements, growth in the average forest can be doubled. Therefore, the amount of carbon dioxide removed from the atmosphere by that forest will also be doubled. With a maximum effort, it looks like we could fertilize enough forests in the next five years to get the carbon dioxide level down to preindustrial levels within forty years, certainly no more than fifty instead of 100 years."

Ray looked a bit skeptical. "To apply Gertrude's concept, does each area have to be treated in its own custom fashion?"

Meriwether smiled. "Yes. But in most forests the soils are already very well mapped and don't vary widely over small areas. We just have to make sure that for a given forest area, we apply a rock dust that is high in the missing elements. The rock dust needs to be ground very fine, but fortunately, this is a technology well understood in the cement-making industry."

"All right," Ray said, "Get a meeting together of the directors who will be involved, and let's kick off the program to fertilize the forests on a large scale. Call it Project Rock Dust."

There being no other actions, the various participants went their several ways. Lucille and Roger, still feeling like recently married folk, went off to the beach for a late-afternoon swim.

CHAPTER 31

Project Rock Dust

The initiation of Project Rock Dust occurred one week later and moved in a direction that surprised no one, considering in the long term, it was the only hope to return the earth to anything like it had been before. With help from some of the other directors, Gertrude had produced an integrated plan which she presented to the group, a plan whose magnitude dwarfed anything they had already set in motion.

Using the preparatory work that had been done in the past year, she presented the critical factors that would be involved. To revitalize the different types of forests with their various types of trees, nine different rock-dust soil additives would be required. In the case of a few circumstances, a combination of more than one additive would be necessary. For locations where the soil conditions were unknown, test teams would be needed to be deployed to those locations before logistics planning for them could be started. A critical milestone in the planning for any area would be the decision as to which tree type was to be planted there. This would be more than what was to be done to bring the soil back to a productive state. Fast-growing types were preferred except where a nut or fruit-bearing tree type would serve to produce food for its locale.

Maps had been created showing where new roads would be needed in locations where it was not more effective for the selected treatment to be applied from helicopters. Where already known, the rock-dust additive to be applied was indicated. Separate maps for areas to receive new trees were supplied since new tree planting would have to be accomplished by manual labor on the ground with an intensive support infrastructure needed where none was in existence. Estimates had been made for each future year for the machinery required, the planting labor involved, the support personnel by skill category, and food and other supporting items.

Ray was impressed at the detail of the planning information and commented to Gertrude, "This project looks like it will use up all the unemployed labor currently just standing around and some currently employed in areas of less priority. Some of the areas that are most distant from current civilization will even need new cities built to support so many people. Are you planning for them?"

"Yes," Gertrude answered. "The present inaccessible areas will be serviced last so we have time to get the new building done. This is particularly true in the tropical rainforests, where in some cases, the roads will have to go in before the cities. With the exception of the support personnel, most of the labor will be unskilled, mostly illiterate, and they will need to be taken first to indoctrination camps, where they will be sorted as to potential skills, needed training, screened as to health issues, and then trained for their particular assignment. Language can be a problem, but where possible, ethnic groups will be kept together."

Ray was following Gertrude's plan with insight and then asked, "What about families? Do you intend to keep them from being split up?"

Gertrude had no real answer for this question. "Keeping families together is desirable but not always possible. It may not necessarily be efficient. When we receive them, they may already have been split. I think, on this issue, we should have more input from George Henson with his experience on resettling already done. It is a bigger issue than just involving the forestry workers.

Ray added, "Good Point." There were many other questions and points of advice that ran the meeting an hour past its scheduled time. As the meeting broke up, in an aside to Gertrude, Ray said,

"Maybe in several days, we could get together and review the names of the people you would like to have in key positions to carry out this program. I think in the near future, you should anticipate growing your organization twenty-fold with the goal in mind of eventually involving one-tenth of humanity. Of course, most of those will be in organizations managed by one or other of the states, but nevertheless, it has to be a coordinated effort to get the most CO_2 out of the atmosphere as soon as possible.

"Yes," Gertrude managed to get out, "I find it difficult to visualize 600,000,000 people all devoted to restoring the forests. Of course, maybe half will be in support rolls, but that is a lot of people. To change the subject somewhat, while I have your ear, I would like your opinion on our having given some priority to planting nut—and fruit-bearing trees over the fastest growing varieties which generally don't produce human edible food."

Ray thought for a minute before replying, "That is a reasonable approach. Perhaps a goal of 10 percent for food bearing to start with, and generally put the food trees where they can be serviced by existing communities."

Gertrude responded, saying, "A case in point is the apricot-growing areas on the Andes foothills, which have been in decline for more than a decade. Per capita, they grow five times the apricots grown in the United States. They have heard about our rock-dust program to bring back the forests and would like to know if it could help their apricots. With the removal of the fruit and nuts each year from the orchards at harvest time, trace nutrients are bound to be reduced to a level that will reduce yields and quality. I would like to try a pilot demonstration there. Except for China and North Korea, whose forestry programs we know little about, Argentina has been the worst laggard is responding to our requests. Helping them with one of their key crops might make a difference."

"What a coincidence!" Ray blurted out. "I am planning a trip to Argentina in a month to motivate them to honor their obligations to accept some folks from northern areas that soon will become uninhabitable." Thinking that Gertrude was now a major player in the SWG and that required that he get to know her well, he added, "Why don't you make a trip to visit their apricot country at the same time. I could wind up my business a few days early and join you and together, socially, we could generate some good will. I happen to speak Spanish rather well."

Gertrude, long familiar in recognizing where political power resided responded with, "Oh, that would be great. I will get in touch with the apricot contacts there as well as the reforestation folks and set up a visit. With your Spanish, too bad I can't engage you for my whole trip."

"Too late now," Ray said as they parted, all smiles.

As it turned out, they traveled together on one of the SWG command airplanes as far as Buenos Aires. There was little to do on the trip other than to get acquainted with each other, mainly what had happened in their lives before Gertrude joined the SWG. In spite of growing up in different countries, they had a lot of common interests. Gertrude made sure Ray understood that early on, she had decided she preferred a career over having children, but that did not preclude an interest in men. As the trip wore on, Ray began to think that as his role as the leader of the SWG, he would probably need a First Lady to help host formal functions, and that Gertrude might well be the one even though she was fifteen years younger than he. Without bringing up children, the age difference should not matter. Gertrude, on her part, thought that the closer to political power the better. She couldn't get any closer than being Ray's wife. As far as love and sex went, she sensed it would develop if she encouraged it, which she intended to do at the first opportunity. What better time than away from the busy times at SWG headquarters?

While Ray stayed in Buenos Aires to work the politics of moving more displaced persons to Argentina, Gertrude went on to the apricot country closer to the Andes by a private plane supplied by the government. The Apricot Growers Association was an important supporter of the party in power and wanted to make a good impression on Gertrude. Her two weeks went smoothly and rapidly while Gertrude reviewed the soil-sampling tests that had been done by the forestry team. She largely agreed with their findings, including the recommended mixes suggested by them for the various areas of existing forests.

While the forestry report had been translated into English, as was the protocol for all the SWG, Gertrude had to utilize translators in talking to all the key people who only spoke Spanish.

She next moved on to the Apricot Growers Association as she wanted to have a good hands-on with that situation before Ray joined her for the last several days of her visit. She had done her homework and told them she knew that apricots were an important crop for the country, being five times per capita of what was grown in the United States. She complemented them and said that the slopes on hills below the Andes should be ideal for apricots that normally flourished in hot summers but needed cold winters. She then speculated that their yield decline for the last several decades, in spite of more land planted to apricots, must be the result of depleted soil fertility. While they had been using a good organic fertilizer, they were probably not replacing the trace minerals that left the orchards with each harvest.

She found out that the apricot growers were not aware of using selected rock dusts to replace missing trace minerals. She borrowed a test team of foresters and showed the apricot growers what the missing minerals were in an orchard that was selected at random. She recounted that the farm fertilizer stores in a typical German city would carry at least six different rock dusts for use on soils with various deficiencies. Also how German public forests were regularly fertilized by the German foresters to maintain good yields of lumber. Without such treatments, one could expect eventually for no trees to grow and the soil to get washed away down to bare rock as was the case in many places in Greece and Italy. In the end, Gertrude earned their gratitude by agreeing to have sent to the apricot growers association enough material to treat a ten-hectare plot in the orchard that they had tested.

Ray joined Gertrude for the last two days, which were spent mostly in being entertained. After all, how often does a head of the world government visit a backwater part of a distant state! Ray told Gertrude that he was not needed back in Puerto Rico right away and as an example of not wasting fuel on an airplane ride to return, they would be returning by steamship. They were given the owner's suite and spent a week getting even better acquainted.

CHAPTER 32

Operation Dragon

Several weeks after the climate-review meeting, on returning to his office one afternoon, Ray found a message from Julia asking to see him. Rather than wait for the next day, which was fully scheduled, Ray decided to drop by the Kerensky household where Julia lived, now that she was married to Olav. Both Julia and Olav were glad to see Ray and made room for him at the supper table. Not until after the children had gone off to bed did the conversation turn to business.

Julia broke the ice. "You know we have been concerned for some time that the Chinese won't capitulate until some hundred million or so peasants have starved to death. At such a point, the fabric of the Chinese society would dissolve into chaos, and it would be very hard for even the SWG to pick up the pieces, let alone relocate two hundred million Chinese. With such a disruption it might be a lot more people.

Ray nodded. "The What If has been forecasting such an outcome for nearly a year but with no better alternatives."

Julia went on with her story. "Well, one of our bright, young staff members has been working some unorthodox initiatives on the What If that we might take. The basic problem, of course, is that the old men in power are so afraid for their personal security from any change that they have become absolutely rigid. Our staffer was looking at covert actions we could take that, over a period of time, would lessen the anxiety of the old men and would also provide a rallying point for a change in the society. The answer is religion!"

"Ah yes," smiled Ray, "historically, when religion has confronted the state, it has sometimes won out."

Julia went on, "Our staffer tried several approaches, strengthen Buddhism, revive Taoism, or even start a new religion. The latter goes nowhere. It takes too long to start, and the Chinese are too conservative to try something brand new. The Buddhists have a very explicit code of behavior which counsels ignoring worldly affairs, so their interests would not coincide with ours. The only way the Buddhists could be made into an effective force would be if we could produce a live Buddha. You know what that means?"

Ray said, "I don't think I do, please tell me."

"Well," she retorted, "a real, live Buddha, of even a lesser variety, should be able to walk on water, live without food, predict the future, teleport himself to anywhere, and do any number of other miracles. I don't think our special tricks department is up to that yet."

"That only leaves Taoism," Ray said. "Tell me the angle on it."

"Taoism works out quite differently," she said. "Taoism goes back much farther than Buddhism, no one knows how far. A lot of the Taoist teachings are in very general terms, but many of them are concerned with worldly affairs. Our intelligence in China indicates that the Taoist elements there have parallel concerns to ours about the direction the Chinese society is going, and they would be quite pliable to our interests if provided with resources. The What If predicts that with a Taoist revival, the old men would lose much of their fear and would allow changes that were in the best interests of the masses of the people. They would still have to be prodded to change by some crises such as increasing crop failures."

Ray was elated. "Get your department to work this up as a major SWG operational plan, and if it still looks good, let's go for it."

Julia had the responsibility for carrying out "Operation Dragon" as it came to be named and, for that purpose, controlled the resources that had been transferred from the CIA and the KGB. She had significant contacts and channels into

China, but the key element she needed was for someone to go to China personally and make the contacts there. It had to be someone who spoke a number of dialects and could pass as a native in a veritable police state. Personnel resources had done a search through the SWG and come up with a prime candidate and two alternates. Julia was waiting for the prime candidate, one Moon Sun, to arrive for a personal interview. Moon was currently a branch chief in the Transportation and Logistics Department, but he had qualifications that made him ideal for the job Julia had in mind. His personnel file indicated that he spoke several Chinese dialects like a native. In fact, he had been Chinese before he had escaped through Hong Kong nearly twenty years earlier. Technically, he looked like the ideal candidate. Julia just wanted to size him up in person to get a feel for how he might react under difficult conditions.

Mr. Sun appeared at Julia's office promptly at the appointed time, and as they exchanged introductions, he said, "George Henson asked me to drop by, something about a possible, temporary assignment . . ."

"Yes, that is right," Julia said. "Before we go into the details of the assignment, I would like to know more about you, you know, like how it was growing up in China."

"Certainly," Moon said. "I was born in Shanghai sometime after World War II, and I grew up on the streets. I only vaguely remember my mother. The communists were picking up all the street kids and putting them in orphanages, something I instinctively knew would be very confining. I managed to get a couple to take me in, in exchange for half of what I could find on the streets. Soon I had to go to a government school, but Shanghai had been an international city for several generations, and no one took the communist brainwashing seriously. It soon became clear that only the communists got the better educational opportunities and, later, the best jobs. So I joined the communists early, and that's how it worked out. I studied linguistics, including English, playing the party game. My assignment as an interpreter took me eventually to Hong Kong, where I defected. Soon I was able to go to Singapore, where I made good business connections due to my knowledge of the then current Chinese thinking." Moon thought that he had said enough, and he lapsed into silence.

She said, "Sounds like you are good at living by your wits. You will need that." Changing the subject, she then said, "What do you know about Taoism?"

Moon hadn't been expecting a question like that but rose to the occasion. "Well, of course, there is the usual problem, given someone unknown who lived so long ago was the originator. The same problem presents itself for the Christians. There are, of course, many writings which are attributed to Laozi which have been the inspiration for their religion. Taoism is really the main spiritual and ethical heritage of much of China and was much more fundamental than, say, Buddhism in establishing the moral character and social fabric of pre-Communist China. It includes one's duties to one's family, to the community, to one's government. Also the duty of the government to the governed. These principles had been ingrained in the society for so long that they were taken for granted, generation-after-generation. Two generations of communism has not been able to eliminate it, although many young people today are not learning all of it. There is also a mystical side."

"What of the older people?" asked Julia.

"They have never accepted communism in their hearts, nor have the peasants, young or old. In the countryside, it is hard to brainwash the young people when the communist doctrine is false to the everyday facts that are observed." Moon Sun was beginning to wonder where this was all leading.

Julia was ready to broach the key question. "Moon," she said, "we have a dangerous assignment which we think you are the best qualified to carry out, but it must be for you to decide. If you decline, you must not reveal to anyone what I am about to tell you. Is that agreed?"

She continued after Moon nodded his head, "Our analyses show that the longer China stays outside of the SWG, the more dangerous she will be to us and to her own citizens when she is faced with a serious food crisis. There is a likelihood for fragmentation of the society and the use of her atomic weapons by some of those riding to power in the breakup. There is even a chance of an atomic exchange with the SWG, in which case there would be an extreme loss of life. There is an alternate which we can initiate, under which the Chinese culture is changed and, under those circumstances, the Chinese leaders would be more receptive to change, including SWG membership."

Moon was curious, particularly about what could be done for his country of origin. "What is the SWG planning?"

Julia was glad to see Moon taking an active role in the conversation. "Our What If analyses show that a revival of the Taoist ethics and values in their society, from the inside, would bring about a sufficient change in the attitudes of the leadership so that positive results would follow. We need someone physically present who can catalyze the process as a grassroots revival, someone who understands the people and yet knows what is at stake. Through channels we still have in operation, we are sending in financial resources, but the key initiation must be done in person."

Julia had come to the end of her prepared arguments and waited for Moon Sun's reply. After a long pause, he said, "I don't know what you want me to do in detail. Whatever it is, I can but try."

Julia smiled. "Well, then you are ready for the details of the operation." She pushed a button on her desk. Half a minute later, the door opened and Greta Schmidt of Science and Technology, who had obviously been waiting for this point in the conversation, entered to join them.

"You know Greta?" Julia asked by way of introductions. They both nodded and Greta sat down. "You see," Julia continued, "We are going to initiate a true revival of Taoism in China with the help of some very modern technology. Greta, please explain our new technology to Moon."

Greta picked up the ball. "Taoism's inspiration came from Lao Tzu, an earlier, obscure mystic, who taught the Tao, meaning, The Way. The Way of the Chinese mystics was an inner growing of consciousness, to be experienced largely through introspection and disciplined meditation." Moon nodded, indicating that this was not new territory for him. Greta went on, "A favorite approach for achieving a one-pointed, internal focus was by means of concentration in meditation on geometrical patterns called mandallas. Jung, in the first part of the twentieth century, in the Western world, made much of this discovery. The actual scientific mechanism is still not clearly understood, but apparently there are nerve connections in the brain that are geometrical and when concentrating on the analogous geometrical pattern in meditation, the functions associated with those nerve connections are stimulated. If the reports of individuals experimenting with this are to be believed, this method can be used to unlock many untapped potentials of humanity, including direct knowing. Such individuals also attain great personal charisma and automatically attract a following, unless they don't desire one."

As Greta paused, Moon said, "Yes, this mystic path was common knowledge among the educated in China. It was not severely suppressed by the communists, because it is a work of a lifetime to even begin to succeed at the endeavor. Only a few per generation are successful."

Greta smiled. "Things have changed. It is now possible for a large number of people to reach such states in relatively short periods of time, and with only modest effort." Moon's face reflected surprise and wonder.

She went on, "In one of our esoteric research programs sponsored by SWG, we have learned of passive devices, made from simple electronic components, that can produce the same results automatically through the subconscious channels of the mind. The very difficult discipline of conscious mind control through years of meditation can be greatly shortened to a period of a few months, not a whole lifetime." Greta pulled out a small device from a folder she had brought with her. The device was in the shape of a small saucer with what looked like two petals attached on opposite sides. "Hold this in your left hand for a few minutes, close your eyes, and tell us what you feel."

Moon closed his eyes and brought his awareness inside himself so as to sense his body. Surprisingly, within a minute, his hand began to feel warm, and a tingling ran up his arm to his forehead. Soon he began to see colors swirling around, where, a minute before, he had only been looking into a soft, black void. Deep within himself, he began to hear the sounds of the low notes of an instrument he could not identify, but if he had to describe it, he would have called it a horn. Moon opened his eyes and again became aware of Julia and Greta. The inner sounds and sights faded immediately, but the tingling in his forehead was stronger. "Some gadget," he said as he reported on his experience.

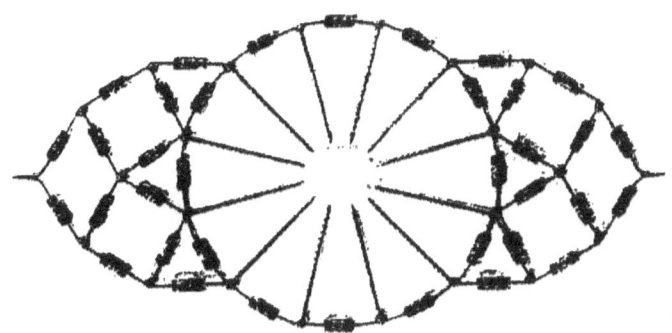

"That one," Greta said, "is configured to stimulate the functions of internal awareness, visualization, and attending, the ones used in conscious meditation. Within a distance of twenty-five feet of one of these devices, concentration in meditation is greatly enhanced. All people are stimulated in its presence, but some, such as you, are more open to what is happening. Over a period of weeks, it is of great aid in concentration for the deliberate meditator. Fortunately for our purposes, we have been able to reduce the electronic pattern in size so that it can be fabricated on a small chip, which will be disguised as a simple button."

Julia took control of the conversation. "You see, Moon," she said, "it will be your mission to introduce these devices to the aspiring young monks of the Taoist monasteries and temples in China so that, within a year, there will emerge a whole legion of charismatic leaders who will put China on a new course. The force and strength of a religion comes from the inner power and knowing of its leaders. They are the leaven around which the masses congregate. Against such forces, no entrenched authority can long prevail. Gandhi was only one in India, and eventually the British Empire had to concede independence. Hopefully, you will have hundreds, maybe a thousand." She laughed. "The old guard won't stand a chance. Instead of several decades, maybe it will all be over in a year."

As Moon drifted into a mental haze at the enormity of what was going to be attempted, he heard Julia continuing, "We have organizations in place that will get you into China and see that you are safely moved around to visit all of the key locations. They will provide contacts for you, but you are the key. It is your job to motivate those you meet."

"A tall order," Moon Sun thought as he left the director's office.

"What do you think?" Julia asked Greta, who had stayed behind when Moon had left. "Do you think he can do it?"

Greta looked pensive. "I'm sure he is our best bet. Being sensitive to the devices will be a great help to him in that he will know of what he speaks when he describes them. Whether he is successful depends on so many other factors which he doesn't control, and we can't even predict. If he fails, we will have to try again with someone else."

One week later, Moon Sun was a member of the crew of a Chinese junk, working its way up the Yangtze River. The time of year was cold and wet. In his clothes were several packages of buttons with a Singapore label. Other means had already been used to send in monetary resources, mostly gold, to each of the monasteries and temples that were on his itinerary. Following the directions they had received from the harbor control ship, they proceeded up the Huangpu to their home dock in Shanghai's busy harbor. Being the junk's home port, there were minimal formalities on arrival. Moon had taken one of the regular crew's place, and he was being escorted by another who took him ashore. Soon he was passed on to a man dressed as a common laborer, and together, they threaded their way through the back streets until they came to a canal full of sampans. On board one, which looked as decrepit as all the others, there were three people, his companion's wife and two monks.

Since religion was being tolerated more in recent times, it had been decided that Moon's best cover would be that of a monk, particularly since his main business would be visiting monasteries. He changed clothes and, soon after dark, three monks emerged from the sampan and made their way on foot to the nearest monastery of their order, a place on the outskirts of Shanghai. It was a wearying walk for Moon, and he was glad for some simple food and a pallet to rest on for the night.

He was not about to sleep. Not only had the day been full of surprises, but a flood of memories came back to him. The Bund did look very different, and much of Shanghai had changed a lot. It was bigger for one thing. In spite of the skyscrapers, the essence, however, was the same.

As he lay on his pallet, Moon reflected that in his early days in China, he had not experienced such relaxation as the soothing atmosphere he found in the monastery. When finally he did fall asleep, it was a restful, dreamless first night.

In the morning, Moon was ushered into the presence of a venerable looking old man, who introduced himself as the head monk. "So," he said. "I have been told by those from a brother monastery that you have the means to bring back the glory of Taoism and return China to the Way of Heaven. How is this to be done?"

Moon chose to quote from *The Great Learning*. "From the loving example of one family, the whole state becomes loving." He paused, and then continued, "Your monasteries will be the family. Bring me your three monks most advanced in meditation, and we shall speed them on the path to True Loving. True Loving is to become one with heaven. The order of Taoism is to become *all loving* and so the state."

The head monk had not heard the quote on True Loving anywhere in his long career, but then what Moon was promising to do was a tall order. If he could deliver, then the quote could no doubt be "discovered" as an old saying, lost in antiquity.

The three monks were brought to Moon in the afternoon, and the head monk stayed to watch. They were located in one of the larger cells of the monastery, and the monks were seated, facing Moon. On questioning, Moon discovered that each of the three, particularly one named Wong Lee, had made some progress on the inner path and had some success in stilling the mind. Good candidates, he thought, as he gave each a button and explained that each of them should keep the button on his person at all times as an aid in his quest of heaven. The head monk asked if he too would get a button, and Moon explained that he did not have any extras, but that the head monk would benefit equally by being near one of the three.

To make sure that they recognized the value of the small buttons and would safeguard them, Moon next had them sit quietly in meditation for two hours. He and the head monk did the same. Afterward, from their eyes and words, there was no question that all, including the head monk, had had very unusual inner experiences and in much greater measure than before in their lives. He told the monks before they left that when they experienced the True Loving, that it was their duty to share it with all they contacted.

The next day the head monk made arrangements for Moon to move west to the next monastery where the process was repeated with similar results. This continued for sixty-five days, until Moon had worked his way around in a large circle ending up in Tsingtao, having distributed all two hundred buttons he had started with. In Tsingtao, Moon became a temporary crew member of another junk, heading for Inchon. The junk made an unusual rendezvous at sea, and Moon was on his way back to the SWG in Puerto Rico.

In his debriefing with Ray, Julia, and Greta, the statement Moon made that stayed with Ray above everything else was, "I learned a lot about Taoism from living it with the monks. It is a way of life that the SWG could do well to adopt for the rest of the world. I think Operation Dragon will have been the high point in my life."

Ray had some interesting news for Moon as well. "While you were gone," he said, "The SWG legislative delegations authorized a new department, to be called The Department of Education. I have been holding the position open for you, because the emphasis that I feel we need to concentrate on is instilling ethics and values in our young people. I think your recent adventure uniquely qualifies you to lead this endeavor."

"I'll be happy to accept," Moon answered, "as long as the educational curricula are expanded to include meditation practice each day."

"Well," Ray said, "if that is what it takes to make responsible and happy people out of our youngsters, then I will vote for it."

Julia laughed. "You know that the only effective teacher is by the example of the adults. Maybe we will have to figure out a way to motivate our adults to meditate as an example for the children. By the way, are we going to make the electronic patterns, you know, the buttons, generally available to the public?"

Ray's face took on a serious look. "Well, we have given out two hundred of them in China, and a number of the SWG staff is experimenting with them. You may check one out from Greta, if you want to join the guinea pigs. This is a Pandora's Box, and we need to know more about the long-range effects before we go public with it."

Within the month, the Chinese leaders noticed an increase in the activities of those who followed Taoism but took no great concern. After all, some of the party principles, though certainly not all, had been borrowed from their more famous sayings. If anything, the Taoist followers seemed more happy and content. What could be wrong with that?

CHAPTER 33

Volcano

On the night of the first full moon after the last atomic warhead had been exploded south of the Bering Strait, a large, inactive volcano on St. Lawrence Island erupted. It was the largest eruption on the North American continent in recorded history. Early reports reaching the Son of NOAH team on the size of the eruption were not encouraging. Meriwether, Roger, and Lucille had gone to the Son of NOAH facility as soon as they had been notified of the event, which was right after breakfast. Ray was quick to join them.

"Well, it looks like one of those random events has caught up with us at a very embarrassing time," Meriwether commented.

Ray asked, "Do you think it erupted from stresses caused by our underwater explosions in the Bering Strait?"

"Hard to say," was Meriwether's response. "In our risk assessment, it did not look overly likely, because the atomic detonations were not near any known active fault zones. The fact that it erupted right at the full moon argues that the stresses had been building up for a long time and the eruption was triggered by the peak gravitational tides that occur at full or new moon. This time of year the moon's orbit would cause the tidal stresses to be near maximum for that location."

Roger turned to Lucille. "Is there an estimate yet of the amount of material that was thrown up into the atmosphere?"

Lucille answered, "We don't know the ratio of steam-to-silica yet, which makes a big difference. For rough working purposes, the observations from our spy satellites give it at half the size of the Krakatau eruption, quite a few cubic miles. Of course, the eruption happened at dusk, and so our observations up to this point are with infrared, which is not as accurate as in the visible spectrum. We should have visible spectrum observations later today."

Lucille continued, "Using the one-half Krakatau-size event, we have started a forward projection for the next ten years to see how the climate is affected. It will be late tonight before the run is completed."

Ray decided to leave and said as he left, "Let's have a directors' meeting first thing tomorrow morning. I want you to give them a detailed projection based on Son of NOAH predictions."

Since Son of NOAH was Lucille's project, it was on her to take the initiative the following morning in the directors' meeting. Her somewhat-haggard face bore mute testimony to the few hours of sleep she had had the night before. While he had no formal responsibility for Son of NOAH, Roger had stayed up with her. Meriwether had come in early to see the results before the meeting was scheduled to start.

Meriwether set the tone for the presentation by summarizing what was known about the eruption. The visual observations had not changed the early estimate of the amount of particulate significantly. Samples of the dust indicated it was an average mix of steam and silica. More details would become available from extended field studies.

Next Lucille went into the implications for the climate. "The wind currents for this time of year will bring the bulk of the very high atmospheric dust into the temperate zone after one revolution of the dust cloud. This will take about a week. The dust will further diffuse after that, but the biggest effect will be from latitude 30° north to latitude 50° north. The dust will gradually settle out, but for the next two years, the average temperate zone temperature will be 2½° Fahrenheit cooler."

Lucille projected a chart. "The chart you see now shows the likely weather conditions for the Northern Hemisphere for this coming summer as we were projecting it before the eruption. This takes into account all the climate modification effects that are already in place. Note that only Canada and some parts of northern Russia were expected to have significant crop failures." Lucille projected a second chart. "Here is the weather projection taking the eruption into account. Because of late frosts in June and early freezes in September, the unsuccessful crop line has moved down to cross the middle of the United States, all of northern Europe, and nearly half of China. The second summer will not be quite as severe as the dust settles."

Ray tried to hide his impatience to get to the bottom line but asked, "What is the long-term effect on the climate?"

Lucille looked up at Ray and changed her chart to the last one. "You can see that the end result is the same as before the eruption, but we get there two years earlier. In other words, we have just lost two of the years of grace we bought with the climate-modification projects. Food stock accounting is not programmed on Son of Noah, but I expect that when Olav works it out, the food surplus we have been carrying for a rainy day will just about be used up in the next two years." Olav nodded general agreement.

Lucille ended her presentation, handing out some packets. "Here are graphs for each year for the next ten years for anyone that needs them. The last graph shows that the permanent snow line ends up about thirty miles farther south than before, but that is within the uncertainty of the data."

Ray asked, "What would happen if another random event of the magnitude of the St. Lawrence Island eruption were to occur in the near future?"

Lucille responded, "We haven't run that one. Based on exercises we have run, it would probably cause even worse crop failures and speed up the eventual changed conditions even more. The probability of such an event is only one chance in two hundred each year, so the risk is very small."

Meriwether put in a comment. "Our model does not yet show the results of accelerated fertilization of the existing forests. Intuitively, that should have an effect before we are completely stabilized in the projections you have seen today and make the results less harsh."

Ray responded to Meriwether, "Lars has promised by the end of next week to give us the rate at which the present forests could be fertilized. As soon as that is available, we should make a Son of NOAH run."

There was considerable discussion among the various directors and also between them and Ray as to how to modify their department plans in the face of the disaster that had befallen them. The general conclusion was that nearly everything had to be accelerated so as to be completed two years earlier than in the previous plan. It was also obvious that the food surplus that had been built up would be badly eroded. All-in-all, it looked like civilization might just be able to squeak by.

Three months later, the coldest June in one hundred years, with many late frosts fulfilled the dire predictions of the Son of NOAH. It was a disaster year for agriculture in the north temperate regions. By July, the Chinese had requested membership in the SWG and turned over their atomic weapons. The Taoist forces had been meditating on the idea of 'One World' and had convinced the old leaders that the Way of Heaven could be achieved only in cooperation with the SWG. The volcanic eruption had been taken as a sign from heaven. "There is only merit to be gained when bowing to the Will of Heaven."

The North Koreans, allies of China, followed their big brother and also petitioned for membership in the SWG.

CHAPTER 34

Man and Woman on the Moon

Monty was sitting comfortably in a lounge chair in the observation dome of the moon base located on the rim of Perry crater, waiting for the takeoff of the resupply module, which was to return to earth, rather low earth orbit. Monty could just at the press of a button make his chair rotate so that he could look out in any direction. Just now, he was viewing the launch pad a short distance along the rim to the West. He thought how well the base planners had laid out everything for the convenience of the base personnel and their operations.

Looking forward to when there would be much traffic throughout the solar system, the Perry base would be the linchpin that made it all possible. First and foremost, the greatest amount of water ice on the moon was located in the crater where there was perpetual darkness: a darkness so cold that the ice could never melt. By fortune, or as some might say, due to the will of Allah, the moon's axis of rotation was perpendicular to the plane of the ecliptic, so the rim of the crater was in perpetual sunlight, an ideal situation for solar power, unlimited power adjacent to unlimited rocket fuel potential. Monty envisioned Perry base becoming the fueling station for all solar system space travel. Well, not quite true, Monty thought, in practice, the fuel needed to be transported to a more convenient place like Lagragian point no. 5, but that was just a detail. The moon would still be the place where the operation center was located. Eventually, it might be where most of the electric power was generated, where the water was mined, and where most of the rocket fuel was produced from water. Rail lines originating at or near Perry would go to many places on the moon. All of this to grow from what was now just a seed. The next step would be to develop the water mining inside the crater so that it could be transported directly rather than to be dragged out by crawler. First would come direct rocket launches from the crater floor and then perhaps cargos flung into space riding on rails up the ramp.

Small as it seemed in comparison to what was to come, what had been done was a feat of great accomplishments achieved by astronauts working mainly in spacesuits and supported entirely by supplies brought in from earth. Not including the mining operation in the crater which was in total darkness, a pure vacuum, and temperatures close to absolute zero, the work at Perry base had been a pushover. Only the vacuum was as difficult as in the crater; on the rim, there was always light which could not be said for other spots on the moon. With a well-designed spacesuit, one was always comfortable while in the sun. Solar power was also always available.

Currently, there were two main areas of the base connected by an underground airtight tunnel, the observation/communication center with the living quarters, and greenhouse, and the garage for the protection of their vehicles with its built-in launch pad. Both areas had their own solar panel farms. The garage also had the processing facility for turning solid ice into a liquid, filtering out any impurities, and by electrolysis, turning part of the water into hydrogen and oxygen. For safety, the hydrogen and oxygen were stored at some distance away.

The launch pad, also acting as the arrival pad, was built into the top of the garage so it could be raised and lowered. When lowered into the garage, a roof could be drawn over the launch pad even when the resupply module was on it, providing pressurization of the main garage. This arrangement allowed work on the resupply module in shirt sleeves and also made for convenience in loading and unloading it. The four vehicles, two track crawlers, and two golf cart-like wheeled vehicles, were housed in separately pressurized bays.

Moon's North Pole

Monty thought of how the division of work was about to change. With the cutbacks in space anticipated to last through the climate-change crises, most building effort was put on hold and the four-person staff was being reduced to just himself and Katherine. The other two were passengers on the resupply module going back to earth. Because with its own power and water, the base was nearly self-sufficient and could expect a resupply visit no more than once a year.

Monty thought of a discovery several years ago which made the work plans for building, once they were reinitiated, much simplified. Artifacts discovered in the Perry crater showed that it had been used before as a supply role for its water by an intelligent race of space-going reptiles originating on earth. Fifty million years ago, they had constructed a ramp along one side of the Perry crater to facilitate hurling water cargos into space, presumably mainly for use as rocket fuel. While for the present, the ramp would be used for bringing up water ice in frozen form with the crawlers; eventually, it was intended to lay tracks on the ramp and with an electric catapult, again hurl water cargos into space.

Monty slowly became aware of a beam of warm energy sweeping back and forth over his brain with a gentle caress. Recognizing Katherine's normal greeting, Monty acknowledged it by sending to her mind his current images of the preparations being made on the launch pad to get the supply module on its way. Water previously mined as water ice from the crater's floor had been converted to hydrogen and oxygen which was being pumped into the tanks of the supply module. Instrumentation Monty was watching showed refueling was complete, and Monty highlighted this in the image he was sharing with Katherine so she would know, if she wanted to observe the liftoff directly, that it was time to join Monty at the observation ports. To imply a sense of urgency, he added another image of her sitting next to him. Katherine was pleased with the warm invitation sent to her and responded with an image of her flying along the passageways to where Monty was. Katherine promptly appeared, and the flexible chair he was sitting in made room for her next to him. Soon the launch count reached zero, and they watched the vehicle take off, first vertically, and then it pitched over to appear to be flying horizontal with the surface. Because hydrogen and oxygen burn with little visible flame, the exhaust was hardly visible as the rocket disappeared over the opposite rim into the black sky.

Recognizing they would now be alone for at least a year, they just sat there for some time, savoring the moment and looking at the non-twinkling stars that were ever so much brighter than when seen from earth. The stars visible never changed as on earth but only rotated around Polaris once a month. The earth's orbit was such that the earth was currently visible, but it would be rising and setting above and below the crater's rim once in a year's time.

Monty and Katherine greatly valued such moments when they were not distracted by outside events which might blur their interchanging of images which gave them the joyous feeling that they were one being occupying two bodies. Their marriage was quite rare in many ways: to start with, being computer arranged. They had not known each other and probably never would have if NASA had not brought them together with the proposal that they should marry. Their type of union was the result of NASA's program to bring the most compatible pairs together after an extensive computer search and testing program as candidates for their long duration missions in space. In the pairing process, NASA soon learned that male/female pairs had much better potential than pairs of the same sex, an eventuality that resulted from the energy flows in the chakras of healthy men and women when pairs were entirely compatible, but not so between persons of the same sex. This established the policy of exclusively using crews on long-term missions consisting of compatible pairs. Another aspect of compatibility was that the members of a pair be in tune with each other telepathically and be personality types that were pleasing to each other rather than grating. Being one in a million if left to chance, NASA adapted the procedure of finding the compatible pairs first, and if they were enthusiastic about their candidate partner, only then investing the resources to make them into astronauts. Usually the candidate couples were identified by a massive screening process at the college senior level.

Monty and Katherine had been brought together at the age of twenty, married a year later, and finished their astronaut training at thirty. They had been on the moon for two years and anticipated finishing their assignment on the moon after being there for a total of five years. The couple that was just now returning to earth had been part of the original team that had built the station. In the team relationship Monty and Katherine had with each other, each knew the other better than any ordinary people possibly could who did not share minds. They also felt that as a team they worked more effectively, because in solving any problem, they had two minds looking at the problem together. If one had an emotional bias, the other likely would be objective. They knew each other so well, there was absolute trust between them, particularly important in emergency situations they would know what the other one was doing.

NASA also had experienced that old dormant emotional traumas, perhaps set down in childhood, but forgotten, could be triggered by some event and then cause alienation in a relationship. To avoid such hidden pitfalls, the NASA training included identifying these potential emotional situations lying dormant in the subconscious and neutralizing them by means of specially developed psychological methods. As a result, no one who had ever been part of a successful telepathic team had ever asked to return to the loneliness of being without their mental partner. The partnership was for life.

With the launch over, Monty and Katherine began a process they took part in each morning, each one portraying a sequence of images representing his or her planned work day. Monty's responsibilities included operation and maintenance of the moon base and its communications with the outside worlds, and he covered his day's plan. In order, it was inspection of the launch pad and garage for possible launch damage, replacement of the inevitably burnt umbilical cable, and an inspection of a crawler to be used in a few days. Katherine had several responsibilities, experiments with lunar materials, growing of food in the greenhouse, operation of various sensors, including earth viewing, and as medical officer. The plan which she imaged was to observe the dust cloud resulting from the volcano eruption from St. Lawrence Island and relay the images to earth. She also imaged some crop harvesting which her personal computer said was due that day.

They embraced with a big hug before they parted to go to their individual tasks, Monty to start on the launch-pad inspection, Katherine to start her harvesting in the greenhouse.

The greenhouse was a structure directly below the observatory level which rotated constantly, if slowly, to present its glazed face to the sun. All other surfaces were super insulated so as to minimize heat loss to the cold of outer space. Because the sun's rays came into the greenhouse horizontally, the plant shelves were stepped going to the back so that the plants nearest to the glazing did not cast shadows on the plants behind them. A large mirror was positioned over the spirulina pond to reflect the horizontal sun's rays down into the water. Katherine harvested a few sweet potatoes and decided that nothing else was ready. There was plenty of produce in their refrigerator for several days of meals. A test of the spirulina pond water showed it would be ready for some harvesting in a day. She then returned back to the observatory, which had completed its observation of the dust clouds on the side of the earth that was visible, and forwarded the images to Perry Base Control on earth. She also tuned in by radio on the progress of the supply module that was soon to rendezvous with a space tug that would take its passengers back to the new Solar Space Station that was in an equatorial low earth orbit. The old Space Station was in a high inclination orbit that was useless from the point of supporting manned space operations to the moon and planets. As Katherine did her work, she regularly tuned in the images Monty was sending her, particularly when he was located in a hazardous work space like the garage with its many doors and hatches that could open to the vacuum of space.

When Monty first reached the garage control room, he viewed the launch pad to make sure it was clear of debris. The launching/landing pad was part of an elevator system so that, on command, it could be lowered into the main garage enclosure. This space was big enough to hold a resupply vehicle on the pad inside a pressurized space. After lowering the pad to the floor of the garage, by remote control, Monty had the roof roll into place and, after it was sealed, went through a pressurization sequence so he could work on the pad while in shirt sleeves. When he did so, he found, as expected, that the umbilical cable had burn damage, but that everything else appeared normal. After replacing the umbilical cable, tests showed that the pad was ready for its next visitor.

Monty next separately inspected each of their four land transporters and their housing bays. Automatic test equipment showed the two dune buggies and track crawlers to be ready for use. He particularly went over the crawler and its equipment that he intended to take down to the crater floor in a few days. Lastly, he made sure there were no air leaks in any of the separate compartments of the garage. Because of the time taken by the day's launch, the scheduled inspection by dune buggy to the two solar panel farms, on which he would be accompanied by Katherine, would be put off until tomorrow.

Katherine, who had been monitoring Monty and sensing he was winding up his work for the day, sent him images of food being cooked and also their smells. Monty responded by starting down the tunnel to their living quarters; looking forward to spending a pleasant evening with her, he sent her a warm anticipatory image, which made her tingle.

Monty and Katherine's later excursion down the ramp to Perry's floor was one of NASA's highlights for the year. At the end of the original construction inside the crater, when the first construction phase was completed, it was not planned to do regular space walks inside the crater with its pure vacuum, total darkness, and near-absolute zero temperature. All planned excursions were to be done from inside the crawlers with any manipulations being accomplished using robotic arms. Exterior lighting and TV viewing provided all the information needed for the most exacting tasks. Returning ice from the floor would be the last task. The main task seemed an unending one of viewing and recording the image messages that had been left them by the prior users of Perry's ice on the walls of the gallery tunnels.

NASA hoped, as a future improvement, to seal off the galleries to be able to provide them with air, heat, light, and elevator access from the living quarters above.

While Monty and Katherine had already processed about half the images engraved on the rock walls of the galleries, there was one sequence they had been holding back on, which began and ended with a majestic figure of a reptilian being wearing more decorative clothing than any other. This also was at the end of a sequence depicting thousands of space ships departing from the solar system, and they both felt there would be something special about the sequence. With each sequence, recording disks, which seemed to be on a diamond media, had been hung on wall hooks nearby. The disks had proven to be particularly helpful as they had studied the format and configured a device to project the contents for detailed study back in the base living quarters. To get the most out of any particular message, Monty and Katherine would meld their minds and record a joint impression. They had already developed a significant vocabulary of the reptilian language but found they achieved a greater degree of accuracy from recreating the messages from the images.

So it was several weeks after the foray into the crater that Katherine was satisfied that they had accurately reconstituted an English language version of what she had dubbed the "Speech of Departure." She and Monty were viewing it together in its final form before forwarding it to earth where they knew it would be viewed by all mankind.

To Those Who Follow

"We salute you as you take your first steps on the ladder to the stars. These disks contain a part of the technology we are leaving you. The rest we have put in safe places on other planets and satellites. You may wonder why we did not use all the water on the moon. We developed a fusion space drive which you will also have someday.

We know not the exact form you will have for your physical bodies. With coming climate changes, you may well be hairy and warm blooded. It matters not, the true form of the human is of the spirit. We are all sons and daughters of the one true being who created us. To be great and worthy is to live in the love of that being.

Be good stewards of the cradle of our mutual birth. For the time it is given to you, care for it and its creatures. Know that we were not the first to travel to the stars and you will not be the last to come after us. Perhaps the ones that follow you will be creatures from the sea."

The voice stopped and the last scene, one of an ocean, faded. Katherine whispered softly, "I wonder what waits for us on Mars and beyond."

*   *   *

CHAPTER 35

Anniversary

The occasion was the twelfth anniversary of the creation of the SWG. The delegations from the member states were convened in a legislative session, and they were being addressed by Ray Carr, who was still the coordinating director of the executive branch of the SWG. He was leaner and grayer and, in addressing the delegations, was also addressing the media and, through the media, all of humanity.

"Ladies and gentlemen of the world, I would like to take this occasion of our twelfth anniversary to review our accomplishments of the last twelve years, and if you will allow me, I would also like to chart where I think we should go in the future. I have reviewed the main points of what I will say to you with my fellow directors, and they are in full agreement on all points. Six of my fellow directors have served you from the start of the SWG.

"As the cause for the existence of the SWG, the climate deserves to be discussed first. The projections of our project NOAH have mostly come about, including the moderation of the glacial period which resulted from our climate-control projects. The permanent ice encroachment originally expected to come as low as the northern United States and most of northern Europe and Asia, has only come half as far. The yearly move southward has slowed to a great extent, and we can expect it to stabilize in about two years' time. This will still be a great challenge, which will be seen when I discuss the world food situation as well as the population moves. These challenges could not have been met without the central leadership of the SWG. Barring another unforeseen incident, such as another St. Lawrence Island eruption or a hit by a large asteroid, the worst is over, and mankind will have survived, essentially intact.

"This brings us to the care of our existing forests and also reforestation. This work must continue unabated at least for another generation, before we can feel that things are back to normal. As the carbon dioxide levels are reduced, the snow line should draw back, and in the lifetimes of many of you now living, it should be possible to repopulate the northern temperate zones we have been forced to abandon. We now know that more than the excess use of fossil fuels by humanity, our basic problem was caused by the dying of the forests due to loss of vital nutrients, mainly trace minerals. As we feed the forests and bring the soils back into balance, the trees have shown that they will become vigorous and healthy. The new young trees that we have planted, and are still planting, will grow better and faster in soils that have been revitalized. It still takes a long time to grow mature trees, even though we have selected mainly fast-growing varieties. Still there is no choice. In the long run, it is the trees that will save us. A large portion of humanity will have to be foresters for generations to come." Ray smiled at Gertrude, his wife of nine years, and now the director of Reforestation.

"Population and the various relocations come next to mind. With the moderation of the glacial period that we have been able to implement, we have had to relocate only three hundred million people, rather than the five hundred million that was first projected. In retrospect, I doubt that we could have mustered the resources necessary for the original challenge. The moves that we did make were still colossal, compared to other endeavors taken on by humanity over the ages, and required much flexibility and patience by all of humanity. At this stage, twenty million still face resettlement, and the cooperation of the entire world is still needed to accomplish the remaining task. Most of these twenty million will be relocated in areas of new housing and food production so that the impact on the rest of the population should be at a minimum. For logistic purposes, the population moves essentially followed our plans: The Canadians to the southwest United States and parts of Mexico, the northern Europeans to the coasts of North Africa, and the northern Asians to Australia. Only a small population in the southern tip of South American has needed to be relocated. Some Africans have had to move because with the changing weather patterns, new drought areas have appeared, and some old drought areas have become productive. Our food surpluses are still rebuilding very slowly, and it will be necessary to hold the total world population constant, no more births than deaths. Eventually, as the fertile segment of the population decreases, the total population will decrease automatically, which will relieve pressure on our food stocks and other facilities that are still in short supply.

"That brings us to the next topic, food. By forcing the whole world to become essentially vegetarians, we have been able to prevent starvation, with much less land under cultivation. The massive plankton farms have augmented the traditional food supplies and, because of the plankton's rich protein content and the introduction of the NASA protein-rich sweet potato, the average human on the planet for once has a good nutritional diet. It is also a more varied and interesting diet due, in large measure, to the contributions from the tropical rain forests. We have much left to learn and do in this area. There are many edible plants that we are not yet harvesting from the rain forests, but we should learn how to do so in the future. We must also protect the food supply from degradation by unnatural means, such as GMOs.

"I know that one area in which the dreams of most of the world are not yet realized is in housing and related infrastructure. Due to the urgency to make the population moves, temporary housing was necessary to a large extent. In other, more-settled areas that absorbed significant numbers of people, it was necessary to double up in existing facilities. Everyone now has basic shelter, which could not have been said twelve years ago. This is an area which also requires our continual efforts for the foreseeable future. Recognizing the apparently innate desire of humans to have their own nests, as housing facilities improve in the future, I see a time when we may be able to move back to a situation of private ownership of the home." At this comment, a loud cheer went up from the world congress delegations. Ray continued, "As a matter of fact, we should probably start moving toward a greater degree of free enterprise in our business world also, but let me save that thought for the second half of this report.

"Energy production and use is a key factor in our progress. While many felt the elimination of most recreational uses of the automobile was a great loss, the gains have been impressive. Energy consumption, worldwide, is now only one-half of that of twelve years ago, and even more significantly, the use of fossil fuels has been reduced by a factor of ten. As of today, almost all automotive power plants use methyl alcohol, generated from biomass, or are run on electric batteries. The economics of scale in solar-voltaic power generation is now so great that the cost of such power from the sun rivals that of hydro-electric installations. All remaining fuel-burning plants should be phased out within seven years' time. The atmosphere is already much cleaner and, of overriding importance, the carbon dioxide content has been reduced by about thirty parts per million since it peaked ten years ago. Our program to replace methyl alcohol with hydrogen as a completely nonpolluting vehicular fuel is well underway, and the first production vehicles to use hydrogen have already been introduced. The delay over our original timetable was necessary in order first to get the hydrogen ground and distribution systems in place. We were able to meet our goals in the use of hydrogen in photo-voltaic power-generation systems as a means for storing energy, particularly through dark or sunless hours.

"We have made much progress in science and technology in general areas I have not mentioned, particularly with help from our predecessors, the intelligent reptiles. The big emphasis is on developing processes and systems that are sustainable indefinitely without destroying the environment. A major principle implemented has been that toxic substances should not be manufactured and introduced into the environment in the first place, compared to our old system of unsuccessfully controlling them after they have been released into the environment. This is particularly true in the farm area where vast amounts of land are involved, and the potential for toxic contamination is greatest. Our success in agriculture has largely been possible by reverting to natural systems of agriculture, sometimes called organic, and by recycling human wastes to enrich the soil. We have also made great progress in our distribution systems so that there are few distribution wastes left over, such as bottling and packaging. Those few that are unavoidable, we have been able to handle by careful recycling. Our widespread fiber optics communications network has made travel for most previous reasons unnecessary.

"A short note on air and sea transport. Both our lighter-than-air vehicles and our use of wind power for driving sea transports have proven to be great successes. These systems are efficient in the use of energy and are non-damaging to the environment. Their use will greatly multiply in the future.

"Moving on to a more humanitarian concern, as a by-product of the entry of the Chinese into the SWG, we have reestablished an ethics and human values system into our society, from which it had been rapidly disappearing. This has had a significant influence, particularly among the younger generation, in focusing on nonmaterial aspects of our human heritage. I attribute the reduction in tensions and conflicts in the current society, which is borne out by statistics, to this swing away from the material life to artistic, intellectual, and spiritual pursuits, engendered by the new ethics and value system that is being widely embraced.

"In closing the first part of my report, I want to touch on security, or what is often called the armed forces. At the time the SWG was created, perhaps 20 percent of the world's resources were being expended on armed forces of all kinds. Small wars between neighboring countries were common, and the world possessed the ability to annihilate itself more than ten times over. At its inception, the SWG reduced all arms drastically and, with the final joining of China and N. Korea, was able to eliminate atomic weapons. Conventional weaponry was also greatly reduced. At the present time, the SWG possesses three active ballistic missile carrying submarines, three armored divisions, and enough defensive armament to defend its island enclaves from surprise attack. The member states of the SWG only possess lightly armed militia for the purpose of maintaining local law and order. No offensive capabilities remain to any of the member states that cannot easily be countered by the small forces of the SWG. Through the threat of its missiles, the SWG rules the world without any challenge.

"This brings me to the second part of my report.

"In saving humanity from certain starvation and annihilating warfare, the SWG has created the most totalitarian system mankind has ever experienced. It is planet-wide. While it has saved our bodies, it has necessarily crushed our souls. Before it becomes an entrenched way of life and before humanity forgets what real freedom is, we must move away from totalitarianism. Now is the time, when the glacial period threat has been recently met and overcome.

"As I see it, the primary problem is that the SWG is a dictatorship of a conglomeration of separate states, each with very different local governments and traditions. Most of these state governments were not selected by the people that they govern. As such, this conglomeration will never grow into a true world government, equally serving all of humanity. Both the SWG and the member state governments that divide our world must soon be abolished.

"In restructuring our society, we can do well to learn from the past. We must install the checks and balances, such as strong and independent judiciary branches, and open media and press, so that we never return to the totalitarianism we are now employing." There was an embarrassed laugh from the delegates present. "On the other hand, we must guard against the excesses of the past, so-called free democracies where greed ran rampant, destroying the environment, exploiting the common man, and enslaving the poor. The ethical standards we have begun to give to our children in the schools must become part and parcel of the fabric of the society.

"I propose that a people's constitutional convention be convened for the purpose of drafting a Federal World Government Constitution as well as model State Constitutions. We must assure world and state governments designed by the people. We must have a government that does not need to defend itself. It should be so loved and cherished by the people that there would be no need for any defense. I would hope to see at least the following ideas addressed in these constitutions:

1. A guarantee of human rights to every individual, man, woman, and child. Free elections on a 'one person, equal vote' basis, without influence by special interests.
2. Elimination of all borders and restrictions of movement of people and goods around the globe.

3. Guaranteed provisions of the basic needs of food, shelter, education, and health services, independent of the ability of the individual to do useful work.
4. Guaranteed employment with both a minimum and maximum income. Recognition of child-care as respected and paid employment.
5. A fair system of incentives which would reward each in proportion to his or her contribution, eliminating the need to conform through the use of or the threat of force.
6. The use of the tools of science and technology for the benefit of humanity and our mother the earth and not for the greed of individuals.
7. An environment of education and learning so that each human has the opportunity to achieve his or her full potential in body, mind, and spirit."

Ray Carr sat down amid waves of applause from all the legislative delegations as well as from the other members of the executive present. He knew it would take time and a lot of hard work to make his vision of a new humanity to come about, but he was convinced that it would be worth any effort. As a recent convert to Taoism, Ray knew that the Way of Heaven would come about through the True Loving, and that was to be gained through meditation. Real changes could not be imposed from above. Real changes would have to be made on the individual level, each one changing himself or herself for the better.

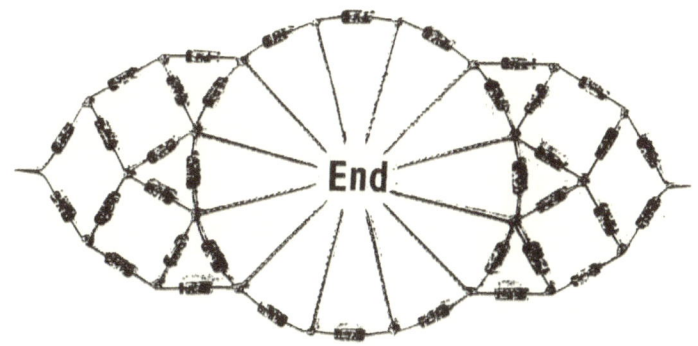

9 781483 696669